JUDAISM, CHRISTIANITY, AND ISLAM

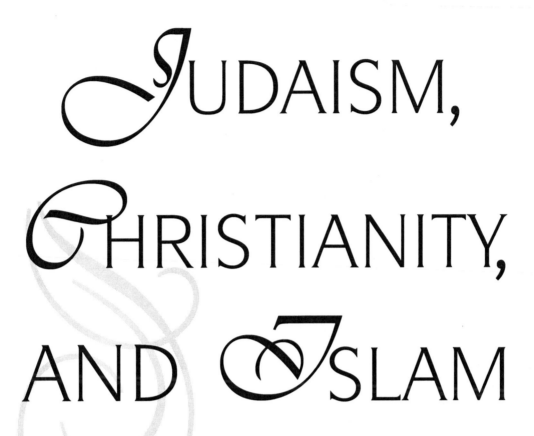

DIFFERENCES, COMMONALITIES, AND COMMUNITY

SECOND EDITION

BY FRITZ WENISCH

cognella®
academic publishing

Bassim Hamadeh, CEO and Publisher
Michael Simpson, Vice President of Acquisitions
Jamie Giganti, Managing Editor
Jess Busch, Senior Graphic Designer
John Remington, Acquisitions Editor
Brian Fahey, Licensing Specialist
Mandy Licata, Interior Designer

First published in the United States of America in 2015 by Cognella, Inc.

Printed in the United States of America

ISBN: 978-1-62131-145-4 (pbk) / 978-1-62661-954-8 (br)

www.cognella.com   800-200-3908

Contents

CHAPTER ONE

Preliminary "Stuff"

Religion Courses at Secular Universities

Tom entered the auditorium. Quite a number of students had assembled already. He looked for a seat in the middle section. It was about ten minutes before class was to start, and students kept on coming in.

He intended to graduate when the current term was over. Two days ago, his academic adviser had noticed that a general education course was still missing from Tom's transcript. He had scrambled to find one; in the end, he had signed up for the course that was about to begin. "I hope I will get by with as little work as possible," he thought.

An elderly man entered with a stack of papers which he placed on the table in front of the room. "That must be the prof," Tom thought. The man fiddled with the electronic equipment, shook his head and left. Several minutes later, he returned with a young lady. She grabbed the portable microphone and did what looked like replacing the battery—and then, "TESTING: ONE … OOPS, TOO LOUD!!" She pushed a button and tried again, "Testing: One, two, three—it works!" She handed the mike to the prof, who spoke into it. "This is Arnold Schwarzenegger, who has come specifically to try this microphone out. Yes, it works, unlike California when I used to be governor." The people in the room laughed. Tom thought, "Although that guy does not look at all like Schwarzenegger, his accent is a bit like the ex-governator's."

Now, class began. The professor handed a syllabus out, introduced himself, mentioned that he was from Austria ("Salzburg, to be specific, where Mozart was born, not the town Schwarzenegger is from"), explained the course requirements, including a strict attendance policy ("Rats! I actually must come to class," Tom sighed), and then, he began teaching …

(I) TWO CHIEF DIFFERENCES BETWEEN THIS COURSE AND RELIGION COURSES TAUGHT AT RELIGIOUS VENUES

For many of you, this is not the first course dealing with religion. It may, however, be the first religion course you are attending at a secular (highbrow for "nonreligious") environment. Let me pick Sunday school (a course in a Jewish or Muslim venue also would work, of course), and explain how it differs from what I will be doing here—besides never teaching on Sundays, of course.

1. Day job (philosophy teacher) intrusion

First, my teaching style will be influenced by my day job, which is philosophy teacher. (My dean and department chair think that I am a philosopher. Do me a favor and do not tell them that I am only a philosophy teacher.) People with that day job look at religion invariably very much from the "systems of thoughts" perspective. I promise, however, that I will try to do my best to get across that religion is also a matter of the will and of the heart; but given my background, the "matter of the mind" aspect will color much of what I am going to tell you over the course of this semester. How does this compare to Sunday school? I doubt that your Sunday school teacher shared my day job.

2. "Appeal to revelation," customary in Sunday school, is "out of bounds" here

More important, though, is a second difference. To understand it, let's ask ourselves where Judaism, Christianity, and Islam derive their teachings from. Suppose you ask a Jew to justify one of his or her beliefs. He or she would refer to the Jewish Holy Scriptures. A Christian would refer to the Christian Bible—Old Testament[1] and New Testament; a Muslim to the Qur'an. If you ask the three of them, "Why should I accept what these Scriptures say," you would be told, "Because they contain messages that ultimately come from God," either indirectly, such as through prophets or heavenly messengers, or directly; "because they are messages 'from the other world.'"

A message of this kind is called "revelation," a word having the literal meaning of "removing a veil." Thus, Judaism, Christianity, and Islam are religions which claim to be based on revelation, on a message "from the other world."

Remember your Sunday school teacher: That person simply assumed that revelation actually had taken place, that its having occurred was a fact, and justified many of the statements he or she made through an appeal to revelation. Those among you who have attended a religion class taught by a rabbi also might remember that he (or she if the teaching took place in a Conservative or Reform Judaism setting) similarly appealed to revelation. The same is true of Islam. You can hear Muslim teachers say, "What I just told you is true because it is stated in the Qur'an, and the Qur'an is the word of God." (Actually, he would say "Allah" instead of God; but this word means the same.)

---

1 As far as content, the Old Testament is pretty much the same as the Jewish Holy Scriptures. Later, the relationship between these two collections of texts will be taken up in detail.

Jews, Christians, and Muslims agree that there has been revelation (although they disagree about where it can be found), and they appeal to the content of what they consider as revelation to support their positions.

This highlights a second—actually, the chief—difference between the course you are enrolled in and religion classes offered at religious schools, churches, synagogues, or institutions associated with mosques. Teachers in these other classes routinely appeal to revelation to support their statements. This involves saying something like, "What I just explained is based on a message from 'the other world.'" In contrast, if I were to appeal to revelation to support the truth of what I am going to tell you, I would be breaking the law as it applies to public schools in the United States. If you were to complain to the dean about it, and if I would not change my teaching even after being called on the carpet by him or her, I would get fired.

This does not mean, of course, that I am not allowed to argue in support of a point of view. There are many points of view, including controversial ones, you will hear me support through arguments, in some cases—when I will be speaking about one of my hobbyhorses—even vigorously. I will, for example, argue in support of the statement "Christians believe Jesus to be the son of God," as well as in support of the statement "Muslims believe Muhammad to be the most important prophet." That Christians believe the first and Muslims the second can easily be supported through historic evidence; I do not need to appeal to revelation—to a message from another world—to justify it.

Would I, however, wish to justify that Jesus *is* the son of God (rather than merely that Christians *believe* him to be the son of God), I would have to say something like, "The New Testament says that Jesus is the son of God, and the New Testament is the word of God"; that is, I would have to use revelation to support that view, and that's off-limits as far as this course is concerned. It would, of course, not be off-limits in a Sunday school class.

To make sure you get a handle on the second difference between Sunday school classes and the course you are attending right now, let me repeat: In a Sunday school class, revelation may lawfully be appealed to for the purpose of supporting a view; in this course, the law does not permit appeals to revelation as support of a belief.

Thus, in this course, I will try to tell you as accurately as possible what Jews, Christians, and Muslims believe—which means, I will try my best to convince you of the statement "It is actually true that they believe these things"; with regard to the question, however, "Are these beliefs actually true (or 'which ones of them are true')," more often than not, I will have to say, "For the purpose of this course, I have no idea."

3. Arguments in support of a view do have a place in this course; only "appeal-to-revelation-arguments" are off-limits

Why did I say "more often than not"? What is the exception? The "no idea" statement applies only in those cases in which the belief of a particular religion can be supported through *nothing but* an appeal to revelation. The "no idea" statement does not apply to those religious beliefs that one can understand as true, not only by an appeal to revelation, but also through one's own thinking, observation, or insight. Take, for example, the statement, "Murder is wrong." All three of the religions we will take up in this course agree with it. In addition, though, one can see independently of the teachings of these religions that the statement is true. Even most atheists agree with it. Consequently, I am allowed to defend it, using supporting reasons such as the following: "Just think about what it means to be human. Then, you will clearly understand that you do not have the right to murder someone." I am, however, not allowed to use the following supporting reason: "It is wrong to murder because the Bible (or the Qur'an) says that it is wrong." This would be using an appeal to revelation to support the view, and as I have stated, such arguments are off-limits here.

Thus, supporting reasons I may use in this class must appeal to what one can see to be true independently of a claim to revelation; I am not allowed to take recourse to an appeal to revelation.

Each of the three religions we will discuss in this course holds many things that cannot be supported by an appeal to our understanding, observation, or insight. Examples are, "There are angels" (held by many Jews, by Christians, and Muslims), "Muhammad is the most important prophet" (held by Muslims), and "Jesus is the son of God" (held by Christians). Someone intending to support these views would, in the final analysis, have to resort to revelation: "The Bible says so and it is the word of God; the Qur'an says so and it is the word of God." Since as a teacher of this course, I am not allowed to base my arguments on a claim that there actually was a genuine revelation, I must refrain from defending any of these and similar views.

(II) WHERE DOES THE PROHIBITION AGAINST APPEALING TO REVELATION COME FROM? IS THERE A CONSTITUTIONAL MANDATE TO SEPARATE CHURCH AND STATE?

This leads to the question "Why is appealing to revelation forbidden to me in the context of teaching this course? Why is it against the law to do so at a public university? Is it an unimportant law, or an important law? Whose law is it?"

1. A politically correct—but factually incorrect—view

I can easily imagine the one or the other of you saying: "You, Fritz, are not allowed to appeal to revelation when teaching this course because of the most important law of the nation, the fundamental law of the United States, aka the Constitution. That document contains a statement demanding a separation between church and state; URI is a state institution; consequently, teachers are not allowed to defend religion in the classroom. Well, Fritz? How about it ... what are you waiting for? Why don't you say it?"

It appears that the speaker expects me to imitate Walter Williams and say, as the latter does in many of his columns, "'Go to the head of the class';[2] you have given a clear and well-informed answer."

Contrary to that, I am saying, "Stay where you are; you have parroted a politically correct and widely accepted prejudice, but it does not correspond to the truth."

---

2 Williams often asks a question in his column, and then, he continues, "If you say xxx [= answer to the question he considers to be correct], go to the head of the class."

The truth is—besides, "Your teacher, Fritz, is one of the most politically incorrect individuals you will ever meet": Whatever the so-called mainstream media and many of my colleagues may say, the source of the prohibition against appealing, at public schools in the United States, to revelation as a support for certain beliefs is not the Constitution as written, but the Constitution as misinterpreted by the United States Supreme Court. The law of the land is, however, the Constitution as presented to us by the United States Supreme Court, even if that interpretation is demonstrably false.

I can hear the guy whom I did not send to the head of the class say now "What do you know, Fritz? Go back to Austria where you came from."

Before sending me home, let's look at some facts—and before doing so, let me insert the following aside.

2. "Yours truly" has no problem with a suggestion to refrain from an appeal to revelation; nevertheless …

Given the variety of religious beliefs among URI students, I would teach this course in a religiously neutral manner even if the U.S. Supreme Court did not tell me to do so. Thus, the following reflections are not meant to present me as saying "Rats, the United States Supreme Court does not let me teach this course the way I would like to"; rather, they are meant to invite you to ask whether what your civics teacher might have told you about the country you live in might not need to be corrected.

3. … The First Amendment to the Constitution does not say what the Supreme Court says it says

Prior to considering what the U.S. Constitution actually says about religion, some background is necessary:

(1) "Civics course background"

If you ever took a civics course, you might remember:

The U.S. Constitution was written by the Constitutional Convention which met in Philadelphia in 1787. In 1788, a sufficient number of states had ratified the document for it to become effective. The following year (1789), James Madison proposed to Congress a number of amendments to the Constitution. (The word "Amendment" refers to changes, additions, or deletions.) They were approved by Congress and sent to the states for ratification. By 1791, ten of these amendments had been ratified by a sufficient number of states. Collectively, they were "tacked on" to the Constitution and are known as the Bill of Rights.

(2) The wording of the First Amendment's Religion Clauses: No "separation talk"

The First Amendment—the one crucial for the issues I am explaining at present—begins with the words, "Congress shall make no law respecting an *establishment* of religion, or prohibiting the *free exercise* thereof." It consists of two clauses or provisions, the first known as the "establishment clause," the second as the "free exercise clause"; jointly, they are known as the "religion clauses."[3]

The language is a bit old-fashioned and can easily be taken the wrong way; so let me make sure that it is properly understood. "Establishment of religion" as used in the Amendment has nothing to do with what is called today "religious establishment," such as church, synagogue, or mosque; rather, it means, "giving legal preference to a religion," such as passing a law according to which a religion is considered as the one officially designated as preferred, or even worse, as the one to which one *must* adhere. "Respecting," as used in the Amendment, has nothing to do with the attitude of respect your teachers demand from you (don't some of them expect you to bow down before them and kiss their feet?); rather, it means "concerning," "regarding," or "having to do with." Finally, I do hope you know that Congress is the federal legislature. Thus, in contemporary language, the First Amendment's religion clauses state, "Congress, i.e. the Federal Legislature, shall make no law having to do with giving legal preference to a religion, or interfering with the free exercise of religion." Thus, the Amendment forbids Congress to enact two types of laws: First, laws giving legal preference to a religion; second, laws prohibiting the free exercise of religion.

Laws enacted by Congress must be religiously neutral; but where is the "separation between church and state" talk?

(3) "Fritz, don't you know about Jefferson?"

Maybe you say, "You ignorant Austrian, if you knew American history, you'd have heard about Thomas Jefferson. He said that the First Amendment to the U.S. Constitution requires a separation between church and state."

True, Jefferson was the first one to use the "Separation between Church and State" language. In 1802 he wrote a letter to the Danbury Baptist Association in Connecticut, in which he stated that the American "legislature should 'make no law respecting an establishment of religion, or prohibiting the free exercise thereof,'[4] thus building a wall of *separation between church and state*."[5] Apart from being sloppy—he meant "separation between religion and government," he is, as shall be shown below, mistaken. Also, it is interesting to note that his involvement with the First Amendment was minimal: He had no part in drafting it, and he did not participate in the involved congressional discussions about it; he was not even in the country when Congress debated the Bill of Rights. To take his statement about the amendment as Gospel truth, as many "church-state separationists"[6] do (although they often scoff at the real Gospels), is unwarranted, even apart from the following arguments showing that the Constitution does not demand the government to be neutral toward religion.

---

3 The Constitution itself—as opposed to one of its amendments—also contains a provision concerning religion. That provision states that there is to be no "religious test" as qualification to any office or public trust under the United States. (See Article VI.) This, and the part of the First Amendment just quoted, are the only instances where religion is referred to in the United States Constitution.

4 Here, Jefferson quotes word for word from the First Amendment to the U.S. Constitution.

5 Thomas Jefferson, *Writings* (New York: Viking Press, 1984), p. 510.

6 I am using Jeffersonian sloppiness, which is very prevalent among the separationists.

(4) Three often-overlooked facts about the First Amendment's Religion Clauses

My arguments chiefly consist of pointing out three facts that are often totally ignored by the "separation between religion and government"[7] enthusiasts:

First, the Amendment begins with the word "Congress," referring, as indicated earlier (as you no doubt knew anyway without me saying it) to the federal legislature consisting of the Senate and the House of Representatives. As indicated, laws made by Congress must be religiously neutral. What the individual states might do in this regard is not addressed in this amendment.[8] They were allowed to have established religions. Several did; the one having an established religion the longest was Massachusetts—yes, believe it or not, Massachusetts, priding itself on its liberalism today. There, state support for the Christian denomination of Congregationalism lasted until 1833, which is 42 years after the Religion Clauses had become a part of the United States Constitution.

Second, the Religion Clauses demand religious neutrality only by the lawmaking function of Congress, the function through which Congress makes rules applying to each and every U.S. citizen. The Clauses do not apply to the rules which each house of Congress makes for carrying out its business. (See Article I, Section 5, of the U.S. Constitution: "Each house [of Congress] may determine the rules of its proceedings.") There is no requirement for these rules to be religious neutral; as a matter of fact, they are not neutral with regard to religion. In the same year in which Congress approved the Bill of Rights, including the Religion Clauses, and proposed them to the states for ratification, each of the houses of Congress voted to begin each of its sessions with a chaplain-led prayer. This is still the case today. There is a House Chaplain and a Senate Chaplain, and both these jobs get you a handsome salary, paid by the taxpayers. There is nothing contrary to the First Amendment's Religion Clauses involved here.

Third, in speaking only about the legislative branch of the federal government, the First Amendment's Religion Clauses do not say anything about the executive branch and the judicial branch. There is no requirement for religious neutrality with regard to the procedures these branches adopt for carrying out their day-to-day work. Prayers during a presidential inauguration (or during other presidential ceremonies, for that matter) are entirely constitutional. Whether or not such prayers are to take place depends, according to the Constitution, only on the decision of the person being inaugurated as president. If Congress would adopt a law demanding such prayers, that law would be unconstitutional as violating the Establishment Clause; were Congress to enact a law forbidding such prayers, that law would be unconstitutional as violating the Free Exercise Clause.[9]

Similarly, there is no constitutional requirement for the United States Supreme Court to be religiously neutral in carrying out its day-to-day work. In fact, each and every Supreme Court session begins with a short prayer. The Court Crier calls out "God save the United States and this honorable Court." Similarly, as stated with regard to the executive branch of the federal government, a law Congress would pass mandating this practice would violate the Establishment Clause; a law forbidding it would

---

7 From now on, I will avoid Jeffersonian sloppiness.

8 Before someone else calls me an "ignorant Austrian" once again, I hasten to point out that I will explain in a little while how First Amendment provisions "came down" to the state level.

9 In addition to violating the Religion Clauses, these laws would also seem to run afoul of the "separation of powers" principle on which the U.S. Constitution is built.

violate the Free Exercise Clause.[10] Whether or not the practice is to be continued depends, according to the Constitution, on nothing but the discretion of the United States Supreme Court.

In short, regardless of what Jefferson has said and what the "separation enthusiasts" may tell you, the U.S. Constitution does not mandate government neutrality with regard to religion as implied by the "separation between religion and government" talk.

(5) How did the First Amendment "get down" to the state level?

For more than 75 years, until 1868, the Bill of Rights—including the Religion Clauses—applied only to the federal government (in the case of the religion clauses, it applied only to Congress). It did not apply to the governments of the individual states.[11] The limitation of the Bill of Rights to the federal government came to an end with the Fourteenth Amendment to the Constitution, adopted in 1868. The crucial portions of this amendment read, "No state shall make or enforce any law which shall abridge the *privileges and immunities* of citizens of the United States; nor shall any State deprive any person of life, liberty, or property, without *due process* of law." The first provision is called the "Privileges and Immunities Clause"; the second is called the "Due Process Clause."

One of the effects of this amendment was to "pull" the provisions of the Bill of Rights "down" from the federal level to the states, the counties, and the municipalities. I am passing over the rather tortured history that was involved until the U.S. Supreme Court finally came to grips with that fact[12] and clearly spelled out that, because of the Fourteenth Amendment, state governments also had to respect the rights that the Bill of Rights granted U.S. citizens vis-à-vis the federal government.

(6) What the situation at the state level would be like if logic were to rule

The application of the Religion Clauses to the state level means that the situation at the state (and local) level is to be a precise mirror image of the situation at the federal level. Let me describe what this mirror image is to look like (I was about to call it a logic teacher's dream; but that would be incorrect, for it was the actual situation up until 1948, including with regard to the role of religion in public schools):

Laws enacted by state legislatures are to be religiously neutral; whatever rules state legislatures devise for carrying out their business need not be religiously neutral—whether or not they are religiously neutral depends on the preference of a majority of the members of the legislature. Similarly, whether or not the state executives and judiciaries wish to maintain religious neutrality in carrying out their day-to-day functions depends likewise on the preference of the officeholders in these government branches.

How do public schools figure into that picture? By no stretch of the imagination can they be considered a part of the legislature, even if they are established by state law. In consequence, it is, in accordance with the U.S. Constitution, to be left up to the discretion of local school officials whether or not—and to what extent—religious activities should go on at a particular school. A state law mandating such activities would be a violation of the Establishment Clause; a state law prohibiting them would be a violation of the Free Exercise clause: State legislatures are to observe in this respect the

---

10 Again, there would also seem to be a difficulty with the Separation of Powers principle.

11 This was explicitly asserted by the U.S. Supreme Court in its 1833 *Barron v. Baltimore* decision.

12 This is another rather inglorious segment of the history of the U.S. Supreme Court.

neutrality imposed on them by the United States Constitution, as applied to them by the Fourteenth Amendment.[13]

What I have just outlined—and almost called a "logic teacher's dream"—was the actual situation in the United States for the 80 years following the adoption of the Fourteenth Amendment, until 1948.

(7) A United States Supreme Court failing to stick to its proper role: the result

What caused the situation to change? In short, a United States Supreme Court that did not stick to its real job, interpreting the Constitution, but took it upon itself to change it, including the Bill of Rights.

Maybe you tell me once again, "What do you know? You are only an Austrian—speak about the Austrian Constitution." Well, I do have a U.S. Supreme Court justice—actually, a chief justice, as my witness: Earl Warren. He was chief justice from 1953 to 1969. In 1955 he made the candid statement, "When the generation of the 1980s receives from us the Bill of Rights, the document will not have exactly the same meaning it had when we received it from our forefathers."[14] Warren was unusually candid in this respect; the Constitution had been changed de facto by Supreme Court decisions before his time already; it also has been changed by the Supreme Court after his time.

Two United States Supreme Court decisions are of particular importance for the teaching of religion at public U.S. schools.

The first is *McCollum v. Board of Education*, handed down in 1948. That decision declared sectarian religious teaching in public schools during regular school hours to be a violation of the First and the Fourteenth Amendments to the U.S. Constitution, even if participation is voluntary. Sectarian religious teaching is instructing that involves the promotion of the viewpoint of a particular religion. Thus, since 1948, it is deemed unconstitutional to teach religion in public schools, such that the point of view of a particular religion is promoted, or such that religion in general is promoted over no religion at all.

The second of these cases is *School District of Abington Township v. Schempp* (1963). The decision declared the Lord's Prayer and devotional Bible reading to be unconstitutional in public schools, but also stated, "Nothing we have said here indicates that such study of the Bible or of religion, when presented objectively as part of a secular program of education, may not be effected consistently with the First Amendment." Thus, the decision allows what the Court calls an "objective" teaching of religion. It permits teachers like "yours truly" to teach religion by way of neutral presentation.

In the United States, the Supreme Court has the final say about the meaning of the Constitution: What that Court says, goes. The Constitution is taken to mean what the Supreme Court says it means. This also holds true when a good case can be made that the Court misinterpreted the Constitution. As I explained, I believe that the United States Supreme Court's interpretation of the Constitution's Religion Clauses is deficient (to put it mildly); but given the role of the Court as the final arbiter, I must comply with its decision, although I may express my disagreement with it. Let me also remind you of an earlier "aside": Even if the Supreme Court had not outlawed what it calls "sectarian" religious

---

13 In contrast to the types of laws just mentioned, a state law ensuring that in the case of minors, parents should be allowed to exempt their students from religious activities, and in the case of older students, the students should be allowed to exempt themselves would neither go in the direction of establishing a religion, nor interfere with its free exercise, would, therefore, seem to be appropriate. One would, however, hope anyway that the school administrators themselves would consider the principle behind that law as policy, even if there would be no such law.

14 Earl Warren, "The Law and the Future," in *Fortune Magazine*, November 1955.

teaching (teaching supporting the viewpoint of a particular religion or of religion in general), I would avoid it anyway, because of the variety of religious backgrounds among students at this university, and given that it is a secular school.[15]

(III) RESTATING PRECISELY WHAT THE NEUTRALITY REQUIREMENT APPLIES TO; FORMULATION OF THE "FOX PRINCIPLE"

It is important, however, to emphasize again what the neutrality requirement applies to, and what it does not apply to. Remember that religious people defend their views by appealing to revelation, which they claim to find chiefly in their scriptures (the Bible and the Qur'an in the case of the religions covered in this course). Whenever we come across a belief that could be supported only by an appeal to revelation, I am not allowed to defend that belief. Views that also can be supported in other ways I am allowed to defend; my defense of these views may involve, however, only arguments appealing to our own understanding, observation, or insight. I may, of course, explain how representatives of a religion support their views through revelation; I may not, however, take a stand on whether or not these attempts at support are successful.

I almost totally forgot to state the following—it should go without saying, anyway: Whenever I defend a view through an appeal to our own understanding, observation, or insight, there is, of course, absolutely no requirement for you to agree with that view. All I can require of you is demonstrating that you understand my arguments.

One additional point: As I said, I am not allowed to support views that can be defended only through an appeal to revelation. In today's intellectual climate, no one would give me any grief, were I to attack the teachings of a religion, especially if I select one that is subject to prejudices against it. It seems unfair to me, though, to attack views in a forum in which nothing can be said in their defense. Consequently, not only will I refrain from defending views that are claimed to be based exclusively on revelation; I will also refrain from attacking them. The neutrality I will adopt will be two-pronged: I will refrain from "arguing for" as well as from "arguing against." If you ask me regarding a religious position that could only be supported through an appeal to revelation, "Is it true or false?" My response will be, "For the purpose of this course, I have no idea." In other words, views that can be supported exclusively through an appeal to revelation will be presented in accordance with what I call the Fox principle: "I report, you decide."[16] At times, I will explain the arguments that religious people use to support their views; if these arguments involve an appeal to what is claimed to be revealed, however, I will not enter into the question of whether or not they are successful.

Well, this brings us about to the end of today's class meeting. Wait … do not walk out on me yet; there are still several brief matters left. We did not cover much religion yet. The background I gave you,

---

15 Even if the U.S. Supreme Court would have gotten matters right, it appears that religion courses taught from the perspective of a religious persuasion should be offered at public universities only as free electives, and their course titles and/or descriptions should clearly specify that the course is taught from the perspective of a particular religion.

16 This is borrowed from the Fox News Channel slogan: "We report, you decide."

though, is important. It helps you reflect on what type of institution you are studying at. It also might help you reflect on what kind of government you live under.

(IV) CORRECTING YOUR CIVICS TEACHER; IMAGINING HOW BENJAMIN FRANKLIN WOULD COMMENT ON THE CURRENT SITUATION

Allow me to conclude with two additional remarks along these lines:

You may remember from your civics course (if you took one, that is) something like the following remark about the U.S. Constitution: "This country's founders wanted to give stability to the government of the United States; therefore, they made sure that the United States Constitution would be difficult to change. To change that document, it is required that each House of Congress approve of the change by a two-thirds majority; and then, the changes must be submitted to the various states for ratification. The amendments become effective only if three-fourths of the states agree with it[17]—very, very difficult to achieve."

I am telling you: Changing the Constitution is very easy—if you belong to the right group of people, that is. The document can be changed by a one-vote majority of a group on nine unelected officials, aka United States Supreme Court Justices.

This reminds me of the kite guy, Ben Franklin. As you might know, he participated in the drafting of the Constitution. After the work was completed, he left the building in which the Constitutional Convention had met. A lady walked up to him and asked, "What kind of government did you give us?" He replied, "A republic ... if you can keep it."

Suppose he would come back to life and become acquainted with today's situation. I am afraid he would say, "You did not manage to keep the republic. You allowed it to be replaced by a tyranny of judges."

See you next time ...

> Tom got up from his seat. He asked himself, "What's the rest of this course going to be like? It looks as if there is going to be quite a bit of material—and a strict attendance policy! Lots of work for a general education course. But at least the guy is funny. Also, unlike my Sunday school teacher, he is not going to tell me, 'You better believe such-and-such, or else!' Why does the university have those general education requirements, though? Things would be much simpler without them ..."

---

17 See Article V of the U.S. Constitution.

CHAPTER TWO

Interlude

*A Discussion at a Student Party About Astronomy and
Introduction to Philosophy (Not a Part of Any of the Classes)*

I am told that conversations like the following hardly ever—maybe never—take place at URI
student parties, but here it is anyway:

It is the second week of September. A large crowd has assembled at a Narragansett house
jointly rented by several URI seniors. One of the renters yells, "Keep it down, or the police will show
up, arrest some of us, and place a yellow sticker on the door."[1]

Jake, a junior, walks up to Beth, a sophomore. He had seen her in his intermediate business course.
"How is your semester shaping up?" he asks. "So far so good," she replies, and continues, "What I
learned today in my introductory astronomy course is truly amazing. When those astronomers thought
they were well on their way to solving all the problems of the universe, entirely new ones appeared—
and they are at a loss for answers."

"How so?" Jake inquires.

(I) THE AWESOME UNIVERSE

"Well," Beth replies, "first, the amazing stuff: The teacher tried to convey to us the absolutely enormous
size of the universe. I kind of had an inkling of it; but hearing it today made me truly aware of what
'awesome' stands for—in its totally old-fashioned meaning (which we students hardly ever use). I knew,
of course, that, compared to our solar system, our planet earth is nothing but a speck of dust. But if one
sets our huge solar system in relation to the collection of stars of which it is a part, the Milky Way, it

---

1 A "yellow sticker?" What's that? Many URI students live off-campus in the town of Narragansett in rented houses, or
"down the line," as it is called in local lingo. Many of the houses are no strangers to loud and otherwise disruptive parties,
which cause neighbors to call the police. In 2007 the town decided to identify such houses with yellow stickers placed on their
front doors. A $100 fine is charged if the sticker is removed prior to the end of the school year. Although the policy has been
legally challenged with the help of the ACLU, so far, it has been upheld as constitutional.

also turns out to be practically nothing. Just imagine: The closest star is about 4.2 light years away from our sun; the diameter of the entire Milky Way is 100,000 light years, with billions of stars. But even so, it is only one of an unimaginably large number of other galaxies."

"Truly amazing," Jake agrees. "But what are the problems you hinted at?"

Beth continues, "I will get to it. First, though, the teacher mentioned what he called the 'static universe' theory. According to it, the universe simply exists. Even though all of it is moving, maybe it just circles around one point, has done so forever and ever during an infinite past, and will do so forever and ever during an equally infinite future. Albert Einstein tried to come up with a mathematical description of the static universe. He was faced, though, with the problem, 'Why does the force of gravity not pull all the components of the universe together so that they collapse at its center?' To handle this difficulty, he stuck what he called the 'cosmological constant' into his formula, a force counteracting gravity. I could not help but think that this was a bit of cheating—a 'fudge factor';[2] but the static universe theory got shot down, anyway. It was given its death knell when the red shift of light coming from distant galaxies was discovered, showing that the universe is expanding, that its various galaxies are flying away from each other, from one spot at which once, maybe something like 14 billion years ago, the entire stuff the universe contains had been crammed together. God only knows what happened that caused it all to fly apart at breakneck speed."

"I think they call it the 'Big Bang,'" Jake interjects.

"Precisely," Beth replies and continues, "but what caused it? How was it all before that? No one knows. Steve Hawkins—I hope I got his name right; we will have to know it for Quiz #1[3]—says, of course, that there was no 'before'; that the Big Bang marks the beginning of time. That strikes me as very odd. It gets even stranger, though: The Big Bang theory came to be deeply entrenched in astronomy and pretty much supplanted the static universe theory. Astronomers tried to be very logical about their new view. One of the absolutely, positively consistent forces in the universe is, of course, gravity. So astronomers reasoned: There may have been a huge explosion about 14 billion years ago, which caused all the components of the universe to fly apart; but the force hurling them apart is counteracted by gravity. This means that the speed at which the galaxies fly away from each other must diminish; maybe at one point, the motion will even come to a standstill—but only for a moment. Because then, the galaxies will be pulled together again by gravity, and fly back at an ever increasing speed to the point in space where they left after the Big Bang. The collision of all that matter at the center of the universe will once again possibly cause a cataclysmic explosion leading—once again—to a flying apart of all the matter—this would be the next 'Big Bang.' There will be again an expanding universe just like it is now, with a subsequent contraction and another explosion, and so forth, forever and ever—and maybe there have been many 'Big Bangs' in the past—and maybe we do have something similar to the static universe theory in terms of an infinite past and future, only not as 'calm' as the previously posited static universe. But all of this required the assumption that the current expansion of the universe be slowing down. Believe it or not, though: This assumption proved to be wrong! It is not even that the rate of expansion stays the same; no, it is accelerating. This flies totally in the face of common sense, of logic, and of the laws of nature as they are known to date. All astronomy can do for an explanation is

---

2 That's how Richard Panek calls it on p. 60 of his *The 4% Universe—Dark Matter, Dark Energy, and the Race to Discover the Rest of Reality* (Boston/New York: Houghton Mifflin, 2011).

3 She got the name almost right; it is "Stephen Hawking."

come up with what they call 'dark energy'—an <u>unknown force responsible for the acceleration</u>, which, verbally, at least, fits together with 'dark matter,' their explanation of the fact that the force of gravity is stronger than it is supposed to be on account of visible matter (that stronger gravity should, of course, place an even more effective break on the expansion of the universe; but the 'dark energy' is turning its nose up on it). When I left the classroom, all I could do is look at the beautiful blue sky and feel totally overwhelmed by what I had heard about the dimensions of the universe, the mysteries permeating it, the many unsolved riddles it contains, and what seems like our total insignificance within it."

They are silent for a moment.

Then, Jake says, "Interesting—when I left my introduction to philosophy course today, I also did so with strong feelings—and I have not been able to shake them even as of now, although the teacher had predicted that they would go away as fast as they had come."

"How so?" Beth asks.

(II) "ARE YOU WASTING YOUR LIFE?"

Jake replies, "The prof asked us, 'Where do you come from? What are you here for?' He added with a smile, 'Don't get me wrong—I am not asking why you are in this room (the simple answer for most of you is to get general education credits), but why you are on this earth. What—if anything—is your task during this life? What—if anything—is the purpose of human existence?' Then, he added, 'Maybe some of you would tell me that they know; I am pretty sure, though, that most of you would have to say—if you wish to be honest—that you have no idea. I invite the ones who have no idea to consider the following story: Two people are sailing out in Narragansett Bay, each of them in his boat. Suddenly, the weather takes an unexpected turn for the worse. Fog rolls in and the wind picks up. It starts getting dangerous, and each tells himself, "I better get out of here." The fog and the shifting winds make it impossible for them, though, to know the direction of the land. One of them takes his compass out, and together with a map and his recollection of approximately where he is, determines the direction in which he must sail. He does so, although it is difficult. The other does not bother with his map and his compass—they stay in their drawer. He simply sails with the wind. Now, the two sailors' paths cross. The first one yells over to the second, seeing that he is sailing in precisely the wrong direction, "Do you know where you are going?" "I have no idea," the other yells back as he disappears again into the fog.' The teacher paused a bit, then he continued, 'Why did I tell you this? Those among you who must say, "I have no idea what the purpose of human existence is"—are they not like the second sailor in my story?

"'Even for the one who knows what the purpose of human existence is, it may be difficult to live in accordance with it; but what are the odds of living up to it if you do not even know what it is? Isn't it likely, then, that you will totally "blow it"? "Blowing it" … picture a freshman away from home for the first time, interested more in parties than in studying (you probably know some of these characters—I do hope none of them are in this room). When his dad wants to see the son's first report card, all of the grades are big, fat Fs. Isn't it a bad experience to have to stand before your old man and admit that you "blew" your first semester?

"'Perhaps, though, this is nothing compared to having to tell yourself at the end of your life, "I have blown it." Wouldn't this, however, be the likely outcome for the one who does not know what the purpose of human existence is, and who does not even make an effort to find out?' The teacher looked around in the room. Then, he continued, 'I can see on the faces of most of you that I caused you some discomfort. I know human nature, though, so let me tell you: For most of you, this uncomfortable feeling is going to disappear just as fast as it came. As you are going to leave this room, give it five minutes, ten at the most, and the majority of you will be able once again to focus on how to have fun over the weekend, rather than being bothered with actually trying to find a map and a compass to determine the direction your lives should go in.' Then, class was over, and I, belonging to those who have no idea about what the purpose of human existence could be, was feeling deeply uncomfortable—and even up to now, I was not able to get rid of this feeling."

Jake takes a deep breath. Beth smiles at him and said, "Then, you are the exception to what your intro to philosophy teacher said at the end."

"Maybe so," Jake replies.

By now, they are sitting next to each other on a bench at the side of the room, away from the din of the party.

"Oh, hi there, Beth," exclaims a young man, walking over to them.

"Hi, Tom," Beth gives back.

Tom asks, "Did you find an alternative for the math course you want to drop?"

She sighs, "All courses fitting in my schedule are oversubscribed—I think I must stick with math."

Tom suggests, "Why don't you try the religion course that Austrian professor is teaching? He seems like a nice guy; maybe he'll let you in."

"You think so?" Beth asks.

"Just come to class with me tomorrow. It doesn't hurt to try," Tom replies.

Jake inquires, "Do you think he might allow me to sign up late also? I'd love to replace my ancient history course with something else."

"As I said, it doesn't hurt to try," Tom repeats.

The following day, the Austrian professor allowed both Beth and Jake to sign up for his religion course.

Chance had it that the next couple of classes dealt with …

… What do Jews, Christians, and Muslims see as the cause of the universe, and as the purpose of human existence?

CHAPTER THREE

Monotheism

The Core of the Faith of Jews, Christians, and Muslims

THE NATURE OF GOD ACCORDING TO JEWS, CHRISTIANS, AND MUSLIMS

(I) The "source of the universe"

After making several announcements, the professor began "lecturing":

Consider what astronomers tell us about the unimaginable dimensions of the universe, in space as well as in time: A size larger than we can comprehend; a time for its existence too long for us to get a handle on. A number of stars, compared to which even the United States national debt appears negligible.

Where did it all come from? If it all started with the Big Bang, how did it happen? Did all of it spring into being from nothing by itself? With no cause? That defies human reason, does it not? Maybe, though, the Big Bang was not the beginning, and there was a "before"—a "before" preceding the enormous stretch of time since the Big Bang. Did the universe perhaps exist forever? That would seem to escape the illogic of something jumping out of nothing all by itself; but is not an actually infinitely long past also a bit hard to swallow?

Now, think about yourself—something that is, compared to the enormousness of the universe, puny (understatement of the millennium).

Where did you come from? Where are you going? What is your purpose? What are you here for?

If this would be a course falling into the area of my day job (philosophy teacher), I would not only be able to report on answers that various philosophers have formulated, but I would even be allowed to defend my own position with solid reasons.

Given that this is a religion course, and given the strange standing of religion courses at public U.S. universities, all I can do is explain how Judaism, Christianity, and Islam answer these questions.

Remember the Fox principle. What I am going to say next is presented in accordance with it, although I will not always bother repeating that it is so. Thus, you are well advised to remember that principle whenever something I say sounds, if taken out of context, as if I were presenting my own view.

Where does the universe come from? Considering this question leads immediately to the heart of the three religions discussed in this course.

The answer to the "origin of the universe" question can be found in the beginning of the Hebrew Scriptures (called the *Old Testament* by Christians):

"In the beginning, God created the heavens and the earth." This sentence claims that the universe ("heavens and earth") was not always "simply there"; it does have a beginning. It did, however, not "pop" out of nothing all by itself; no, it was called into existence. Its being called into existence was in the beginning: this marked the first moment of time. Not only have the things in time been called into existence, but time itself with them. Similarly, not only have the things in space been called into existence, but space itself with them. Had the universe not been called into existence, there would be, except for the one who called it into existence, absolutely nothing, not even empty space; not even empty time. We do have a hard time thinking of absolutely nothing; usually, we think of it as totally empty space. Empty space is far from being nothing, though: As soon as there is empty space, there is something to which all the laws of geometry actually apply, and those of you who have studied geometry know that this is quite a lot.

As it is, there is not absolutely nothing except for the one about whom it is said: "In the beginning, God created the heavens and the earth"; for God called the universe into being. Everything existing besides him is dependent on him.

(II) Imagining and thinking

This leads, of course, immediately to the question, "Who is the one who created the heavens and the earth? Who is God?"

Right off the bat, it is said about him that he is unimaginable. Many who hear this say, "Well, that's the end of it—if he is unimaginable, nothing can be said about him anymore."

Not so fast: One of the heroes of my day job, the French philosopher René Descartes, pointed out that thinking is different from imagining, and that what cannot be imagined can still be thought about. To demonstrate this, he invites us to imagine first a polygon with 100 sides, known as a hectagon, and then, a polygon with 1,000 sides, known as a chiliagon. In both cases, the mental picture your imagination produces will be the same: A polygon with very many sides. In other words, it is impossible to imagine what makes the two different from each other. Nevertheless, all of us clearly understand (or so I hope) what makes a hectagon different from a chiliagon.

Similarly, although likely, no one can avoid having a "mental picture" when speaking about God, this is not what counts. What counts is what I am inviting you to think about: Someone outside of time, beyond space, someone more powerful than anyone could imagine: He is able to call the universe and everything in it into existence, thus changing the state of "nothing" into "something" (actually, "quite something" if we think once again about the vastness of the universe). Not only did he call the planets, the stars, and the galaxies, together with all that is between them—not only did he call those items into existence, but you and me also, each individual human being.

(III) Creating does go together with sustaining

How do I relate to the one who called the universe into being, including me? To appreciate this fully, it is <u>necessary to think about one often neglected aspect</u> (i.e., side) of God's "calling things into being." Usually, we think about it in terms of an artist creating a work of art, a painting, for example. While the artist works on it, his mind is fully preoccupied with it. Then it is finished. The artist looks at it; perhaps, thinking, "Not bad—not bad at all"; then he puts it to the side, and begins to paint something totally different—another work of art. Applying this thought to God, we think, "God has called me into being 19, 20, 21 years ago (in your case; I am not going to give you even a hint how long ago it was in my case). It was then that he was intensively concerned with me; but now, he has put me to the side, similar to what the artist did with the finished painting, and moved to other things to be called into existence—I am at the back of his mind at best." That latter thought is a frequent misunderstanding. Properly understood, _creating_ includes _sustaining_—<u>keeping in existence</u>.

Think of an image projected on a screen. If the projector is turned off, the image will disappear. The same force that placed the image on the screen in the first place must continuously be applied to keep it there; removing the force will make the image go away.

Similarly, the same power that calls the universe into existence in the first place must keep it in existence. Were God to withdraw this power, the universe would disintegrate into nothingness.

This need for the continuous presence of God's sustaining power does not apply, of course, only to the universe as a whole; it applies—it actually primarily applies—to each and every individual item in the universe, including me, my personality. God called it into existence however many years ago, and now, he keeps it in being. I am not like a work of art the painter put to the side to get on with other matters; no, the same intimate concern with which I was called into existence is present to me at any moment to keep me in existence; otherwise, I would "dissolve" into nothingness. What applies to me in this respect applies also to you and to everyone else who exists.

But there are more than seven billion of us! How can one being simultaneously be intimately concerned with all of them—with each of them even more intimately than a painter is with the work of art he is creating? Well, make that about 80 billion—the number of humans who supposedly existed since humanity began (as will be explained in greater detail later, the religions we are discussing in this course do not consider death the end of the existence of the human personality), and add each and every other item in the universe, including the billions and billions of stars with all their parts. Superficially, one is tempted to ask, "Doesn't this give multitasking a new name?" Less superficially, whenever you think of the one who created the heavens and the earth, you must think of someone outside of space and time—a nonspatial and nontemporal being—who has the power to call each and every individual thing into being and keep it there. This might make one appreciate at least a little what is meant by "almighty," a property ascribed to God.

What was called into existence (or, with respect to what I am going to talk about next, better "made effective") includes, by the way, the laws of nature: He made and sustains material substances such that they exert gravitational forces upon each other; he made and sustains protons and electrons such that they attract each other; he made and sustains electrons such that they repel each other. He also established the so-called "constants" of the universe, and keeps them what they are.

Thus, what you are to think about when you hear the word "God" is rather different from the superficial images the word evokes for many: The bearded guy in heaven, the "old man upstairs."

It is because of him that the universe exists.

But nothing forced him to call the universe into existence. Had he not done so, there would be nothing but him; he is, however, totally self-sufficient, not in need of anything besides him. The universe was not called into existence because he had a need to satisfy.

(IV) What God (supposedly) is like

What is this being like—this being called "God"? If after my explanation, you say, "Impossible to imagine," I would remind you first that I urged you to put your imagination to the side and focus on thinking. If you were to reply, "But it is even hard to think about it," I would tell you, "Jews, Christians, and Muslims would say at this point, 'Join the club.'" Whatever is said about God, it is never possible to "get one's mind around it" (the way you can "get it around" the nature of a square or a pentagon); for us, there always remains darkness; even more darkness than light.

But he is there, keeping everything in existence—or so Jews, Christians, and Muslims assert.

1. The "in God's image" help

Jews and Christians claim, however, that we are given an enormously important help with respect to thinking about God. This assistance comes from the words in Genesis that God created humans in his image. (Gn 1.26–27)

Consider what "being an image" means: Someone shows you a painting of a face. You ask, "Who's that?" He replies, "Your friend Bill, of course." Suppose, however, that there is absolutely no similarity between that image and Bill. You would reply, "Whoever that is, it's not Bill." This makes clear that for something to be truthfully called an image of something else, there must at least be some similarities between the two. Thus, if humans are in the image of God, there must, in spite of all the enormous differences, also be at least some similarities between humans and God. Consequently, thinking about human nature—the image—must give us the one or the other clue about God, in whose image human nature is.

Think about it in terms of the following analogy:

A friend invites you to a party. "I'd love to come; but you must give me directions to your place," you reply. He begins telling you how to get to his house. You are not that good at following directions, and get lost after the second sentence. He starts out again, and you get lost again. After a third fruitless event, he rips a sheet of paper out of his notebook and draws you a little map. Later that day, you use the map as you drive to his house and have no difficulties finding the place. The differences between the scratchings on the piece of paper and the landscape you are to drive through are enormous, far greater than any similarities between the two; if the map is drawn correctly, though, it gives you valuable clues about the "real thing."

Judaism and Christianity claim now that it is similar with human nature and God: Human nature takes the place of the scratchings on the piece of paper; God corresponds to the landscape. Just as looking at the scratchings on the piece of paper gives the person important clues about the landscape, so does considering human nature give important clues about God—because humans are "in the image" of God. We can look at certain features of human nature and say, "God is somehow like that." (The word "somehow" is used to make clear that in this case, wherever there are similarities, there are always differences far greater than the similarities.)

Here are some of the things human nature allows one to recognize about God, as Judaism and Christianity see it:

2. God as a person?

Looking at our nature, we realize about ourselves that, unlike lifeless matter, we do have consciousness. Through it, we are aware of things other than ourselves (our surroundings) and of ourselves. In addition, we do have the ability to make free choices, rather than being determined in everything by forces outside of ourselves.

Thus, the being in whose image we are, the one who called the universe into existence and who keeps it there is "somehow like this": It is true to say of God that he is aware of things other than himself and of himself, and that he is free (the latter manifests itself in that nothing forced him to create the universe, or this universe rather than a different one).

Being aware of things other than oneself and of oneself and having the power to make free choices are the central features of beings who are persons.

Since Judaism, Christianity, and Islam apply these features to God, it is said that these religions believe that God is a person. This makes their "supreme being" different from "Brahman," the "ultimate reality" of Hinduism. In this case, not even an "image relationship" between us humans and "ultimate reality" is assumed; "ultimate reality" is assumed to be in every sense and in all respects totally different from us. Thus, for many Hindus, Brahman even goes beyond the awareness-unawareness distinction; it is neither aware, nor unaware.

3. Trying to "overcome" Muslim hesitancy

It should be noted that Muslims do, perhaps because of their great reluctance to claim knowledge of God's nature, have reservations with regard to calling the God they believe in a person. (They also might be reluctant, by the way, to apply the Genesis image talk to God.)

I remember, however, the following conversation with a Muslim student a number of semesters ago: Following the class in which I had stated that Jews, Christians, and Muslims believe in a God who is a person, he came up to me and said, "We do not believe that God is a person." I asked, "Do you believe that God knows about you (is aware of you), about other humans, and other things in the universe?" "Of course," he replied. I continued, "Do you think that God has self-knowledge?" "How could it be different?" he gave back. "Do you believe that God is free?" I asked. "Naturally," he exclaimed. I stated, "Calling God a person means nothing but saying that these three things are true of him." "OK," he stated, "then we believe that he is a person," and walked away.

Another reason for a reluctance to apply the concept of "person" to God may be that some consider it as meaning pretty much the same as "human." The reason for this is that humans are the only persons known to us from experience. We are, however, *finite human* persons. Since we are the only types of persons known to us from experience, it might easily happen to us that by mistake, we "shift" some of the features that characterize us as *finite* or as *human* into God. This leads to a need of "refining" the "God as a person" understanding.

4. "Refining" the "God as a person" understanding and summary

Jews and Christians (and to some extent Muslims) hold that features characterizing us as persons apply also to God, in a manner of speaking. They also hold, though, that nothing of what defines us as *finite* persons applies to him; equally, nothing that defines us as *human* persons applies to him.

As *finite* persons, we are temporal—beings in time; but God is, as stated earlier, outside of time; time is one of his creations.

As *human* persons, we do have a physical body; God, being even beyond space, does not have a physical body. Human persons are either male or female; the male-female distinction does not apply to God, however. God is neither a man nor a woman—something that is obscured by the fact that the male personal pronoun is traditionally applied to him.

To summarize: Jews, Christians, and Muslims believe in a God who is the creator and sustainer of the universe, who knows everything (who is omniscient), including our most secret thoughts (after all, our minds, what does the thinking in them, as well as the thoughts themselves must be kept in existence by him). God is almighty in the sense that he can do everything that is logically and metaphysically possible; he is just, and he is a person in the sense explained earlier.

5. How do we know about God according to Jews, Christians, and Muslims?

There are the following two additional questions:

First, how do we know about God? Second, precisely how does he relate to humans—besides having created them, and keeping them in existence?

First, the "knowledge question":

My day job contains a field called "metaphysics." One of the questions discussed there is, "Does God exist? Can we even know an answer to that question?" Many philosophers claim that it is possible for us to know through human thinking, through our own reason, that God exists. They claim that there are "proofs of God's existence." These proofs are, however, rather complicated and involved—they are not for "simple-minded people" (at least in one sense of "simple-minded").

Judaism, Christianity, and Islam claim, however, that God has come to the assistance of human reason by telling us that he exists and what he is like (to the tiny extent to which we can follow such an explanation). He also supposedly has told us "what he wants from us."

Thus, according to these three religions, humans do not have to rely on their weak reason with regard to knowing about God. Their knowledge about God comes from what is called "revelation" (remember: literally a "removing of the veil" so that one can see what is hidden behind it); in its nonliteral meaning, it is "information provided by God to humans" (a message given to humans by God).

Thus, Judaism, Christianity, and Islam claim to be based on revelation. (I do hope you remember that I talked about this during the first class meeting already.) The information supposedly coming from God is not limited to his existence and his nature, but includes many other matters—the final destiny of humans, for example. Also, this information does not always directly come from God; at times, it comes through persons functioning as his agents. It supposedly was direct when God spoke to Moses out of a burning bush (Ex 3.4–23); it was through an agent when Gabriel announced the birth of Jesus to Mary (Lk 1.26–38) or when, as Muslims claim, the same angel recited the Holy Book of Islam, the Qur'an, to Muhammad.

Thus, how do we know the things about God that I told you?

Remember: I must say, in light of the Fox principle, "For the purpose of this course, I have no idea what can be known and how it can be known"; Jews, Christians, and Muslims would say, however, that we know it through revelation.

CHAPTER FOUR

The Relationship Between God and Humans

(I) DOING GOD'S WILL?

What does revelation say about the relationship between God and Humans?

Humanity does <u>have</u> a <u>definite beginning</u>—it began with Adam. Each and every individual human being also does have a definite beginning. While many contemporary nonreligious people believe that each and every individual human being also does have a definite end—at the moment of death, Jews, Christians, and Muslims disagree. For them, death is not the end of the human personality; rather, it is through death that one finally and definitely is enabled to enter into the very relationship with God for which one has been created in the first place, for which this life is supposed to be something like a "practice," a "preparation."

This leads us on to the "purpose of human existence" point. What have humans been created for? For entering into a relationship with God. What kind of a relationship?

Some of you might respond, remembering what you have heard in religion courses not taught according to the Fox principle, "We are to do God's will," and some of you might add, "That means, for the most part at least, not doing things we would like to do, and doing things that are hard or boring."

Judaism, Christianity, and Islam might respond, "True, we are to do God's will; but he does not want us to obey his commands in a legalistic manner. God's will is that we enter into an intimate, close relationship with him—that our hearts respond appropriately to him in view of who he is, but also in view of the intimate and close relationship he has toward us. True, doing his will in the sense of obeying his commands, even when it is hard to do so, is a part of it—it is the 'training' for responding as we are supposed to; but it is not the 'heart of the matter.'"

(II) HOW DOES GOD RELATE TO HUMANS?

What, then, is the "heart of the matter?"

Judaism and Christianity would once again take recourse to the "it is somehow like this" argument—remember the thought of humans being in the image of God. They would call attention to a relationship among humans we are familiar with and say, "God relates to us 'somewhat like this' already now; and we are to respond in kind."

What is that relationship?

Jews and Christians might tell you, "Read the book (part) of the Bible called 'Song of Songs' (or 'Song of Solomon' or 'Canticle of Canticles')—this might give you a clue about how the relationship between God and humans is to be."

Following this advice might initially confuse you, for that book is a poem describing a passionate love between a man and a woman, a man and a woman who are, as someone lacking the proper understanding of this kind of relationship would say, "madly in love" with one another, "just plain crazy" about each other. How is this to help?

Jews and Christians would say, prefacing their explanation with a reminder that wherever God is similar to humans, there are even greater differences, "God's relationship to each individual human being is, of course, totally different from all relationships between humans known to us; but the human relationship coming closest to the way he relates to us is that of a man to a woman with whom he is 'madly in love.'"

"Come again?"

"Yes, that's how it is."

"You mean to tell me that God is 'in love' with me?"

"That's what Judaism and Christianity would say; although they would add the, 'in a manner of speaking' qualification."

The "Song of Songs" is to give us an inkling of how God relates to each and every human being—with a love characterized by an intensity going beyond anything we can imagine; and of all human experiences, the love of a man for a woman with whom he is in love is most similar to this love. Muslims might be a bit squeamish about that comparison; but that God loves humans, they would agree with.[1]

(III) HOW HUMANS ARE TO RELATE TO GOD

1. How it should be, and how it really is

This might help us understand what Jews, Christians, and Muslims believe about the purpose of human existence. In prosaic terms, we exist "to do the will of God." To get at the non-prosaic side: What does a man wish of a woman with whom he is in love? Why, for her to love him back, of course—to love him more than anyone else.

---

1 "Surely Allah loves those who turn much (to him) and loves those who purify themselves" (Qur'an 2.222, based on Ali). "Yes, whoever fulfills his promise and keeps his duty—then Allah surely loves the dutiful" (Qur'an 3.76, based on Ali).

What, then, does God want, given how he relates to us?

If you say, "for us to love him back," you got it.

But given the nature of the love with which he loves us, try to understand what "He wants us to love him back," really includes: That you love him back with a love that compares favorably in intensity and intimacy with the love a woman has for a man with whom she is in love.

That's how your love for God is to be.

So I invite those among you who happen to be religious to compare their actual relationship to God with how it is supposed to be, according to the religions this course deals with. Does the intensity and intimacy of your relationship to the God you believe in compare favorably to the intensity and intimacy that exist between persons in love with each other? If LOL ever was a proper response to a question, it likely is so at this point. I am sure that many in this room who believe in God must admit that their relationship to God hardly even deserves to be called love; those bold enough to say, "I do love God," will probably have to add, "But in intensity and intimacy, it falls far short of what exists between a man and a woman in love with one another."

This makes us "stumble" from considering the purpose of human existence to our task on earth—at least according to Judaism, Christianity and Islam.

First, to repeat, the purpose for which we have been created is to experience an intensive and intimate love relationship with God, and to be forever happy in this experience. Our task is related to the realization that love is a two-way street. This love exists already from the side of God. But what is there from your side leaves a lot to be desired—and that is once again the "understatement of the millennium." Thus, your task is learning to requite God's love; changing yourself into a person who truly loves God back—this is your task during this life, according to Judaism, Christianity, and Islam.

This task is spelled out in a passage of the Jewish Holy Scriptures, considered by many Jews as the most important part of their Bible—a passage known as the "Shema Israel," two words meaning, "Hear O Israel." The passage derives its name from the first two words of the Hebrew version of the passage:

> Hear O Israel, The Lord our God, The Lord is One! **Therefore, you shall love the Lord, your God, with all your heart, and with all your soul, and with all your strength.** Take to heart these words which I enjoin on you today. Drill them into your children. Speak of them at home and abroad, whether you are busy or at rest. Bind them at your wrist as a sign, and let them be as a pendant on your forehead. Write them on the doorposts of your houses and on your gates. (Dt 6:4–9)

2. How to get oneself to accomplish the goal of human existence

Love is an emotion, a feeling, a response of the heart. There is hardly anything concerning which there is more confusion today than about emotions and feelings. If this would be one of my day job courses, I would now go into many details concerning a clarification of the nature of "feelings" as one can find them in the philosophical writings of one of my heroes, Dietrich von Hildebrand.

For the purpose of this course, I must confine myself to some essentials, and mention first the fickleness of the human heart; how difficult it is for us to respond with the appropriate emotions to the persons, things, and events around us.

Here are some examples:

Imagine meeting someone who is even better than you in an area in which you excel (sports, mathematics, playing an instrument, whatever—fill in what corresponds to your situation). What *should* your heart's response be? Isn't it admiration, being happy for that person? How does your heart *actually* respond, though, in many such cases? Isn't it with envy, jealousy, and resentment—maybe even hatred?

Or think of Irving who is looking forward to a baseball game on TV. There are some holdups at work, though, and he leaves later than usual. A glance at his watch lets him know, "If I drive fast, I will be home when the game starts." He steps on the gas, hoping that no cops will be lurking by the side of the road.

On the interstate, there is a traffic tie-up. He gets angry as it becomes clear that he will miss the beginning of the game. Now, several emergency vehicles, including three ambulances, make their way past the traffic on the shoulder of the road, and Irving must squeeze to the left.

"All of this will take forever," he curses.

Three ambulances—does that not tell Irving that something terrible must have happened a couple of hundred yards ahead of where he is? Several people must have been injured; maybe there was even loss of life!

Compare missing part of a ballgame—or even all of it—with several people being involved in a serious accident. What is worse? Isn't it clear that the first one does not even deserve to be mentioned in comparison to the second?

If Irving's heart was "in the right place," would he not be full of compassion for the people who must be suffering very much through what seems to be a serious accident? Instead, all his heart manages is anger about being made late for a ballgame.

Also, often, when our heart *should* respond in a certain way, it seems to be dominated by the "who cares" attitude. Think about the many cases in which you remained unmoved when you learned about other people's misfortunes, including those of acquaintances, relatives, even friends.

With regard to God, the "my heart is unmoved" phenomenon is especially frequent.

What to do? If my heart is unmoved, it does not help for me to decide, "Be moved"; my heart is not under the direct control of my will. It is, however, not entirely removed from that control either: My will does have some indirect influence over it. Think of people in poverty. Appropriately, we should feel compassion for them; but actually, our hearts may be cold. However, what if we acted toward them *as if* we had compassion with them; that is, if we actually were to go out of our way to help them when we can? We might then notice that slowly—ever so slowly—our hearts would limp after our will; and over time, something like a genuine feeling of compassion might develop.

This also works with regard to other matters; Judaism, Christianity, and Islam claim that it also works with regard to God.

Tell your will to make the kinds of decisions you would make if you would love God, admitting to yourself (and to others, if indicated) that actually, your heart is cold (otherwise, you would be a hypocrite); and slowly, over time, your heart's coldness will diminish, and maybe even genuine love for God will develop.

That's where doing God's will comes into the picture.

Remember: To move ourselves into the direction of loving God, we must act "as if" we loved God.

Think about a man at work who has a task he dislikes. Whenever he can skip it without his boss noticing, he skips it; whenever he must do it, he does it with inner resentment. One day, he finds out, however, that the woman he loves finds it important for him to carry that task out. From now on, he will never skip it again and will even do it with joy, knowing that it will make his beloved happy. Generally, if a person loves someone else, he or she will do what the other person wants him or her to do.

Remember: The person whose heart is cold with regard to God is to act as if he or she loved God—which means, as the example shows, doing what God wants him to do, or, expressed in a more formal way, "doing God's will."

Doing God's will is, for the cold-hearted person, the surest way to learn loving God.

What does doing God's will involve?

Jews reply, "Follow the law as stated in the Torah." (Details will be provided when we get to Judaism. Then, we will also see that the chief groups of Judaism differ from each other with regard to the laws of the Torah they continue to find mandatory.)

Christians state, "Follow the moral laws stated in the Torah as interpreted and amplified by Jesus." (Again, details will be provided in the Christianity segment.)

Muslims would say, "You must carry out the duties spelled out in the Qur'an; especially important are those known as the 'Five Pillars of Islam.'" (Their nature will be explained in the Islam segment.)

Let me end today's class with a real question and an answer that is, in light of the importance of the question, rather awkward—but we are "stuck" with that answer, given the role of religion at secular schools in the United States:

Question: Does God exist? (Given what we have gone over, can you think of a question more important than that one?)

Answer: "Not for me to say as a part of this course."

Tom, Beth, and Jake left the auditorium together. Tom remarked, "The kind of God he talked about in there is very different from what I got out of my Sunday school class. I was made to think about him more as someone 'out to get me' rather than someone … someone who …" Beth asked, "Someone who loves you?" "Precisely," Tom replied. Beth said, "Wouldn't it be awesome if such a God really existed?" "Kind of," Jake said. "'Kind of?' Only 'kind of?' What do you mean?" Jake did not reply. "Do you think he exists?" Beth asked. "Do you?"

CHAPTER FIVE

The Faith of the Jews

From the Beginning of Judaism to A.D. *136*

(I) ABRAHAM

For most of the existence of the Jewish religion and in many quarters today, Judaism concerned itself chiefly with a small segment of humanity, a people special to God, selected by him from all other nations. That people descended from Abraham, born in the 20th or 19th century B.C. The descent is traced over Isaac (whose mother was Sarah), Abraham's younger son, and his grandson Jacob. They were called Hebrews, until after the Babylonian Captivity (see below) only by other nations, possibly meaning "Those who crossed over" (Haran, where Abraham had lived for many years, is, from the perspective of Canaan, where he settled later in his life, on the other side of the Euphrates River). They were also called Israelites, derived from "Israel," a name given to Abraham's grandson Jacob after he had wrestled for a whole night with an angel representing God—the name might mean, "The one who struggled with God and man." Today, they are called "Jews," a word derived from Judah, the name of one of the 12 tribes of the Israelites, one of only 3 tribes that continued to exist after the destruction of the (northern) Kingdom of Israel (see below). The other two tribes are Levi and Benjamin.

Abraham, originally named Abram (I will use this shorter name until I get to the change—very soon), was born in a town called Ur (the Bible refers to it as "Ur of the Chaldeans"—Gn 11.31), situated in what is today southern Iraq. His father, Terah, took Abram, his wife Sarai (later named Sarah) and some other relatives, including his nephew Lot, out of Ur. They intended to travel to Canaan (the biblical name for Palestine, the region in which parts of the contemporary countries Israel and Jordan are located), but settled in Haran, a town in what is today southeastern Turkey, not far from the present-day town of Sanliurfa.

After Terah had died, God told Abram to journey to their original destination, promising that he would make him the father of a great nation, and that all nations on earth would be blessed in him (Gn 12.1–3).

Abram and his relatives left Haran and settled in Canaan. Although God had promised that a large nation would stem from Abram, his wife Sarai was childless and old. Thus, she suggested that Abram have intercourse with Hagar, according to Genesis, an Egyptian maidservant of theirs (Gn 16.1). Hagar bore Abram a son, who was named Ishmael. About 13 years later, God made a new agreement with Abram in the course of which he changed his name to "Abraham." He gave Abraham and his descendants the land of Canaan as a permanent possession. He commanded circumcision to be the outward sign of the covenant he had entered into with Abraham and his descendants. He also promised that Sarai, whose name was to be changed to "Sarah" (both "Sarai" and "Sarah" mean "princess"), would bear Abraham a son. This promise caused Abraham to laugh within himself because of Sarah's and his own advanced age; he asked that God might bless Ishmael. He was not ready to believe that he would actually have a son with Sarah. God straightened him out, however, and affirmed once more that Sarah would have a son, to be named Isaac. While Ishmael would have many descendants, including 12 princes, God states about Isaac, "But my covenant I will maintain with Isaac, whom Sarah shall bear to you by this time next year." (Gn 17.21)[1]

The following year, Sarah gave birth to a son to whom the name Isaac was given, as God had commanded.

(II) ISAAC, JACOB AND HIS 12 SONS—TO EGYPT

Isaac had two sons, Jacob and Esau. As noted earlier, Jacob was later in his life given a second name, Israel. He had 12 sons. They are the ancestors of the 12 tribes, or clans, of the Israelites. Joseph, one of Jacob's sons, was his father's favorite. This caused his brothers to be jealous of him. Once, when they were pasturing their father's sheep, the father sent Joseph, who was not required to be with the sheep, to inquire how his brothers were doing, and bring a report back to Jacob. When their brothers saw Joseph (whom they resented), they decided to kill him; but their brother Reuben suggested that they throw him into a dried-out cistern, from where he intended to save him later. They followed Reuben's

---

1 Looking ahead to Islam, this is a difficult passage for Muslims. As we will see, they trace the lineage of Arabs back to Abraham over his older son Ishmael (as becomes clear from what is written in the text, Jews trace their lineage back to Abraham over Isaac). This in itself is not the difficulty I am referring to. Rather, the difficulty emerges when one realizes the Muslim claim that the covenant God made with Abraham did not include the descendants of Isaac, but those of Ishmael. In Maulana Muhammad Ali's *The Holy Qur'an with English Translation and Commentary*, there is a lengthy footnote arguing this point, presenting as a chief consideration that a covenant is made with Abraham and his descendants prior to any mentioning of the birth of Isaac, where the covenant actually could go either way—even Abraham first understood it that way, doubting the promise that Sarah would have a son, as made evident by the text paragraph to which this footnote is appended. Ali also presents several subsidiary arguments in support of the Muslim view. I was curious what he would say about the passage quoted above which is quite explicit in identifying Isaac's rather than Ishmael's descendants as those with whom the covenant is being entered. Well, Ali does not mention the passage, even though he mentions several others from the same chapter, including the verse immediately preceding the one quoted above. He might, of course, simply apply to Gn 17.21 what is done by Muslims in many other cases in which the Qur'an's understanding of Judaism is in conflict with the Jewish Holy Scriptures: That in their original version, these Scriptures conformed to the Qur'an, and that whatever is in conflict with the Muslim understanding is due to changes made by copyists of these Scriptures. In this case, that type of consideration would, however, weaken Ali's own argument; for if Gn 17 is unreliable with regard to that one verse, what does give him the confidence to rely on the verses he needs to make his case? (Incidentally, Ali's commentary to which this footnote applies concerns Surah 2.124 and appears on pp. 56–57 of his Qur'an edition.)

suggestion. A short while later, Midianite traders came by, on their way to Egypt. Judah, another of the brothers, proposed that Joseph be sold to them. They followed that suggestion, and told Jacob that a wild animal must have killed Joseph.

Thus, Joseph came to Egypt and became the slave of a certain Potiphar. His master's wife tried to seduce him; but he resisted, and she claimed that he had attempted to rape her. Consequently, her husband had him thrown in prison. There, he correctly interpreted the dreams of two of his fellow inmates, both of whom were servants of the pharaoh (title of the king of Egypt). After one of them had been allowed once again to return to his position, the pharaoh had a dream that disturbed him very much. The servant remembered Joseph's correct interpretation of his own dream, and told the pharaoh about it. Joseph was brought from prison, and his interpretation of the pharaoh's dream impressed the latter so much that Joseph was not only set free from jail, but appointed as a high government official.

Joseph had stated that the king's dream predicted seven years of plenty and seven years of famine. As a government official, he saw to it that during the years of plenty, enough provisions were set aside for the lean years.

The lean years were not limited to Egypt, but also affected Canaan. Jacob and his sons heard that there was enough food in Egypt. So the sons decided to travel there to see whether they would be able to buy some. They were led to the government official, Joseph, their brother. They did not recognize him; he, however, knew right away who they were. To make a long story short, he tested whether they had changed; the test turned out positive; he forgave them and identified himself to them. They moved with their father and their families to Egypt to settle there; at the time, they numbered, according to Ex 1.5, about 70 persons.

Some generations later—the 70 had multiplied into a large people—when the Egyptians had forgotten about Joseph, they became concerned about the foreigners living in their land, enslaved them, and the pharaoh ordered that all their male children born be killed; only the girls were allowed to live.

(III) MOSES, THE EXODUS, THE GIVING OF THE LAW, AND 40 DESERT YEARS

The pharaoh's daughter, however, adopted the Hebrew child Moses as a child of her own, saving his life, and raising him. When he had become a young man, he witnessed an Egyptian abusing one of his Hebrew kinsmen. Moses came to his countryman's defense and killed the Egyptian. The matter became known, though, even to the pharaoh, so Moses fled Egypt and went to Midian, east of the Sinai Peninsula, across the Gulf of Aqaba. There, he married a local woman. After what the Book of Exodus calls "a long time" (Ex 2.23), when he was tending the sheep of his father-in-law, God spoke to Moses from a burning bush, ordering him to go back to Egypt to lead his people out of slavery.

Moses returned to Egypt, but the pharaoh—a successor of the one who had been in power when Moses had fled—had no intention of letting the Hebrews go, not even after God had struck Egypt with nine plagues. It was only after the tenth plague that he relented. It involved the death of the firstborn of each Egyptian family. At the twilight of the evening before that plague was to strike, the Israelites were to slaughter an unblemished lamb and roast its meat, to be consumed. Some of the lamb's blood was to be applied to the doorpost and the lintel of each house in which an Israelite lived as a sign to the angel of death so that he might "pass over" that house and not kill the firstborn in it. For Jews, this is the origin of the Passover Feast.

Now, the Israelites were allowed to leave Egypt—according to Ex 12.40, this was about 430 years after Jacob, his sons, and their families had settled there. A little while later, though, the pharaoh regretted that he had allowed his cheap labor to leave the land, and pursued them. His troops caught up with them at the Red Sea. God divided the Red Sea for the Israelites, however, and they escaped through it. When the Egyptians pursued them, the water flowed back, and the pursuers were drowned. The Israelites were now safe from the Egyptians.

During the third month after they had left Egypt, they reached Mount Sinai, and it is there that God gave the law to the Jewish people, including the Ten Commandments.

Since the Ten Commandments are of crucial importance for Judaism as well as Christianity (Rabbi Joseph Telushkin calls them "the cornerstone document of Jewish and Western morality"[2]), I am including them here as Telushkin states and summarizes them (the relevant Bible passages are Ex 20.2-14 and Dt 5.6-18):

> (1) I am the Lord your God who brought you out of the land of Egypt, the house of bondage. (2) You shall have no other gods besides Me. [You shall not make any graven images.[3]] (3) You shall not carry [take][4] the Lord your God's name in vain. (4) Remember the Sabbath day to make it holy. (5) Honor your father and mother. (6) You shall not murder. (7) You shall not commit adultery. (8) You shall not steal. (9) You shall not bear false witness against your neighbor. (10) You shall not covet your neighbor's house; you shall not covet your neighbor's wife, or … anything that is your neighbor's.[5]

Telushkin points out that (1) is a statement, not a commandment, and continues, "That is probably why, in Hebrew, these words are called … the Ten Statements, and not … the Ten Commandments."[6]

Looking ahead to Christianity: Just like Jews, Christians consider the Ten Commandments fundamental for human conduct. There are, however, differences between the manner in which various religious groups combine the commandments into 10: Catholics and Lutherans consider the first commandment to be, "I am the Lord your God … you shall not have other Gods besides me … You shall not

---

2 Joseph Telushkin, *Jewish Literacy—The Most Important Things to Know About the Jewish Religion, Its People, and Its History* [henceforth referred to as Telushkin, *Literacy*"] (New York: William Morrow and Company, 1991), p. 55.

3 This is not included in Telushkin's summary, but in the Bible text he summarizes; I am including it here in anticipation of the manner in which Christians organize the commandments.

4 Telushkin insists on the translation, "You shall not *carry* the Lord your God's name in vain," interpreting the commandment as chiefly meaning that one is not to use God as a justification in selfish causes. Usually, however (as Telushkin also observes), the translation is, "You shall not *take* the Lord your God's name in vain," meaning that one is not to use the word "God" in trivial contexts.

5 Telushkin, *Literacy*, p. 55.

6 Telushkin, *Literacy*, pp. 55-56.

make any graven images," that is, they combine what are the first two commandment (or "statement") according to the Jewish understanding into one. They still end up with ten commandments, though, because they separate what is (10) in the quotation from Telushkin into two commandments: "(9) You shall not covet your neighbor's wife; (10) You shall not covet your neighbor's goods." Most Protestants and Eastern Orthodox Christians consider the first commandment to be "I am the Lord your God who brought you out of the land of Egypt, the house of bondage. You shall have no other gods besides Me," and the second, "You shall not make any graven images." Then, they follow the manner in which Telushkin presents the commandments.

Concerning the Fourth Commandment (the Third according to the Catholic and Lutheran count), it also should be mentioned that most Christians consider the day to be kept holy to be Sunday rather than Saturday.

After the Ten Commandments had been given to the Israelites, they continued their journey towards Canaan, the land that God had given to Abraham and his descendants through Isaac. When they arrived at the borders of the region they were to occupy, they sent spies who returned with frightening reports about the size and strength of the people living there. So the people became furious with Moses, complained about having been led out of Egypt, and instead of trusting that God would help them as he had done in the past, they lost confidence in him. Thus, God did not allow the people who had left Egypt to enter the Promised Land, except for the children. As far as the rest were concerned, they had to wander in the desert for 40 years, until all of them had died. It was only then that God allowed the Jewish people into Canaan.

(IV) SETTLING THE PROMISED LAND; THE PERIOD OF THE JUDGES; THE UNIFIED KINGDOM; AND THE DIVIDED KINGDOM

The Jews occupied Canaan under Joshua's leadership. The area was divided among the tribes of Israel, except for the tribe of Levi, whose male members were responsible for the worship services; no land was assigned to them. They were to be supported by the members of the remaining tribes. If, however, one looks at a map of Israel representing that time, one finds 12 names associated with areas. Two of them are Ephraim and Manasseh, the descendants of Joseph's two sons. At times, they are referred to as "half-tribes."

For a little over two centuries, these tribes lived as a loose association without a formal centralized authority. At times, leadership (moral, not formal) was exercised by impressive personalities called judges. The most popular among them was perhaps Samson; the final one was Samuel. When Samuel was judge, the Israelites began clamoring for a king. Samuel was skeptical of the idea, but in the end, he acceded and anointed Saul as king. Saul's successor was David (although he had to fight for several years until he became acknowledged as king of all of the Israelites). Under him, Jerusalem was conquered—until that time, it had been a holdout of a non-Jewish people, the Jebusites. David made that town into the capital of the kingdom. David's successor was Solomon. Under him, the unified kingdom reached its largest extension and the climax of its power. Solomon also had the first temple in Jerusalem built, around 950 B.C.

After him, the rivalry between the Jewish tribes, which had caused difficulties for David at the beginning of his reign, caused a permanent break-up of the Jewish nation into two kingdoms. In the north was the kingdom of Israel,[7] with its capital Samaria; in the south was Judah, with its capital Jerusalem. The border between the two kingdoms was about ten miles north of Jerusalem.

The kingdom of Israel, the northern kingdom, was destroyed in 722 B.C. by the Assyrians.[8] It comprised ten of the 12 tribes of the Jews. Its destruction gave rise to various legends about the "ten lost tribes of Israel," although the Second Book of Kings of the Jewish Holy Scriptures (17.6) states that the people were "deported to Assyria." Many of the lower-class people presumably stayed behind, and over time, mingled with pagan peoples the Assyrians settled in the area. The Samaritans descended from that amalgamation. From the perspective of Judaism, their religion is a mixture of the Jewish faith and paganism.

(V) THE BABYLONIAN CAPTIVITY; RETURN OF THE CAPTIVES; EZRA AND NEHEMIAH

Jerusalem, the capital of the southern kingdom, was destroyed in 586 B.C. by the Babylonians, and the members of higher classes of people were deported to Babylon (located in what is today the area of southern Iraq). The temple built under Solomon was destroyed with the destruction of Jerusalem.

In 539 B.C. the Persians[9] conquered Babylonia. Unlike the Babylonians, who had deported the Jewish elite from Jerusalem, Cyrus, king of Persia, allowed conquered peoples to stay in their own territory. In keeping with this, he gave the Jews living in and around Babylon the option to return to their ancestral home. While many remained in Babylon, a sizable number returned, and "reestablished a Jewish state under Persian rule."[10]

In 516 B.C. the Jerusalem Temple was rebuilt.

Important Jewish leaders falling into that time period are Ezra and Nehemiah. Ezra spoke out against intermarriage between Jews and non-Jews, occurring so frequently that, if it would not have been checked, it might have led to a complete assimilation of Jews to other peoples. Nehemiah made Jerusalem once again into a fortified city, by seeing to it that defensive walls were built around it.

---

7 When I use the expression "Israel" or "people of Israel," I refer to the Jewish people as a whole; for the northern kingdom, I will use the expression, "kingdom of Israel."

8 Assyria was an ancient kingdom centered in the northern and middle part of Mesopotamia (the area between the Euphrates River and the Tigris River). The country has a history going back as far as the third millennium B.C. For our context, the period beginning with the ninth century B.C. is of special importance, when Assyria expanded into a large empire. In 612, the town Nineveh, which was then its capital, was destroyed, and Assyria was conquered by the Babylonians with the Medes as their allies.

9 The center of Persia was situated in what is present-day Iran.

10 Telushkin, *Literacy*, p. 110.

(VI) ALEXANDER THE GREAT, THE PTOLEMIES, THE SELEUCIDS, THE MACCABEES, HEROD THE GREAT, AND THE ROMAN EMPIRE

General history's next important leader was Alexander the Great (he lived from 356 to 323 B.C.). He succeeded his father as king of Macedonia[11] (336 B.C.). In a short time, he established a vast empire that included much of the Asian continent. By 330 B.C. he had defeated the Persian Empire. Thus, the area around Jerusalem turned from a province of Persia into a part of Alexander's empire.

Following Alexander's death, his "officials took over his kingdom, each in his own territory, and … they all put on royal crowns" (1 Macc 1.8–9). Alexander's empire was divided into several kingdoms. One of them was that of the Ptolemies, centered in Egypt. They dominated the area around Jerusalem until 198 B.C. Another was that of the Seleucids, who ruled ancient Syria[12] (called here "ancient Syria" to distinguish it from the contemporary state Syria). They began controlling the area around Jerusalem in 198 B.C. The Seleucid king Antiochus Epiphanes (ruled 175–162 B.C.) instigated cruel persecutions of the Jews, attempting to force them to accept Pagan practices.

Under the Maccabees[13] the Jews staged an uprising, which finally was successful in 142 B.C. In that year, the Jews achieved, for the final time prior to the founding of the contemporary state of Israel, political independence, at least for a part of the area they consider as their ancestral home, shaking off domination by the Syrians. This was to last, however, only until 63 B.C. In that year, a civil war broke out among the Jews between a faction led by Hyrcanus II and one led by his younger brother, Aristobolus, concerning who should rule the region. The brothers invited Pompey, the Roman general who was in the process of expanding Roman rule to ancient Syria, to mediate their dispute. He arrived with a Roman army, occupied Jerusalem, and decided in favor of Hyrcanus II, whose rule was from now on dependent on Roman support, making the area around Jerusalem, in effect, beholden to the Roman Empire and dependent on it.

A little later, the Herod Dynasty came to power, with Roman help. The clan stemmed from Idumea, located south of the area around Jerusalem, and was not of Jewish origin. Rather, during the end of the second century B.C., the Jews—following the Maccabean revolt, free from foreign domination for the last time in their history prior to the founding of the state of Israel—had subjugated the Idumeans and compelled them to live as Jews. In 37 B.C., Rome appointed Herod, known in history as "Herod the Great," to be king of Judaea. He ruled until 4 B.C. He tried to curry favor with the Jews by enlarging the Jerusalem Temple in a magnificent way. He was unspeakably cruel, ordering, among other executions, that of his first wife's grandfather, of her brother, of herself, her mother, and three of his sons; the latter supposedly made the Roman emperor Augustus exclaim, "It is better to be Herod's pig than his son." (In the Greek language, which Augustus is said to have used for this utterance, the word for "pig" sounds very similar to that for "son.") Herod wished his kingdom to be divided among three of his remaining sons: Archelaus was to rule the southern part, including Jerusalem, Herod Antipas was

---

11 Today, a country north of Greece is called "Macedonia," as is the northernmost province of Greece.
12 Ancient Syria included much of the territory that Assyria had once controlled.
13 These uprisings are described in detail in the two Books of Maccabees, which form a part of the Catholic Old Testament. They are, however, not included in the Jewish Holy Scriptures or the Protestant Old Testament.

to rule Galilee, and Philip was to rule the area east of Galilee. Following Herod's death, the Romans acceded to this wish.

Archelaus was removed from his position by the Roman emperor Augustus in A.D. 6, pursuant to many complaints about his rule received from the Jews, and the area he had governed was turned into a Roman province, headed by a procurator (governor). The most well-known of them is Pontius Pilate. He ruled the area from about A.D. 26 to about A.D. 37, and was the fifth person in this office. He was the one who sentenced Jesus to death.

The year A.D. 66 marks the beginning of a Jewish revolt against the Roman occupation force. In response, the Romans first devastated Galilee; then they laid siege to Jerusalem; after having taken it under the leadership of General Titus (nine years later, he became Roman emperor), they destroyed it completely, including the Temple, in A.D. 70.

In 132 the Jews living in Judaea staged another revolt under Bar-Kokhba, who was at the time regarded by some as the Messiah. Although over the course of this rebellion, heavy casualties were inflicted on the Roman army, the revolt was finally put down in 135 after large numbers of Jews had been killed. Joseph Telushkin writes about the Bar-Kokhba revolt and the earlier revolt leading to the destruction of Jerusalem and the Temple, that in the opinion of many Jewish historians, they are "the greatest catastrophe to befall the Jewish people prior to the Holocaust."[14]

Following the Bar-Kokhba rebellion, in 136 the Roman emperor Hadrian ordered the ruins of Jerusalem to be razed to the ground. He had a Roman city, called Aelia Capitolina, built over these ruins; Jews were forbidden from entering the area, and non-Jews were settled there.

---

14 Telushkin, *Literacy*, p. 146.

CHAPTER SIX

A Jump Across Many Centuries (and the Big Pond)

Next, we must jump across many centuries and the "Big Pond" (aka the "Atlantic Ocean"): I am going to tell you about the history of Judaism in the United States.

(I) BACKGROUND

Prior to considering how Judaism came to this country, some background information must be filled in, including items concerning secular history.[1]

During the Babylonian Captivity already, Jews had settled in many places of the then-known world outside of Palestine. After the destruction of Jerusalem by the Romans, and especially after the Roman emperor Hadrian had ordered Aelia Capitolina to be built over the ruins of Jerusalem, issuing an order that Jews were never again to be permitted to enter that town, the dispersion of Jews into various parts of the world intensified.

The first arrival of a Jewish community in North America relates to an event in Spain that occurred in 1492, the same year in which Columbus arrived at these shores. In the very same month that Columbus was commissioned to "discover the Indies," King Ferdinand and Queen Isabella of Spain issued an edict telling the sizable population of Jews living in their domain that they either had to become Christians or leave. The Jews were given four months to comply with that edict.

Many of them decided to leave. They were allowed to take their property with them; but those among them who owned land had to sell it in haste, far below the actual value. Thousands of them died

---

1 If I would be uncharitable to the American educational system, I would say that all of you should have been made familiar with the secular history items during your high school years. As it is, I am keeping my mouth shut—except for saying that similar comments would have been in order at many points in the previous segment.

during the flight. They settled in various parts of North Africa, Western Asia, and Europe, including in Italy, joining a Jewish community south of Rome. They did so with the explicit permission of Pope Alexander VI, which shows that Spain did not have the leadership of the Catholic Church on its side when expelling the Jews.

Other Jews sincerely converted to Catholicism.

For our context, a third group of Jews is particularly important: Those who pretended outwardly to convert, but in their hearts, they stayed true to the Jewish faith. They participated in Catholic rituals—but only "for show." Secretly at home, they continued practicing their Jewish faith, kept the Sabbath, celebrated the Jewish holy days, and kept kosher. Since they pretended to be Catholic, however, they were subject to the jurisdiction of the Inquisition;[2] their lives were in danger if their continued adherence to the Jewish faith were discovered by the authorities, and if they were to refuse renouncing Judaism. They were called "Marranos," a word meaning "pigs." This was, of course, a slur meant to express contempt; but it also indicated that one could "ferret them out" by their refusal to eat pork. A more appropriate designation for them is "crypto-Jews," literally, "secret Jews," and that's the term I will use.

In 1496, four years after the Jews had been expelled from Spain, Portugal, the country to the west of Spain, did likewise. Thus, crypto-Jews also began existing in that country. In both Spain and Portugal, they secretly practiced the Jewish faith for many generations.

The first Jewish community in North America originated from the Portuguese crypto-Jews. Prior to continuing, the "secular history matters" announced earlier need to be taken up.[3]

(II) SOME MATTERS OF SECULAR HISTORY

Columbus's arrival in North America gave a strong additional incentive to European colonialism—the practice of European countries to bring areas outside of Europe under their dominance. At the end of the 1400s and during most of the 1500s, Spain and Portugal were the only "game in town," as far as European colonialism is concerned. It was only during the late 1500s and the early 1600s that other European powers started participating in this endeavor. At the 1494 Treaty of Tordesillas, Portugal and Spain divided the non-Christian lands outside of Europe between themselves by drawing a north-south line though the Atlantic Ocean. Areas west of that line were Spanish; areas east of it were Portuguese. This meant that all of North America and most of South America were considered as belonging to Spain, the exception being the eastern part of what is now Brazil, which was considered to be under Portuguese jurisdiction.

In the 1530s Portuguese settlers moved to the eastern part of South America, establishing, among other places, Olinda; nearby Recife (the latter town is currently the capital of the Brazilian province Pernambuco) was founded in 1548. A number of Portuguese crypto-Jews settled in Recife, hoping that, far away from the Portuguese center of authority, it would be easier and less dangerous for them to live in accordance with their faith.

---

2 The jurisdiction of the Inquisition was limited to Christians who deviated from the official teaching of the Catholic Church.

3 If I were extremely uncharitable to the American educational system, I would now refer back to an earlier footnote.

In the early 1600s, three European countries besides Spain and Portugal founded colonies in the Americas, ignoring the provisions of the Treaty of Tordesillas, in which they had not participated anyway. These countries were England, France, and Holland.

The first permanent and successful English colony in North America was Jamestown, in what is today Virginia, founded in 1607.[4]

In 1608 Samuel the Champlain founded Quebec as a French colony.

In the following year (1609), Henry Hudson, searching at the behest of the Dutch East India Company for the elusive North-east Passage to India, sailed up the river named after him today. In consequence, the Dutch (people from Holland, aka the Netherlands) claimed the area for their country, calling it New Netherland. The first settlement was established in 1624, which marks the beginning of New Netherland. That settlement was called Fort Orange, near the site of today's Albany. In the following year (1625), a fort was established on the southern tip of Manhattan Island. Negotiations were started with the Manhattan Indians for a purchase of the island from them; these negotiations were successful the following year, and the island was purchased for what legend calls 24 dollars' (60 guilders') worth of trinkets. Even if inflation may have significantly changed that number—I have read an estimate according to which in today's dollars, the price would amount to $1,000.00—it was doubtlessly vastly underpaid; perhaps the Louisiana Purchase is the only land deal similarly advantageous to the buyer.

(III) BACK TO THE BACKGROUND ...

In Europe at that time, religious freedom was virtually nonexistent. In keeping with the 1555 Augsburg Peace of Religion, the ruler of a region had the right to determine which religion the people living there had to adhere to. This meant that Catholics living under a Protestant ruler had either to adopt Protestantism or emigrate to a Protestant part of Europe; Protestants living under a Catholic ruler had either to emigrate to a Catholic part of Europe or to adopt Catholicism. A notable exception to this was Holland, where, beginning around the time of its declaration of independence from Spain in 1581, religious tolerance was practiced. This tolerance extended not only to various forms of Christianity, but also to Jews. In consequence, Jews moved to Holland from various parts of Europe where they were persecuted, and in general, they were favorably disposed toward Holland.

It also bears mentioning that religious conformity often was enforced to a lesser degree in the colonies than in the mother country. At times, this was simply due to the fact that it is easier to get away with more when one is far away from the centers of authority; at times, that was even intentional. England, for example, officially allowed people to practice in its colonies religions which were not permitted in the home country.

Moving to the Americas again, I remind you of Recife, the Portuguese town in which crypto-Jews lived. In 1630 the Dutch took the area away from the Portuguese. They brought their religious tolerance to the region. In consequence, the Jews living there no longer had to practice their religion in secret; they were able to do so openly. Many European Jews moved there from parts of Europe where Judaism was oppressed. A thriving Jewish community developed; two synagogues were built.

---

4 A colony on Roanoke Island established in 1587 at the behest of Sir Walter Raleigh was intended to be permanent; it was, however, not successful.

This was to last, however, only until 1654, when Portuguese forces retook the colony. Once again, the Jews were expelled. Some moved to Holland, some moved to the Dutch Antilles (aka the Netherlands Antilles), and some decided to travel north to the Dutch colony New Netherland. They arrived in New Amsterdam in 1654.

(IV) FINALLY IN NORTH AMERICA—EVEN IN AN AREA TO BECOME PART OF THE UNITED STATES

1. A small group of Jews: 1654 to 1825

The 1654 arrival of Jews in New Amsterdam marks the beginning of the oldest Jewish community in North America, known to this day as Shearith Israel, meaning "A remnant of Israel."

Actually, the director general (governor) of the colony, Peter Stuyvesant,[5] did not want the newcomers to stay. They were advised, however, to appeal his decision to the West India Company in Holland, in charge of the colony. It took until 1655 for the company's decision to arrive. It was favorable to the newcomers: They would be allowed to stay, provided they would be able to take care of their own.

New Netherland was a Dutch colony until 1664, when it was captured by England.[6] Its name was changed to New York, and New Amsterdam became New York City. The Jews continued living in that town, and looking ahead, the group of Jews living there[7] today is the largest in the world, outside of the state of Israel.

Rhode Island also figures prominently in the early history of Judaism in this country. In 1658 "fifteen Spanish Portuguese Jewish families"[8] settled in Newport, founding the second Jewish community in North America. That they are of Spanish and/or Portuguese extraction is evident by their names. It is assumed, however, that they did not directly come from these countries, but spent some time elsewhere. There is no unanimity, however, where they lived before coming to Rhode Island. "The view most widely held … is that they came from Curaçao, in the West Indies."[9] Curaçao, an island north of Venezuela, has been under Dutch rule since 1634, except for two brief periods of English rule, 1800–1803 and 1807–1815.

Thus, while Rhode Island cannot boast having the very first North American Jewish community, we do have a close second. We also have a genuine "first": The oldest North American synagogue still

---

5 Prior to that appointment, he had served as governor of Curaçao in the West Indies. During a military campaign against St. Maarten, at the time controlled by Portugal, he lost a leg (hence his nickname "Peg Leg"). Subsequently (1647), he was appointed director general of New Netherland, where he ruled in an autocratic fashion. When a board of nine advisers he had appointed complained about him to the Dutch government, he dismissed them. The Dutch government judged the complaint to have merit, though, and instituted a municipal government for New Amsterdam (1653). When England launched a surprise attack in 1664, Stuyvesant surrendered the colony to them. He continued to live on his farm on lower Manhattan Island. He died in 1672, and was buried in a private chapel on his farm. Today, the site, at Second Avenue and Tenth Street, is the location of an Episcopal church, St. Mark's-in-the-Bouwerie.

6 It was recaptured by the Dutch in August of 1673, but returned to England in November of 1674.

7 Naturally, today, there are Jewish communities in New York City besides Shearith Israel.

8 "Touro Synagogue—National Historic Site," in *Newport History*, summer 1975, vol. 48, Part 3, p. 281.

9 *Ibid.* As the same publication states, some think that these Jews came from Holland; others assume that they came from New York (at the time, of course, still called New Amsterdam).

existing is in Rhode Island. It is known as the Touro Synagogue, located on Touro Street in Newport. "Touro" is not to be confused with "Torah," the designation of the first five books of the Jewish Holy Scriptures. The synagogue's name is derived from the Touro family. Isaac Touro was spiritual leader of the Newport Jewish congregation when the synagogue was dedicated in 1763, still during the colonial era. (The New York community had built a synagogue in 1730 already, located on Mill Street in lower Manhattan, but it is no longer standing.)

The Touro Synagogue proudly displays an important document concerning religious liberty in the United States: General George Washington had visited Newport in 1781,[10] to confer with French general Rochambeau (the French forces, allied with the Americans during the War of Independence, had their headquarters in that town). Washington also visited the town as president, in 1790. During that visit, the warden of the synagogue, Moses Seixas, made a formal presentation to Washington, to which the president sent a written reply. A facsimile of the reply is posted on the West Wall of the interior of the synagogue.[11] The document contains the sentence, "For happily, the Government of the United States, *which gives to bigotry no sanction, to persecution no assistance*, requires only that they who live under its protection, should demean themselves as good citizens, in giving it on all occasions their effectual support." (Emphasis added. Bigotry is an extreme form of intolerance.)

Around the year 1800, toward the end of what I have called the "small group of Jews" period, only between 2,000 and 3,000 Jews lived in the United States. Besides the two oldest Jewish communities in New York City (formerly New Amsterdam) and Newport, Jewish congregations existed in Savannah, Georgia (founded 1733), Charleston, South Carolina (founded 1741), Philadelphia, Pennsylvania (founded 1745), and Richmond, Virginia (founded 1789).[12] Thus, six Jewish communities existed at the time.

2. German immigrants: Bringing the number of Jews up to 250,000 (1825–1880)

Beginning around 1825, large numbers of Jews from Germany (as well as from areas culturally influenced by Germany) came to the United States. The reason for this immigration can be explained as follows: When Napoleon had expanded his dominance over much of Europe through the "French conquests, the Jews of central Europe had become in some measure 'emancipated.'"[13] Following his final defeat at the Battle of Waterloo (1815) and his banishment to the island of St. Helena, though, central Europe went back to the old ways in many respects. Jews were once again treated as second-class citizens. This caused many of them to leave and come to the United States. In central Europe itself, Jews also attempted to become more similar to the majority population, among other things by changing their religious practices. The German Jews brought these reform tendencies to the United States, and the American brand of Reform Judaism originated among these immigrants. They also participated in the westward expansion of the United States taking place at that time.

---

10 He had been in Rhode Island at two earlier occasions, in 1756 and 1776.

11 The original was kept for some time in the B'nai B'rith Klutznick National Jewish Museum in Washington, D.C.; when the museum ran into financial difficulties in 2002, the letter was, together with many other items, placed in storage. Currently (since 2012), it is on loan to the National Museum of American Jewish History in Philadelphia, PA.

12 Jewish immigrants had begun to settle in the Richmond area as early as the 1760s.

13 Nathan Glazer, *American Judaism* (Chicago and London: The University of Chicago Press, 1972), p. 26.

By 1880 the number of Jews in the United States had grown to about 250,000.

3. East European immigrants: Boosting the number of Jews even further (1880–1921)

In Eastern Europe during the late 1800s and early 1900s, the situation of the Jews was significantly more desperate than it had been in central Europe during the time of the German Jewish immigration into the United States. In the east, there were persecutions, murders of Jews, and pogroms, defined as "organized riots accompanied by murder and pillage of the Jewish community."[14] To escape from this dreadful situation, large numbers of Jews fled the area, many of them immigrating to the United States. Around 1920 the number of U.S. Jews had grown to about 2,000,000.

4. The United States stems the flood of immigrants (1920s)—Jewish immigration comes to a near-standstill

The immigration of Jews from eastern Europe virtually came to a halt in the 1920s, when the U.S. Congress enacted laws placing severe restrictions on immigration.

The first of these laws was the Emergency Quota Act of 1921. It limited the number of immigrants allowed to come from an individual European country to 3% of the number of persons from that country in the United States in 1910.

A further restriction was enacted with the 1924 National Origins Quota Act. It limited the number of immigrants allowed to come from an individual European country to 2% of the number of persons from that country in the United States in 1890.

Further modifications of immigration laws were enacted in 1929. The various laws favored immigration from countries that had many immigrants in the United States (northern and western Europe), and discouraged immigration from countries with relatively few immigrants (southern and eastern Europe).

Thus came to an end the period that Emma Lazarus had described in her poem engraved on a tablet within the pedestal of the Statue of Liberty in New York City: "Give me your tired, your poor, your huddled masses yearning to breathe free, the wretched refuse of your teeming shore. Send these, the homeless, tempest-tost to me, I lift my lamp beside the golden door!"

---

14 Telushkin, *Literacy*, p. 246.

CHAPTER SEVEN

The Chief "Denominations" of U.S. Judaism

Next, we "jump" to the present—Judaism as it exists today in the United States—although here and there, some items belonging to earlier history (mostly the late 1800s) will have to be taken up, and the Jewish Holy Scriptures, as well as other important Jewish writings, will be considered.

Contemporary U.S. Judaism is not monolithic. Among observant Jews, three major groups are to be distinguished. They are: Orthodox or Traditional Judaism; Reform or Liberal Judaism; and Conservative Judaism. Conservative Judaism occupies a middle position between Orthodox and Reform Judaism. The three groups differ from each other with regard to their origins, their practices, and their beliefs. Thus, each denomination of Judaism will be divided into three segments, one dealing with the origin, one with the practices, and one with the beliefs.

(I) "INSERT": THE TORAH, THE JEWISH BIBLE, AND OTHER WRITINGS IMPORTANT FOR JUDAISM

As I have stated, one respect in which the three contemporary chief denominations of Judaism are different from each other concerns their practices—that is, the extent to which they obey the Jewish law. That law is formulated in the Torah, the first five books of the Jewish Holy Scriptures, identical with the first five books of the Christian Old Testament. Thus, a word or two (actually, many more) about these books shall be included here. Naturally, this leads to speaking also about the rest of the Jewish Holy Scriptures, as well as to other writings important for Judaism.

1. The Torah

The word "Torah" comes from a Hebrew word meaning "teaching." The five books of the Torah (as well as the first five books of the Christian Old Testament) are (using the names by which they are known in the English language), Genesis, Exodus, Leviticus, Numbers, and Deuteronomy.[1]

The title "Genesis" is derived from a Greek word meaning "origin." The book's name is derived from the fact that it speaks about the origin of the universe, of humanity, and of the Jewish nation.

Exodus comes from a Greek word literally meaning "way out." The book has this name because it describes, among many other things, how the Jewish people were led out of Egyptian slavery.

The name of the book Leviticus is derived from one of the 12 tribes of Israel, the one stemming from Jacob's son Levi. Moses and his brother Aaron belonged to this tribe. The descendants of Aaron were to serve as priests (kohanim); the other male members of that tribe were to assist with the worship services—they were known as Levites. The third book of the Bible contains many of the laws that are particularly important for these worship services; thus, the book must be heeded in a special way by the members of the Levi tribe. This is reflected in the book's title.

The book of Numbers derives its name from the fact that it begins with an account of a census of the Jewish people—it literally begins with many numbers.

"Deuteronomy" is derived from the two Greek words *deuteros*—"second," and *nomos*—"law." Literally, the name means, therefore, "the second law." Two reasons are given for this name: First, in it, Moses repeats and summarizes many of the laws that are stated in earlier books (including the Ten Commandments, which can be found in Ex 20.1–17 and Dt 5.6–18); thus, it is a "second version" of the Torah laws. Another reason is: Deuteronomy has in common with Leviticus that it contains many, many laws. Thus, it is the "second book heavy on the law," after Leviticus.

2. A general remark on the Jewish Holy Scriptures

At this point, a general remark on the Jewish Holy Scriptures is to be made. The Jewish Holy Scriptures contain all the materials that can be found in the Christian Old Testament.[2]

Before saying anything else, a remark on the word "book" is to be made: That's what the parts of the Bible are called. Why?

The parts of the Bible were written by many different authors over many centuries. Thus, they originated as independent units. That they are collected, bound between two covers, and handed to people as one volume is a comparatively late development. Calling the parts of the Bible "books" harks back to their origin, to the time when they really were books independent of each other—not books in our sense, to be sure, but scrolls. They were written on long strips of papyrus (the material used to write on in ancient times, made from a plant with the same name) which were rolled up on two wooden sticks.

Traditionally, the Jewish Holy Scriptures are said to contain 24 such parts (or books), divided into three groups: the Torah; the Prophets, called "Nevi'im" in Hebrew; and the Writings, called "Ketuvim"

---

1 Their Hebrew names, derived in the case of each of these books from the first or second word of the Hebrew text, are Brei'sheet, Sh'mot, Va-Yikra, Ba-Midbar, and Devarim.

2 As will be pointed out in the Scripture part of the Christianity segment, the Roman Catholic Old Testament contains seven books in addition to the ones included in the Jewish Holy Scriptures and in the Protestant Old Testament.

in Hebrew. The Hebrew names give rise to the following acronym for the types of Scriptures the Jewish Bible consists of: "Tanakh."

The **Torah** books are (to repeat their names, together with common abbreviations) Genesis (Gn), Exodus (Ex), Leviticus (Lv), Numbers (Nm), and Deuteronomy (Dt).

The **Prophets** are divided into the *Former Prophets* and the *Latter Prophets*; the Latter Prophets are further subdivided into the Major Prophets and the Twelve. The Former Prophets are Joshua (Jos), Judges (Jgs), Samuel (Sm), and Kings (Kgs). The Major Prophets (first set of books belonging to the Latter Prophets) are Isaiah (Is), Jeremiah (Jer), and Ezekiel (Ez). The Twelve—traditionally only one scroll in the Hebrew Scriptures—will be listed separately (together with common abbreviations for the individual prophets) in the "Scriptures" segment of the text part on Christianity, which traditionally considers them as twelve books (or scrolls).

The **Writings** are Psalms (Ps), Proverbs (Prv), Job (Jb), Song of Songs (Sg), Ruth (Ru), Lamentations (Lam), Ecclesiastes (Eccl), Esther (Est), Daniel (Dn), Ezra-Nehemiah (Ezr), and Chronicles (Chr).

In the Protestant Old Testament, Samuel, Kings, and Chronicles are divided into two scrolls each, as opposed to being only one; thus, making up six scrolls instead of only three; Ezra-Nehemiah is divided into two scrolls, one being Ezra, the other being Nehemiah; and the Twelve are divided into 12 scrolls. Thus, if you do the math, you will see that the Protestant Old Testament contains 39 scrolls rather than only 24; this does, however, not mean additional content, but a different organization of the material.[3]

3. The Mishna and the Talmud

Besides the Bible, there are other writings important to Judaism. They are referred to as the Talmud.

How does the Talmud relate to the Torah? Telushkin writes that the Torah contains "the backbone of all later Jewish law."[4] It is maintained, however, that from the beginning, there was an oral tradition applying the law to many concrete situations, and explaining and interpreting it. Around A.D. 200, this oral tradition was written down by a man known as Rabbi Judah the Prince. This written version of the law is known as the Mishna. As Telushkin writes,[5] many generations of rabbis debated the Mishna. Finally, the content of these debates also was set down in writing, comprising the Talmud. Actually, there are two such written collections resulting from these debates. One was written down in the fifth century A.D. by rabbis in Palestine. This document is known, therefore, as the Palestinian Talmud. The other was written down in the sixth century A.D. by rabbis in Babylon. It is known as the Babylonian Talmud.

---

3 For the Catholic Old Testament, see the previous footnote, as well as the Bible segment in the Christianity part of this text.
4 Telushkin, *Literacy,* p. 23.
5 See Telushkin, *Literacy*, p. 152.

(II) ORTHODOX JUDAISM

1. Meaning of the word; a remark on the group's origin

Next, we turn to Orthodox Judaism. The word "orthodox" is derived from two Greek words, *orthos*—meaning "right," and *doxa*—a word with several meanings, one of them being "judgment," and a bit more freely rendered, "belief." Thus, Orthodox Judaism is "right belief Judaism." By calling itself that way, it sets itself apart from the other two forms of Judaism through a claim that it is the group with the correct beliefs; the implication is that wherever Reform and Conservative Judaism disagree with Orthodox Judaism, they are mistaken.

Concerning its origin, Orthodox Jews claim to go back to the very beginning of Judaism; that one need not look for a special origin of the group. They claim to have preserved the original beliefs of Judaism, and to the extent this is still possible today, the original practices. "To the extent it is still possible today" is to take into consideration that there are many practices prescribed in the Torah which cannot possibly be observed today anymore; for example, those referring to the activities to be carried out in the Temple in Jerusalem: Since the destruction of that Temple in A.D. 70, there is no location anymore where they could be observed.

2. Practices

This brings us to the practices of Orthodox Judaism.

(1) General remarks

These practices are prescribed in the Torah, the first five books of the Jewish Holy Scriptures. When asked, "How many commandments are there in the Torah," many people reply, "Ten." True, the so-called Ten Commandments are a part of the Torah laws; but they are only the famous "tip of the iceberg." There are 613 individual prescriptions, called *mitzvot* ("laws"; singular *mitzvah*). An Orthodox Jew is obliged to adhere meticulously to all of them to the extent to which they apply to him or her. The "to the extent" clause is not a loophole; rather, not all laws apply to all humans; some apply only in special circumstances. As I have pointed out earlier, none of the laws regulating the worship services to be carried out in the Jerusalem Temple currently apply; the same holds true of the laws governing the priesthood. Thus, the number of laws that contemporary Orthodox Jews observe is significantly smaller than 613. In the words of Telushkin, "A great Eastern European rabbinic sage, the *Haffetz Hayyim* (1838–1933), computed that fewer than three hundred *mitzvot* are still practiced today."[6]

Further, there are laws that apply only to males and laws that apply only to females. Suppose I decided to become an Orthodox Jew, and said, "I want to be ultra-orthodox. I will observe all of the 613 laws." Well, in my case, good luck with the laws applying to women during the days after they have given birth. (See Lv 12.1–8 for these laws.)

---

6 Telushkin, *Literacy*, p. 496.

Although fewer than 300 laws apply to contemporary life, too many still remain to discuss all of them. By way of example, I will take up two types of laws, those relating to food, and some of those relating to the Sabbath.

(2) Dietary prescriptions

The basics of the food laws are stated in Chapter 11 of Leviticus, the third book of the Torah. That chapter distinguishes between foods that may be eaten—called "kosher" today—and those that may not be eaten. It divides the foods to which the kosher-nonkosher distinction applies into four groups: Land animals, sea animals, birds, and insects (at the time the Torah was written, insects were still a regular staple of the diet).

For a land animal to be allowed as food, it must have split hooves and "chew the cud," i.e., be a ruminant. Ruminants are animals that swallow their food (only plants) quickly without chewing it, and later, regurgitate it, chew it, and swallow it again. Cows, sheep, and lambs belong to this group, and are kosher, therefore. Horses, camels, rabbits, and dogs belong to nonkosher animals, as do pigs, for although the latter ones do have split hooves, they are not ruminants.

Sea animals must have fins and scales. (Scales are platelike structures covering the skin.) Thus, trout, cod, salmon, bluefish, or haddock are allowed; lobster, shrimp, or shellfish are not.

Concerning birds, instead of providing general categories, Leviticus gives only a long list of non-kosher birds. From that list, one can deduce that birds of prey and scavenger birds are not allowed. If a bird belongs to neither of these two groups, it is kosher. According to ancient Jewish traditions, chicken, turkey, duck, pheasant, quail, and goose belong to the kosher birds.

Since insects are not a part of our diet anymore, I am skipping them.

Besides the general rules applying to types of food that may and may not be eaten, there are two other important dietary proscriptions.

One is derived from Gn 9.4, which prohibits eating "flesh with the life blood still in it." Thus, the consumption of blood is prohibited. Meat even from kosher animals must, therefore, be properly prepared. This begins with the slaughter of animals. They must be killed with a quick stroke to the neck, severing the carotid artery, to make sure that as much blood as possible is lost. Then, the flesh must be treated with salt to remove the remaining blood.

A second additional rule goes back to the following prohibition, stated three times in the Torah: "You shall not boil a kid [here, a young goat] in its mother's milk." (See, for example, Ex 23.19.) Apparently, the flesh of a baby goat cooked in its mother's milk was a delicacy among the pagan people surrounding the ancient Jews; perhaps to make sure that imitating the diet of these people might not lead to imitating their pagan religious practices, it was forbidden for Jews to consume this type of food. Today, that three-fold prohibition survives in a prescription against combining meat and dairy products at the same meal. After a meat dish, one must wait for quite some time before one can eat dairy products. According to many rabbis, the wait is as long as six hours; some set it at three hours (a tradition among Jews coming from Holland orders only a one-hour wait). After a dairy dish, one must wait for about half an hour before one is allowed to consume meat.

To prevent even an accidental mixing of the two foodstuffs, kitchens in Orthodox Jewish homes have two sets of cooking utensils: one for dairy products, and one for meat products.

Fish (not regarded as meat), fruits, vegetables, and eggs may be eaten with either meat or dairy products.

(3) Justification of "seemingly arbitrary" prescriptions

Many people ask at this point, "What's the reason for these (and many other similar) laws? Are they not totally arbitrary?"

No doubt they are different from laws against stealing, lying, committing adultery, or murder. Concerning these latter laws, one can recognize that they apply quite apart from what the Torah says. Even many atheists would acknowledge that they simply express how human beings deserve to be treated because of what it means to be human.

In contrast, that rabbit or shrimp may not be eaten can be known only from the Torah. What is the reason for these seemingly arbitrary prescriptions?

At times, health reasons are given to justify these laws. This does, however, not seem sufficient. It might have applied in the past to eating pork from which one could get trichinosis; but even then, it did not apply to many other nonkosher foods, and today, in our part of the world at least, getting diseases even from pork is rare.

Orthodox Jews use different justifications. One is: "Someone believing in one God who has created us out of love and wants us to love him back—such a person's life must be different from that of a person who does not share this belief. Because of our weak nature, we need signposts reminding us of the kind of life we are to lead. That's where the seemingly arbitrary laws come into the picture. Continuously having to act differently from how others are acting is a powerful reminder that our lives must be different from those of other people. What counts is, of course, not the outward observance, but the change of heart to which the outward observance is to help and guide us. This is in keeping with the reason the Torah itself gives at one point for such a law: 'For you are a people sacred to the Lord your God.' (Dt 14.21)."

(4) Sabbath observance

As promised, here are some remarks about the Sabbath. It is the weekly Jewish holy day, kept on Saturday, the seventh day of the week. The Torah says about this day, "For six days work may be done; but the seventh day is the Sabbath rest, a day for sacred assembly, on which you shall do no work. The Sabbath shall belong to the Lord wherever you dwell." (Lv 23.3) Thus, Orthodox Jews are not allowed to do any kind of work on the Sabbath. No fires are to be lit (flicking a switch is considered lighting a fire); no business is to be conducted—an Orthodox Jew is not even allowed to carry money in his pocket on that day, and travel is forbidden. This includes using a car for driving to the synagogue; one can attend the Sabbath services taking place there only if one lives in walking distance.

The service in the synagogue is conducted in Hebrew, and men and women are seated separately.

By the way, Orthodox Jews never use the word "temple" for the synagogue; at times, they call it *shul* Yiddish for "school" or "synagogue."

(5) "Where life is at stake"

Are all of the Torah laws absolutely binding in all circumstances, or are there situations in which an Orthodox Jew can set them aside?

The answer to this question is derived from the following passage in the Torah: "Keep my statutes and decrees, for the man who carries them out will find life through them. I am the LORD." (Lev 18.5) Suppose that there is a conflict between a Torah law and human life; that obedience to that law in a given situation would have the loss of a life as its consequence. If that law would be observed in these circumstances, it would no longer be true that one would "find life" through it; rather, it would lead to death. Thus, most Torah laws may be set aside if keeping them would lead to the loss of human life. This is known as the "Where life is at stake" exception.

In keeping with that exception, an Orthodox Jew is allowed to drive a desperately ill person to the emergency room, even on the Sabbath; soldiers may, on the same day, participate in activities necessary for their country's defense, even if doing so involves activities normally prohibited on the Sabbath; if there is a severe famine and people would starve to death unless they eat nonkosher food, they may eat that food.

There are, however, three types of law which are not even overridden by a need to preserve one's own or another person's life. These are laws against murder, idolatry, and adultery.[7]

Concerning murder, one may not save one's own or another person's life through the intentional taking of the life of another innocent person. Two key words in this statement are "innocent" and "intentional." Capital punishment and killing in self-defense or to protect another victim of an attack are allowed, because in these cases, the life taken does not qualify as innocent. Further, in the case of defensive warfare, civilian casualties, including the death of innocent civilians, even the loss of life of innocent children, are often unavoidable. The lives of these persons are, however, not taken intentionally and deliberately, but as an unintended, albeit unavoidable consequence of the defensive actions. Thus, the non-applicability of the "Where life is at stake" exception to murder does not preclude defensive warfare, even if civil casualties are likely to occur.

Next, we turn to laws against idolatry, defined as the worshipping of false gods, such as the many gods the pagans living around the ancient Jews believed in. The non-applicability of the "Where life is at stake" exception to laws prohibiting idolatry means that one must be willing to die rather than participate in idolatrous worship.

The non-applicability of the "Where life is at stake" exception to laws against adultery does not mean that a married woman must resist to the point of death to being raped. Rape is, after all, something she is suffering, not something she is doing. It means, however, as Telushkin writes, "that Talmudic law forbids men and women from engaging in incestuous or adulterous relationships, even if doing so would somehow help keep them alive."[8]

3. Beliefs of Orthodox Judaism

Remember: Origin—practices—beliefs. I have spoken about the origin of Orthodox Jews—they claim that they do not have a special origin, like the other two branches of Judaism; that they go back to the very beginning of Judaism. I also have said a few words about the practices of Orthodox Judaism. Now, I must address the beliefs of this group of Jews.

Their most fundamental belief, I have dealt with already—it is the belief in one, and only one, God who has created humans out of love, and wants them to love him back. This belief is, however, not limited to Orthodox Judaism, but the other groups of religious Jews share it. What are the beliefs characteristic for Orthodox Jews?

---

7 See Telushkin, *Literacy*, p. 523.
8 Telushkin, *Literacy*, p. 522.

(1) Judaism and a creed—Moses Maimonides

At this point, the following "insert" may be appropriate: There are religions which do have a creed or creeds. The word "creed" is derived from the Latin word *credo*, which means "I believe." A creed is a concise summary of the beliefs of a religion, having official or authoritative character for the members of the religion in question. Many groups of Christians consider the Apostles' Creed or the Nicaean Creed as authoritative. In my Islam presentation, we will speak about the Muslim creed—among the shortest creeds of any religion.

There is, however, no official creed of Judaism, not even of Orthodox Judaism. The closest Judaism ever came to having a creed was in a brief work by Moses Maimonides, *Thirteen Articles of the Jewish Faith*.

Who was Maimonides?

For starters, don't confuse him with the Moses of the Bible, who lived around 1200 B.C. Maimonides lived about 2,500 years later, during the Middle Ages. Maimonides was born in A.D. 1135 in Spain (Cordoba). Because Spanish Jews were, at the time, persecuted by the Muslims who were then in power over much of the Iberian Peninsula (that's the peninsula on which Spain is located), he fled the country, first to Morocco in Africa, then, to Israel, then, to Egypt. Although Egypt was also governed by Muslims, unlike their Spanish counterparts, they were tolerant, and Maimonides became private physician at the court of Saladin, the Sultan (ruler) of Egypt, whose residence was in Cairo. Maimonides' nickname is "Rambam," standing for "Rabbi Moses ben Maimon." He died in 1204.

Maimonides wrote many books, including a work of great importance for philosophy, entitled, *The Guide for the Perplexed*.

For our context, the work concerning the articles of the Jewish faith is particularly important.

Maimonides considered adherence to these 13 articles as mandatory for a Jew. This becomes clear from the following words the work contains: "When a man believes in all these fundamental principles, and his faith is thus clarified, he is then part of this 'Israel' whom we are to love, pity, and treat, as God commanded, with love and fellowship. ... But if a man gives up any of these fundamental principles, he has removed himself from the Jewish community."[9]

According to Telushkin,[10] a popular summary of the 13 articles is contained in many Jewish prayer books. But even so, they cannot be called "The Official Creed of Judaism," not even for Orthodox Jews. (Reform Jews disagree with several of these provisions.)

(2) Four beliefs characteristic of Orthodox Judaism

There are four important beliefs that set Orthodox Jews apart from Reform Jews.

The first one has to do with the hereafter. Today, practically all observant Jews believe in a life after death.[11] Orthodox Jews, however, also believe in a resurrection of the body; they hold that even the physical side of a human being will at one point be included in the hereafter. Two of Maimonides' Thirteen Articles are relevant in this context. One is the Eleventh Article, which states that "the greatest reward is the world to come." It implies only that there is a hereafter, a "life to come." The other is

---

9 See *A Maimonides Reader*, edited by Isadore Twersky [henceforth referred to as "*Maimonides Reader*"] (New York: Behrman House, 1972), p. 422.

10 Telushkin, *Literacy*, p. 177.

11 This was not always the case. The Sadducees at the time of Jesus, for example, denied that there was an afterlife.

the Thirteenth Article, which clearly affirms the resurrection: "the Thirteenth Fundamental Principle is the Resurrection of the Dead."[12] Further, a book of the Jewish Holy Scriptures, known as the Book of Daniel, says, "Many of those who sleep in the dust of the earth shall awake" (Dn 12.2). Orthodox Jews can cite this as biblical evidence in support of their belief in the resurrection.

Second, many Orthodox Jews hope for a restoration of the ancient animal sacrifices that were once offered to God in the Jerusalem Temple. This would, however, require that the Temple be rebuilt, exactly on the site of the original site. Today, a Muslim structure, the Dome of the Rock, stands on this location, already built during the first century of Islam. Although, as Telushkin says, even many Orthodox Jews have ambivalent feelings about the idea of the restoration of these sacrifices, "the Orthodox prayer book … repeatedly reiterates the hope that the Temple will be rebuilt, and sacrifices offered there again."[13]

Third, Orthodox Jews hope for the coming of a great religious and political leader, the Messiah. The word *Messiah* literally means "the anointed one," going back to the practice of anointing the kings of ancient Judaism with oil. Thus, the Messiah will be the "king of kings." This great leader will be a descendant of David, become political leader of Israel, cause all the Jews living all over the world to move back to Israel, and establish peace among all the nations of the world. Concerning the Messiah, Maimonides writes, "We are to believe as fact that the Messiah will come."[14]

Fourth, Orthodox Jews consider the dispersion of Jews all over the world as something negative. They think that Jews should live in Palestine, the area of the world that God has given to Abraham and his descendants as a permanent possession. To buttress their claim to Jewish ownership of that area, they refer to the following words God speaks to Abraham according to Genesis: "The whole land of Canaan, where you are now an alien, I will give as an everlasting possession to you and your descendants after you; and I will be their God." (Gn 17.8) As mentioned earlier, "Canaan" is the word the Bible uses for the area called "Palestine" today.

If an Orthodox Jews is asked, "Why do you not move immediately to Palestine—to the state of Israel—if you think that that's where Jews should live?" he might reply, "Don't get me wrong—I am glad that Israel exists as a place of refuge for Jews who are still persecuted in many places of the world. Israel as it is organized today is, however, a secular state. Things will change when the Messiah will come; and if I am still alive then, rest assured that I will hurry to Israel."

(III) REFORM JUDAISM

Next, we will discuss Reform Judaism.

1. Origin

As was briefly mentioned earlier, this group of Judaism has its origin in Germany in the 1800s. German immigrants who arrived between 1825 and 1880 brought it to the United States. Thus, we must briefly jump back in time and across the Big Pond—to Germany in the 1800s.

---

12 *Maimonides Reader*, p. 433.
13 Telushkin, *Literacy*, p. 62.
14 *Maimonides Reader*, p. 433.

Unfortunately, Jews were treated there as second-class citizens. They tried to assimilate as much as possible to the majority population. While they did not abandon their chief religious convictions, they attempted to make their religious observances as similar as possible to that of the Christians who surrounded them, for the most part Lutherans.

In keeping with this, they changed the architecture of the synagogue to include stained glass windows with actual pictures in them rather than only ornaments; during the synagogue service, the German language was used instead of Hebrew, and organ music was introduced into the service, very much to the displeasure of traditional German Jews, since musical instruments may not be played on the Sabbath.[15]

In the United States, the Jewish immigrants from Germany liberalized their practices further.

A key U.S. document for Reform Judaism is the so-called Pittsburgh Platform, put together and approved by Reform rabbis in 1885, named after the town in which they met. Another important document is the Columbus Platform of 1937, modifying some points contained in the Pittsburgh Platform, especially the Pittsburgh document's assertion that Judaism is primarily a religion, and its stance against Judaism as a peoplehood. In light of the horrendous crimes that were being perpetrated against Jews in Nazi Germany, the peoplehood character of Jews was emphasized in the 1937 Platform.

2. Practices

To understand how Reform Judaism looks at the law formulated in the Torah, it is helpful to distinguish two types of laws. One is the moral law, the other is the nonmoral law.

The moral law includes prescriptions with regard to our duties towards God and humans. With respect to God, we are to recognize that there is only one God, that he is the lord of the universe, and that we are to love him with all our soul and all our strength. With regard to humans, we are to love our neighbor as ourselves, and treat others in accord with the prescription of those of the Ten Commandments which concern others. Besides the law to love God, to love our neighbor, and the Ten Commandments, there are numerous other moral prescriptions in the Torah.

The nonmoral law comprises prescriptions like dietary norms, laws relating to purity, and similar matters—most of the laws that would appear "arbitrary" to a non-Jew belong to this group.

According to the Pittsburgh Platform, the moral law is mandatory. Nonmoral laws, however, are not mandatory. The Platform even discourages observing it, stating that they are "apt rather to obstruct than to further modern spiritual elevation." Over the more than a century since the adoption of the Pittsburgh Platform, Reform Judaism seems to have weakened its stand against the observance of at least some of the nonmoral laws. They continue to be considered as non-obligatory, though.

3. Beliefs

Among the beliefs setting Reform Judaism apart from Orthodox Judaism, there is first a denial of the resurrection of the body. Death is, however, not considered as the end of the existence of a human being. The state of this world and God's justice and goodness require there to be a hereafter, in which the scales of justice are set right. Given that in this life, those who try hard to live justly and uprightly

---

15 For this last point, see Telushkin, *Literacy*, p. 231.

often suffer, while those who are guilty of all kinds of misdeeds are seemingly well off, the universe would be worse than a cruel joke if death would be an absolute end to a human being's existence: An Adolf Hitler would come to the same end as his innocent victims. In keeping with this, the Pittsburgh Platform states, "We reassert the doctrine of Judaism that the soul is immortal." Concerning resurrection of the body, the document says, however, "We reject the belief … in bodily resurrection."

Second, contrary to many Orthodox Jews, Reform Jews do not hope for a restoration of the ancient animal sacrifices to be offered up once again in the Jerusalem Temple. As Telushkin writes, any reference to them is dropped from Reform prayer books; Reform Jews view these "sacrifices as a primitive stage in Jewish religious development."[16]

Third, they do not believe in a Messiah as an individual person who will usher in peace all over the world. The belief in the Messiah is replaced by a hope for a bright future of humankind, when peace and justice will prevail. This is, however, not to be brought about by a Messiah sent by God, but through human efforts. In keeping with this, Reform Judaism encourages involvement in causes of social justice.

Fourth, in contrast to Orthodox Judaism, Reform Jews do not see the fact that Jews live all over the world as something negative. This is closely connected with the preceding point: They feel called to contribute to the coming about of the bright future of humankind; and how could they do so if all Jews were banded together in one corner of the earth?

This does not mean, however, that Reform Judaism is opposed to the State of Israel. When political Zionism, the movement aiming at the establishment of a Jewish homeland in Palestine, was inaugurated by Theodor Herzl in the late 1800s, Reform Jews were opposed to its goals. Several decades later, however, as a consequence of the Nazi persecution of Jews and in conjunction with the emphasis that even Reform Jews began placing on the "peoplehood character" of Judaism, their attitude changed. Israel is seen as a place at which Jews, persecuted in many places of the world, can find refuge; but still, there is no pressure on the part of Reform Judaism that Jews not experiencing persecution move to Palestine.

(IV) CONSERVATIVE JUDAISM

I turn to Conservative Judaism, and first talk about its origin.

1. Origin

In the late 1800s, U.S. Judaism was dominated by Reform Judaism. This extended also to the first rabbinical seminary that was founded in the United States. A rabbinical seminary is a place of higher learning one must attend in order to become a rabbi. The first such seminary in the United States, named Hebrew Union College, was founded in 1875 in Cincinnati, Ohio. Prior to its founding, men who were to serve as rabbis in the United States had to be brought over from Europe.

The dominance Reform Judaism had over Hebrew Union College became dramatically clear during an 1883 graduation dinner at the school. The first course served was shrimp, a totally nonkosher food. Many of the guests were scandalized, got up, and left. The school's excuse that the whole matter was the caterer's fault sounded about as plausible as many a student's excuse for having submitted an assignment

---

16 Telushkin, *Literacy*, p. 62.

after the due date. At any rate, the event was the catalyst for the establishment of Conservative Judaism by a group of Jews who were upset about the extreme developments within Reform Judaism, but who at the same time considered Orthodox Judaism as too strict and unbending.

The new group's seminary, known as Jewish Theological Seminary, located in New York City, opened its doors in 1887.

2. Practices

Concerning practices, Conservative Jews consider both the moral and the nonmoral law as binding; they allow, however, adaptations and changes of the law to account for new circumstances and situations that were unanticipated, often even unimaginable, at the time the law was given. Orthodox Jews do not allow for such changes. (As explained, Reform Jews consider only the moral law as binding.) About Conservative Jewish adaptations of the law, Telushkin writes, "most notable are … decisions to permit driving to synagogue on the Sabbath, calling women to the Torah for aliyot [explained in the next paragraph], and more recently [1983], permitting women to be invested as cantors and ordained as rabbis."[17] (Reform Jews began allowing women to be rabbis in the early 1970s.)

What does the word *aliyot* mean? It is the plural form of *aliyah*, which, literally translated, means "going up." During each Sabbath service, seven segments of the Torah are read. Before a segment is read, a member of the congregation is called up to bless the Torah. During an orthodox service, only men are allowed to participate; in Conservative synagogues, women also are allowed to take part. (They are, of course, also allowed to participate in Reform Temples.)

3. Beliefs

The following may be an apt description of the beliefs of Conservative Judaism: "Conservatism refuses to commit itself to a definite platform of principle and dogma."[18]

---

17 Telushkin, *Literacy*, p. 397.
18 H. D. Leuner, "Judaism," in *The World's Religions*, Sir Norman Anderson, ed. (Grand Rapids, MI: Eerdmans Publishing Co.), third American printing, p. 79.

CHAPTER EIGHT

Miscellaneous Items

(I) ADDITIONAL GROUPS OF U.S. JUDAISM

In addition to the three main groups of U.S. Judaism, there are other groups, such as Hassidic Jews, Reconstructionist Judaism, and people who are "just Jewish."

1. Hasidic Jews

One group of Jews often heard about is the Hasidic Jews (at times spelled Chasidic Jews, to come closer to the correct pronunciation). They can easily "be recognized by the eighteenth- and nineteenth-century black coats and hats worn by most of their male adherents."[1] In terms of their stand on Jewish law and beliefs, they are similar to Orthodox Jews, at times even referred to as ultra-Orthodox. Telushkin designates them as the "conservative stalwarts of Orthodox Judaism."[2] Their distinguishing characteristic is the great emphasis they place on the "joy of performing a commandment."[3] One is to obey the law, not reluctantly, or even with a sour face; one is to do so joyfully. The same applies to prayer and worship. Both activities are to be permeated with joy and happiness. Risking a comparison of apples and oranges, I might say that in their attitude, they are similar to charismatic Christians.

2. Reconstructionist Judaism

Another group of Jews is Reconstructionism. The "patriarch" of the movement, Mordecai Kaplan (1881–1983), grew up as an Orthodox Jew and later joined Conservative Judaism. He practiced it for the rest of his life, although he abandoned a belief in a personal God different from us humans.

---

1 Telushkin, *Literacy*, p. 218.
2 Ibid.
3 Ibid.

Many of his followers, who established Reconstructionism as a separate Jewish movement, returned to a belief in a personal God. Concerning Jewish ritual, Reconstructionists "permit rabbinical students much greater latitude"[4] than is allowed in Conservative Jewish circles.

3. Those who are "just Jewish"

In addition to the groups mentioned, there are those who identify themselves as "just Jewish." This might include persons who take their faith seriously, but are reluctant to declare official membership with one of the Jewish groups mentioned or with another group. It also includes those who do not practice their faith and are, as it were, Jewish in name only; it also includes persons who come from a Jewish background, but have abandoned their faith.

(II) THE JEWISH CALENDAR

The Jewish calendar is neither purely solar, as is our civil calendar, nor purely lunar, as is the Muslim calendar, but, in a manner of speaking, a combination of the two calendar types. Thus, it is useful first to explain the solar calendar and the lunar calendar.

1. The solar calendar and the lunar calendar

The civil calendar used in the United States and the Western world is called "solar," a word derived from the Latin word *sol*, meaning "sun." The objective of a solar calendar is to keep the year aligned with the seasons, which are determined by the earth's position on its path around the sun. Thus, the length of the solar year is to correspond as much as possible to the time it takes the earth to circle the sun once, which is about 365½ days. In keeping with this, the solar year has 365 days; every four years,[5] an extra day is added, generating a leap year—that is, a year with 366 days.[6]

The Muslim calendar is called "lunar," a word derived from the Latin *luna*, meaning "moon." In such a calendar, the length of the month is based on the time it takes the moon to go through its phases once. This is about 29½ days. Thus, in a lunar calendar, the length of the months alternates between 29 and 30 days. Like the solar year, the lunar year contains 12 months. A year with six 29-day months and six 30-day months has 354 days, which is the "baseline length" of the lunar year.[7] Since this is about 11 days shorter than the time it takes the earth to complete its path around the sun, the parts of such a year "slide" around the seasons.

---

4 Telushkin, *Literacy*, p. 422.

5 Exceptions are the century years (years ending with a "0," as 1900). They are leap years only if they are designated with a number divisible by 400. See the segment referred to in the next footnote for a more detailed explanation.

6 The calendar segment contained in the later Muslim section of this text has additional comments on the Western civil calendar, including on the difference between the contemporary Gregorian calendar and the Julian calendar used prior to the Gregorian one.

7 As will be explained in the more detailed segment on the Muslim calendar, some Muslim lunar years do have leap days, with 355 days to the year.

2. The Jewish lunisolar calendar

In contrast to our civil calendar and the Muslim lunar calendar, Jews use a combination of a solar and a lunar calendar called a lunisolar calendar. The calendar's lunar aspect comes into play with respect to the determination of the length of the months, which is to correspond to the duration of the moon's phases, beginning at the point of the new moon. The length of the months alternates between 29 and 30 days, leading, as in the case of the Muslim year, to a year's baseline length of 354 days. For the purpose of keeping the year roughly in step with the seasons, the Jewish calendar's solar aspect comes into play. Occasionally, a leap month is added to the year, bringing the total number of months to 13 months. Each series of 19 years includes seven years with leap months.[8] The leap month has 30 days; consequently, the baseline length for the 13-month year is 384 days. There are also two months that alternate between 29 and 30 days. One of them, named Heshvan, is regularly 29 days, but in some years, it has 30 days. The other, named Kislev, is regularly 30 days, but in some years, it has only 29 days. Thus, years without leap months have 353, 354, or 355 days; years with leap months have 383, 384, or 385 days. This means that there are six possible lengths for the Jewish year. Addition and/or subtraction of days of individual months is to ensure, among else, that the beginning of the months continue to coincide roughly with the new moon,[9] to keep Yom Kippur from falling on a Friday or Sunday (it is not to occur next to a Sabbath), and to prevent Hoshanah Rabbah (the seventh day of Sukkot) from falling on a Sabbath.

The series of months in the Jewish 12-month year is (number of days shown in parentheses) Tishri (30), Heshvan (29 or 30), Kislev (30 or 29), Tevet (29), Shevat (30), Adar (29), Nisan (30), Iyar (29), Sivan (30), Tammuz (29), Av (30), and Elul (29).

In the years with leap moths, Adar is "split up" into Adar I (30 days) and Adar II (29 days). Adar II, which does have the "regular" Adar length, is the more "important" of the two, in the sense that it contains the holy days scheduled for Adar and that anniversaries falling in Adar are to be observed in Adar II.

(III) SOME JEWISH HOLY DAYS

I guess I should say at least one or two words about some of the most important Jewish holy days.

1. The Sabbath

When I told you about the practices of Orthodox Judaism, I made a few remarks about the Sabbath observance. I mentioned that the Sabbath is the weekly Jewish holy day kept on the seventh day of the week. This day goes back to the first creation account in Genesis. There, God is said to have created the world in six days. Then, we read, "Since on the seventh day God was finished with the work he had been doing, he rested on the seventh day from all the work he had undertaken. So God blessed the seventh day and made it holy (Gn 2.2–3)."

---

8 Years 3, 6, 8, 11, 14, 17, and 19 of each 19-year cycle have leap months.
9 The calendar segment in the Islam part of this text explains in detail why alternating 29-day months with 30-day months is not sufficient to keep the beginning of the month coinciding with the new moon.

One of the Ten Commandments states, "Remember to keep holy the Sabbath Day. Six days you may labor and do all your work, but the seventh is the Sabbath of your Lord and God. No work may be done then either by you, or your son or daughter, or your male or female slave, or your beast, or by the alien who lives with you (Ex 20.8–10)." This passage contains the essentials of what is not to be done on the Sabbath.

The Sabbath begins on Friday at sunset and lasts until sunset Saturday. The custom to let the day begin with the evening rather than at midnight goes back to the very first chapter of Genesis, where something like a refrain occurs at the end of each of the six segments stating what occurred on the six days of creation: "… Evening came and morning followed, the first day … evening came and morning followed, the second day … evening came and morning followed, the third day … (See Gn 1)": The day begins with evening.

2. Passover

According to our secular calendar, Passover takes place in March or April. It commemorates the deliverance of the Jews from Egyptian slavery. The name, *Pesach* in Hebrew, is derived from what is stated in the Scripture book Exodus: The Angel of Death, sent to kill all the firstborn of the Egyptians, "passed over" the houses in which the Jews lived, who had marked the door posts and lintels of their houses with the blood of the lamb they had slaughtered, as they had been commanded.[10] The ceremony commemorating the exodus from Egypt is called a Seder (Hebrew for "order"). A festive meal is part of the Passover celebration.

3. Shavuot

Exactly 50 days after the second day of Passover, Shavuot takes place. It is a celebration of the first fruits—the first things to be harvested from the fields, as well as a commemoration of the giving of the Ten Commandments.

4. Sukkot

The name of the Sukkot feast is derived from *sukkah*, designating a temporary dwelling to be erected during the feast, symbolizing the tents in which the Jews had to live during their sojourn in the desert between their departure from Egypt (exodus) and their settling of the Promised Land. Sukkot is also a harvest thanksgiving festival.

5. Rosh Hashanah

Although marking the beginning of the seventh month of the Jewish calendar, Rosh Hashanah is the Jewish New Year, occurring in September or October of our secular calendar. It also marks the beginning of a somber period of Jewish life, one during which one is to remember one's weaknesses and wrongdoings, and feel remorse for them. The period culminates in …

---

10 See (III) of the segment, "From the beginning of Judaism to A.D. 136."

6. … Yom Kippur

Yom Kippur (Day of Atonement) occurs ten days after Rosh Hashanah. The day involves a strict fast. One is to repent of one's sins, pray to God for mercy, resolve sincerely to avoid sin, and commit oneself to return to God.

7. Hanukkah

Hanukkah (Festival of Lights), occurring in November or December, commemorates the victory of the Maccabees over the Seleucids,[11] as well as the rekindling of the lights in the Jerusalem Temple, which that victory made possible.

(IV) STATISTICS[12]

Almost 15,000,000 of the more than 7 billion people estimated to live on earth belong to Judaism.

The current population of the United States is about 319,000,000. About 6,200,000 to 6,500,000 of them—that is, about 1.9% to 2%—are Jewish. About 10% are Orthodox Jews; about 35% are Reform Jews; and about 26% are Conservative Jews. The remainder belongs to other groups, including, of course, the ones I mentioned earlier.

---

11 See (VI) of the segment, "From the beginning of Judaism to A.D. 136."
12 Based on *The World Almanac and Book of Facts 2014* (New York: 2013) and the U.S. & World Population Clocks of the U.S. Census Bureau.

CHAPTER NINE

The Faith of Christians

Remarks on History; the Christian Bible

(I) BACKGROUND HISTORY

Christianity begins with Jesus of Nazareth. Why "of Nazareth"? Because he spent most of his life in Nazareth, a town situated in Galilee, close to the southern border of that region. He was born in Bethlehem, a town in Judaea, about five miles south of Jerusalem. He died in Jerusalem. According to the Gospels, many other parts of the New Testament, and the testimony of an early second-century work by a non-Christian historian (Tacitus, lived about A.D. 55 to 120[1]), his death happened by execution.

As has been explained in the segment on Judaism, in 63 B.C., Palestine, where Jesus spent his entire life, had become dependent on the Roman Empire, and in 37 B.C., the Romans had made Herod of the Idumean region king of the area. According to the Gospels of Matthew and Luke, Jesus was born prior to the close of Herod's reign, which ended in 4 B.C. Thus, although our system of counting years uses "B.C.–A.D.," standing for "Before Christ" and "Anno Domini," the latter meaning "In the year of the Lord [the Lord being Jesus]," Jesus' birth did not occur at the beginning of the year A.D. 1: Since Herod was still alive when Jesus was born, the latter's birth could not have been later than 4 B.C. Likely, it occurred 6 B.C., or even a little earlier.[2] The mistake in our count of years goes back to the ancient

---

1 "Christ ... suffered the extreme penalty during the reign of Tiberius at the hands of one of our procurators, Pontius Pilatus." Tacitus, *Annals* 15.44, available on the Web: http://www.perseus.tufts.edu/hopper/text?doc=Tac.+Ann.+15.44&redirect=true.
2 What Matthew writes in his Gospel tends to support that Jesus was born around 6 B.C.: When wise men, called magi, visited Herod and inquired about a newborn king of the Jews whose star they had seen in the east, Herod was terrified, because he considered their words a threat to the continued rule of his dynasty. He told the magi to look for the child; and let him know where the newborn "king" could be found. He did not tell them that he intended to kill the child. The magi found Jesus in Bethlehem, but were warned in a dream not to return to Herod. When the king found out that the magi had left without giving him the information he had requested, he ordered all male children in Bethlehem two years and younger to be killed. Why two years? Likely, the time line given by the magi implied that the sign they had seen had appeared to them two years prior to their arrival, thus indicating that by the time of their visit, the "newborn king of the Jews" was two years old.

historians Dionysius Exiguus (c. 470–c. 544), who introduced the new counting system. He incorrectly assumed Jesus' birth to have occurred several years later than it actually did. When historians realized the mistake, no change was made, chiefly because it is unknown precisely how the error should be corrected, as the precise year of Jesus' birth is not known.

The life of Jesus falls into the reign of two Roman emperors, Augustus (ruled 27 B.C. to A.D. 14) and Tiberius (ruled 14–37). As stated earlier, at Jesus' birth, Palestine was ruled by Herod the Great. After Herod's death (I am repeating some of the historic information also contained in the segment on the faith of the Jews), the area he had ruled was divided. The part surrounding Jerusalem was assigned first to Herod the Great's son Archelaus (4 B.C. to A.D. 6); subsequently, it was turned into a Roman province headed by a governor. At the time of Jesus' death, the governor was Pontius Pilate, who ruled from 26 to 37. Galilee, which until 4 B.C. had been a part of the area ruled by Herod the Great, was, for the entire time Jesus lived in that region, governed by Herod Antipas, one of the sons of Herod the Great. Antipas ruled from 4 B.C. to A.D. 39.

(II) THE CHRISTIAN BIBLE

Christians take all of their information about Jesus from a part of their Bible which they call the New Testament, in particular from the four Gospels. At one point, I must provide some information on the Christian Bible. What better occasion is there for this than right now? So here goes …

1. Two Testaments

The Christian Bible is divided into two segments, the Old Testament and the New Testament. In these titles, the word "testament" is used in its original meaning: "Pact," "agreement," "contract," or, a bit more highbrow, "covenant." Except for the expression, "Last will and testament," this word hardly is used today in any other context. The books Christians denote as "Old Testament" chiefly concern the agreement God supposedly made with the Jewish people. Christians call that agreement "old," because according to them, it has been superseded by an agreement God made with all of humanity through Jesus. This is the "new agreement," and the collection of books about it is called the "New Testament." "Old Testament" means, therefore, "Sacred Scriptures of the old covenant"; "New Testament" means "Sacred Scriptures of the new covenant."

2. The Old Testament

The Old Testament contains the entire Jewish Holy Scriptures. Christians arrange its books into groups in a manner different from the arrangement found in the Jewish Bible, several Jewish Holy Scripture books are divided into two separate Old Testament books, one (The Twelve) is even divided

---

(Herod had younger boys also executed, probably to be "on the safe side.") If one assumes that the murder of the Bethlehem children took place late in Herod's life, perhaps during the year of his death, which occurred in 4 B.C., the year of Jesus' birth would have been about two years earlier, which is about 6 B.C. Jesus escaped Herod's evil designs because his stepfather, Joseph, also had been warned in a dream, and had fled to Egypt with his family. Upon hearing that Herod had died, the family returned to Palestine and settled in Nazareth when Jesus was still a child.

into twelve books, and the sequence in which the books are arranged in the Old Testament is different from their sequence in the Jewish Bible. Moreover, the Catholic Old Testament contains seven books not included in the Protestant Old Testament or in the Jewish Bible.

As stated in the segment on the Jewish Bible, Jews arrange the books of Scripture into three groups, called the Torah, the Prophets, and the Writings. The books of the Christian Old Testament are arranged into four groups: (1) The Pentateuch, which is the name Christians use for the five books Jews call the Torah; (2) the Historical Books; (3) the Wisdom Books; and (4) the Prophetic Books. The word *Pentateuch* literally means "Five Sheaths," the word "sheaths" designating the containers in which the five scrolls of the Pentateuch were kept in ancient times. (Remember that at the time, what was called a "book" were long sheets of paper, like rolls of paper towels [no kidding], covered with writing, and rolled up on two wooden sticks.)

Below is a listing of the Old Testament books, with standard abbreviations used for them. Books in bold print and underlined (a total of seven) are contained in the Catholic Old Testament, but Protestants and Jews do not include them in their Bibles. The two books which are underlined without being in bold print contain comparatively short segments included in the Catholic Old Testament, but not found in the Protestant and the Jewish Bible. The Protestant Old Testament contains 39 books; the Roman Catholic one contains 46.[3]

The *Pentateuch* includes Genesis (Gn), Exodus (Ex), Leviticus (Lv), Numbers (Nm), and Deuteronomy (Dt).

The *Historical Books* are Joshua (Jos), Judges (Jgs), Ruth (Ru), First Book of Samuel (1 Sm), Second Book of Samuel (2 Sm),[4] First Book of Kings (1 Kgs), Second Book of Kings (2 Kgs),[5] First Book of Chronicles (1 Chr), Second Book of Chronicles (2 Chr),[6] Ezra (Ezr), Nehemiah (Neh),[7] **Tobit (Tb)**, **Judith (Jdt)**, Esther (Est), **First Book of Maccabees (1 Mc)**, **Second Book of Maccabees (2 Mc)**.

The Wisdom Books are Job (Jb), Psalms (Ps), Proverbs (Prv), Ecclesiastes (Eccl), Song of Songs (Sg), **Wisdom (Wis)**, **Sirach, aka Ecclesiasticus (Sir)**.

The Prophetic Books are Isaiah (Is), Jeremiah (Jer), Lamentations (Lam), **Baruch (Bar)**, Ezekiel (Ez), Daniel (Dn), Hosea (Hos), Joel (Jl), Amos (Am), Obadiah (Ob), Jonah (Jon), Micah (Mi), Nahum (Na), Habakkuk (Hb), Zephaniah (Zep), Haggai (Hg), Zechariah (Zec), and Malachi (Mal).[8]

3. The New Testament

The second part of the Christian Bible is the New Testament. It consists of 27 books (scrolls). The first four are known as the Gospels, dealing with the life and teachings of Jesus—they are identified by the names of the persons who wrote them, according to a second-century tradition. The fifth is called Acts of the Apostles, recording the history of the early Christian community; then, there are 13

---

3 Recall that the Jewish Bible contains 24 books. The material contained in it is, however, the same as that included in the Protestant Old Testament. The difference in numbers of books is accounted for by the fact that parts considered as different books in the Old Testament are combined in the Jewish Bible, as indicated in the subsequent footnotes.

4 In the Jewish Bible, 1 Sm and 2 Sm are combined into one scroll.

5 In the Jewish Bible, 1 Kgs and 2 Kgs are combined into one scroll.

6 In the Jewish Bible, 1 Chr and 2 Chr are combined into one scroll.

7 In the Jewish Bible, Ezr and Neh are combined into one scroll.

8 In the Jewish Bible, the prophets from Hosea to Malachi are combined into one scroll, called The Twelve.

letters ascribed to Paul (the last one, called "Letter to the Hebrews," is traditionally ascribed not to Paul himself, but to one of his followers), one letter by James, two by Peter, three by John, one by Jude, and finally, the Book of Revelation, aka Apocalypse.

Here is a list of the 27 New Testament books, with customary abbreviations:

Gospel according to Matthew (Mt), Gospel according to Mark (Mk), Gospel according to Luke (Lk), Gospel according to John (Jn), Acts of the Apostles (Acts), Letter to the Romans (Rom), First Letter to the Corinthians (1 Cor), Second Letter to the Corinthians (2 Cor), Letter to the Galatians (Gal), Letter to the Ephesians (Eph), Letter to the Philippians (Phil), Letter to the Colossians (Col), First Letter to the Thessalonians (1 Thes), Second Letter to the Thessalonians (2 Thes), First Letter to Timothy (1 Tm), Second Letter to Timothy (2 Tim), Letter to Titus (Ti), Letter to Philemon (Phlm), Letter to the Hebrews (Heb), Letter of James (Jas), First Letter of Peter (1 Pt), Second Letter of Peter (2 Pt), First Letter of John (1 Jn), Second Letter of John (2 Jn), Third Letter of John (3 Jn), Letter of Jude (Jude), and Book of Revelation (Rv).

The original language in which all New Testament books were written was Greek, with the possible exception of the Gospel according to Matthew, which may have been written in Aramaic.

4. The authors of the Gospels: An ancient tradition

A second-century tradition states that the authors of the Gospels were Matthew, Mark, Luke, and John. About the identities of these authors and other important matters, the same tradition says:

Matthew's Gospel was written first, possibly in Aramaic, the language which the Jews generally used from the Babylonian captivity on. We do, however, have only a Greek version of that Gospel. This is either a translation of the Aramaic version, or itself the original—the tradition does not allow with certainty to know whether the original was in Aramaic. Matthew, aka Levi, was a tax collector prior to responding to Jesus' call to follow him (see Lk 5.27–32, a passage in which Jesus also states a chief purpose of why he has "come"). A little later, Jesus included him among twelve followers he selected and whom he called "apostles." That word is derived from the Greek *apostellein*, meaning "to send"; that Jesus gave the Twelve that title indicates that they were to be "sent out" in a special way. (See Lk 6.11–16 for Luke's account of the appointment of the Apostles.)[9] Also, beginning with the time of their appointment as apostles, they were continually with Jesus. Thus, Matthew was an eyewitness of most of what he recorded.

Mark, whose second name was John (see Acts 12.12), was, for the most part, not an eyewitness of what he wrote. Supposedly, he was the son of the woman who owned the house in which the Last

---

9 "Wait a minute—I just looked both Luke passages up that are mentioned in this paragraph. In the first passage—the one about the tax collector—the man is called Levi; but barely half a page later, when Luke reports the names of the apostles, he mentions a Matthew, without even giving the slightest hint that this is the person whom he called Levi. So I think that Levi and Matthew are two different people." Good point, but here are two counterpoints: First, that Matthew is the tax collector becomes clear from Mt 9.9, which recounts the same event as does Lk 6.11–16, Jesus' asking a tax collector to follow him. In Mt 9.9, the name Matthew is used for the person whom Jesus asks to follow him. Moreover, that Luke uses different names for the same person without giving a hint that he is talking about the same person becomes clear from the second of Luke's works included in the New Testament, the Acts of the Apostles (Acts). Mark, the reputed author of the second Gospel, also had two names: John and Mark. Luke calls him "Mark" in Acts 15.39; in 13.13, he calls him "John." In neither case does he indicate that he is talking about a person with two different names. In Acts 15.37 (as in 12.12), he calls him by both names: "John, who was called Mark" (two verses later, he calls him only "Mark").

Supper had taken place. Both the woman—named Mary—and the house are referred to in Acts 12.12. Mark is said to have accompanied the Apostle Peter, on whose preaching the second gospel is based.[10] Peter, one of the 12 Apostles, was an eyewitness of Jesus' words and deeds. There is a passage that might indicate that Mark himself was an eyewitness of at least some of the events he wrote about. After the Last Supper, Jesus went with his disciples to a place named Gethsemane on the Mount of Olives, and there he was arrested by people sent by the Jewish authorities. After Mark had mentioned that all of Jesus' followers left him and fled, he writes that a young man following Jesus was wearing nothing but a linen cloth; the people who had arrested Jesus grabbed the young man, but he left the cloth behind and ran off naked. Why is this "side note" included? It cannot possibly be to add a touch of humor to what he is writing; given the dreadful seriousness of the events communicated, that would not fit at all. If, however, it would be Mark's self-portrait—if he was that cowardly young man—then, the inclusion would make sense: "At the time, even I was a despicable coward—although all of us are to be ready to die for Jesus."[11]

Luke, a physician by profession, was not an eyewitness of anything he wrote—he became a Christian only after Jesus had been crucified. Also, he likely converted to Christianity from a non-Jewish background. He claims, however, to have consulted eyewitnesses (see Lk 1.2). He does not identify them; it is, however, surmised that one of them—by no means the only one—is Mary, the mother of Jesus: After Luke gives an account of events before, during, and shortly after Jesus' birth, he states, "And Mary kept all these things, reflecting on them in her heart." (2.19) Further, after Luke's account of an event that occurred when Jesus was 12 years old, he writes, "His mother kept all these things in her heart." (2.51) This has been understood to be an identification of the source of the information—both accounts ending with the words quoted concern matters about which a child's mother would be the best witness. As a "side note," Luke also was associated with Paul—himself not an eyewitness of Jesus' activities—whom he accompanied on several missionary journeys.

John was, like Matthew one of the 12 Apostles, consequently, also an eyewitness of most of what he wrote. The ancient tradition summarized here identifies him with the man called several times in his Gospel "the disciple whom Jesus loved" (see, for example, Jn 13.23), thereby indicating a special friendship between John and Jesus.

This brings us to the question as to whether the Gospels are credible.

Non-Christians reply, "Of course not." They would first observe that many of the matters told in the Gospels, such as numerous miracles, are hard to believe; second, they would point to the theories about the origin of the Gospels, to be explained in the next segment, that are quite different from the ancient tradition presented in this segment.

Christians accepting the ancient tradition would reply, "Two of the Gospel writers were eyewitnesses; one clearly states that he was not, but claims to have spoken to eyewitnesses; and one wrote down what an eyewitness said about Jesus. Isn't the result eminently credible?"

I say, "Fox principle."

---

10 At the end of his first letter, Peter refers to Mark as his "son" (see 1 Pt 5.23), indicating the closeness between the two.
11 Later in life, Mark became bishop of Alexandria in Egypt—Coptic Christians look to him as the founder of their denomination. It was there that he died a martyr's death: He was ordered to be dragged through town tied to horses until he died.

5. The most fashionable contemporary theory about Gospel origins: The Two-Source Hypothesis (aka 2SH)—watch out, a hobbyhorse!!

Those holding what I call the most fashionable contemporary view about Gospel origins do not agree that the Gospels were written by the authors mentioned in the previous segment. For the sake of convenience, though, the traditional way of referring to the Gospels is maintained—they continue to be called Matthew, Mark, Luke, and John, although their authors supposedly are unknown—as a minimum, an examination of the content of the Gospels makes their ascription to the traditional authors questionable.

The view considered at present begins with an observation obvious to any reader of the Gospels: Matthew, Mark, and Luke are very similar to each other, and different from John. They often report the same event in almost identical, at times even totally identical, language—so similar in fact that any professor observing corresponding similarities among term papers submitted by three of his students would seriously doubt that the students worked independently of each other. Matthew, Mark, and Luke also frequently place events they write about in the same sequence.

Because of these similarities, they are called the synoptic Gospels, meaning that comparing them (especially easy to do if they are written in three corresponding columns), allows one to see "at a glance" ("glance" = *opsis* in Greek) what they do have in common. This supposedly establishes that the writers of the Gospels did not work independently of each other; rather, just as the students in the term paper example, somehow, they copied from each other and/or from the same sources. They did a "glance" (*opsis*) "together" (*syn* in Greek); this is another reason for which they are called "synoptic Gospels."

Who is dependent on whom or what, however? To answer that question, one needs to look at the fact that most of what is contained in Mark is also contained in Matthew or Luke, or both (in fact, very much of the Mark content is in both Matthew and Luke). There is very little that is contained only in Mark. This makes obvious—or so the fashionable view says—that Mark's Gospel was written first, and used as a source by both Matthew and Luke.

Further, if one compares Matthew with Luke, one will find a large amount of material that can be found in both of them, but is not contained in Mark. Thus, Matthew and Luke did not get it from Mark. Where did they get it from? The most plausible solution is—at least according to the fashionable theory summarized here—that Matthew and Luke used, besides Mark's Gospel, the same additional written source. This source, consisting mostly of sayings of Jesus, has been lost. It is called "Source Q," the letter "Q" being the first letter of the German word *Quelle*, which means "source."

Thus, Matthew and Luke based their Gospels chiefly on two sources from which they copied. One of them is Mark's Gospel; the other is "Source Q." Since Matthew and Luke chiefly used two sources for the composition of their Gospels, the fashionable view summarized here is called the "Two-Source Hypothesis," or 2SH. That's how I will refer to it from now on.

It is important to emphasize: The 2SH does not maintain that Mark and Q are the only sources for Matthew's and Luke's Gospels, but the chief sources. There are also items reported which can only be found in Luke—much of what he includes in his account of the infancy of Jesus, for example. This comes from a special source. The same applies also to Matthew. Thus, Luke had additional sources not used by Matthew, and vice versa. The bulk of the information in both Gospels supposedly comes, however, from Mark and from the "Source Q."

It bears mentioning also that people accepting the 2SH, which applies only to the synoptic Gospels, do not agree that John the Apostle was the author of the fourth Gospel.

6. Your teacher's skepticism (understatement!) about the Two-Source Hypothesis (the hobbyhorse continued)

(1) Not a "purely religious" question; the challenge

A teacher's hobbyhorse is not supposed to dominate a course on a subject matter much more general than the former; but that the "horse's" neighing is heard at least a little is understandable and seems appropriate. Permit me, therefore, to include at least some critical comments on the Two-Source Hypothesis, which, as you possibly can guess from my remarks, has become my hobbyhorse.

It is important for me to emphasize, though: Whether or not the 2SH is correct is not a purely religious question (although of course important for religion), but a matter chiefly concerned with the linguistic record and with the question of whether or not particular instances of presenting arguments are logical. For this reason, the Fox principle does not apply, and I am allowed to "take sides," which is in this case a "decisive stand against." (Remember that you are totally free to disagree with my stand.)

At this point, the more cautious 2SH defenders might say, "But Fritz, we use our hypothesis to explain a problem badly in need of explanation—that presented by the far-reaching similarities between Matthew, Mark, and Luke. Maybe how we solve the problem is not perfect; but just try to come up with your own solution. We predict that you will wind up saying about the 2SH what Churchill said about democracy: 'It has been said that democracy is the worst form of government except all the others that have been tried.'"

Well, I am ready to take up that challenge.

(2) Introducing the expression "pericope"

Prior to starting in on the arguments, I must introduce an expression that will be used in what follows: "pericope." Raymond F. Collins defines the word as follows: "A unit of biblical material, such as a single parable or a single miracle story."[12] Longer presentations, which are neither miracle stories nor parables, such as speeches Jesus gives, consist of several pericopes. In this case, a single pericope is a brief sequence of sentences forming a thematic unit.

(3) Recap of the arguments allegedly supporting the priority of Mark's Gospel

Turning to the first assumption on which the 2SH is based, that Mark's Gospel is one of the sources for Matthew and Luke, I ask, "Does it make sense to hold that Matthew and Luke copied from Mark"? That it is so is one way to account for the similarities between the three;[13] adding the observation that there are hardly any pericopes contained only in Mark, but not in Luke and/or Matthew, as well as

---

12 Raymond F. Collins, *Introduction to the New Testament* (Garden City, NY: Doubleday, 1987), p. 423.

13 At times, there is a similarity only between Matthew and Mark; Luke would have "skipped" copying the passage in question. Also, there are cases of similarities only between Luke and Mark; Matthew would have omitted copying these passages. Those "skipped passages" also are a matter the 2SH does not have a satisfactory explanation for; but I let it go by.

that there are many pericopes contained in Luke and/or Matthew, but not in Mark strengthens the evidence that Mark was primary and used by Luke and Matthew.

Many who espouse the 2SH expound on the arguments just given, often through showing the similarities between the three synoptic Gospels with impressive side-by-side columns. The difficulties their hypothesis encounters are frequently ignored, though.

Let me attempt a step-by-step development of these difficulties.

(4) Difficulties with the theory that Matthew and Luke used Mark

Among the many pericopes that can be found in all three of the synoptic Gospels is the one concerning Jesus' calming of a dangerous storm while he was in a boat with his disciples. (See Mt 8.23–27, Mk 4.35–41, Lk 8.22–25.) Mark is the only one who mentions that, when the storm broke out, "Jesus was sleeping on a cushion in the stern of the boat." In the Greek original, this is a ten-word sentence. If Matthew as well as Luke copied the pericope from Mark, why did both of them happen to omit the same sentence? By chance?

Another similar example is a pericope which reports that Jesus heals a blind man (Mt 20.29–34, Mk 10.46–52, Lk 18.35–43) Mark is the only one who mentions the blind man's name (Bartimaeus). If Matthew and Luke copied the pericope from Mark, why did both of them happen to omit the name? By chance? Further, with regard to the same pericope, Mark is the only one who describes how Jesus' disciples call the blind man, how he jumps on his feet, and throws his cloak away. If Matthew and Luke copied that pericope from Mark, why did they both omit these same details? By chance?

It might now not go beyond reasonable odds that Luke and Matthew would omit in three cases by chance the same passage from the text they used for the composition of their Gospels; maybe eight such cases, or even ten, or even 15 might be in the realm of what is possible—but 250? That's the actual number of such cases. Thus, the 2SH defenders want us to believe that Matthew and Luke omitted by chance and in 250 instances the same passages from the original they were working with. If a person wishing to defend the 2SH would meet Matthew or Luke, he should urge them to buy a mega-jackpot lottery ticket.

This is not even the end of the matter, though. In addition to the 250 identical omissions, there are 230 cases in which not only Matthew's text differs from Mark with respect to changes in the wording used and/or additions to the text, but Luke's text differs in an identical way from Mark. Thus, the 2SH people want us to believe that independently of each other and by chance, Matthew and Luke made about 230 identical changes of wordings and/or additions of phrases to Mark's text. This brings the total of identical alterations (omissions + changes) to almost 500[14]. If this was by chance, Matthew and Luke ought to be encouraged to buy lottery tickets for the mega-mega-jackpot.

To be serious: The part of the 2SH that wants us to believe that Matthew and Luke copied from Mark is unrealistic, especially in view of the fact that there is another plausible explanation of the similarities between the synoptic Gospels. Prior to taking it up, though, I must say a word about the second major part of the 2SH: The "Source Q."

---

14 For the omissions, see Hans-Herbert Stoldt, *History and Criticism of the Marcan Hypothesis*, translated and edited by Donald L. Niewyk (Macon, GA: Mercer University Press, 1980); Eta Linnemann, *Is There a Synoptic Problem?* Translated by Robert W. Yarbrough (Grand Rapids, MI: Baker Books, 1992). Stoldt documents about 180 omissions; Linnemann adds another 78. For the so-called "minor" agreements between Matthew and Luke over against Mark, see Ben C. Smith's webpage http://www.textexcavation.com/agreementlist.html.

(5) Difficulties with the "Source Q"

The "Source Q"—what is it? I have mentioned before that it is assumed to be a document containing mostly sayings of Jesus. As was explained, it is introduced to account for the many pericopes which Matthew and Luke share, but which are missing from Mark. Where is that document? No one has ever seen it. There is not even a shred of historic evidence that it ever existed—a feeble attempt to point at an instance of historic evidence is based on a mistranslation of a Greek sentence from an ancient work.[15]

Moreover, since that elusive source is to explain the agreements between Matthew and Luke with respect to matters not in Mark, all of a sudden, it must even be assumed to contain at least one of the sayings of John the Baptist (see Mt 3.12 and Lk 3.17, reporting words the Baptist is said to have spoken, but which are not found in Mark[16]).

More importantly, though, there are many cases in which the 2SH defenders wish us to believe that Matthew and Luke used the same Source Q, but even only superficially comparing Matthew's pericope with that of Luke makes more than unlikely that they actually used the same document. By way of example, let me use the so-called Beatitudes, one of the most well-known segments of Jesus' teachings. These are statements of Jesus beginning with the words, "Blessed are …," such as, "Blessed are the poor in spirit, for theirs is the kingdom of heaven." (Mt 5.3) The word "beatitude" comes from the Latin *beatitudo*, meaning "the condition of happiness, felicity, or blessedness."

---

15 This so-called "historic evidence" in support of Q is contained in a work of a certain Papias, bishop of Hierapolis (a town in Asia Minor) around A.D. 130. The original of Papias's work is lost, but passages of it are quoted in other works, in Eusebius's *Church History*, for example. (Eusebius lived from A.D. 260 to 340.) The passage as quoted by Eusebius is "Matthew recorded in the Hebrew language the sayings [of the Lord]." (Eusebius, *Church History*, III/XXXIX. The quotation given in Eusebius does not contain the words, "of the Lord"; but the context in which Eusebius places the sentence quoted makes obvious that Papias was referring to the sayings of Jesus, at least as Eusebius understood him.) Some Source Q defenders argue, "What this Papias quotation speaks about is not to be confused with the Gospel of Matthew as we do have it today. Our Gospel is, after all, not limited to sayings of Jesus, but also contains accounts of his supposed deeds. Papias is speaking about an earlier document, perhaps really written by Matthew, that is limited (or perhaps mostly limited) to sayings of Jesus and does not include (or does hardly include) accounts of his deeds. That's precisely what we take the Source Q to be. Thus, although that source is lost today, the Papias quotation provides historic evidence supporting the thesis that once, that source existed." On the face of it, this seems a persuasive argument—until one considers the actual use Papias makes of the expression translated in the quotation as "sayings." He uses the Greek *logia*. Often, it is translated as "oracles"; in the Greek Papias used (called *koine*), it can also be rendered as "words" or, as it is rendered in the quotation, "sayings." It is now important to realize that Papias uses the very same expression in the title to his own book from which Eusebius takes the quotation. That title is, "Explanation of the *sayings* of the Lord." (Emphasis added.) Numerous quotations from that work have been preserved (remember that the original is lost), and they make clear that Papias himself, in spite of the title he gave to his work, does not limit his account to what Jesus said, but includes what he did. Thus, when Papias uses the expression *logia* ("sayings"), one cannot conclude that he has in mind only "what is said." This must also be kept in mind with regard to his statement about Matthew's work. When he says that Matthew recorded the sayings of the Lord, one may not assume that he wishes to convey the idea that Matthew wrote a work consisting only (or mostly) of what Jesus said. Moreover, there is a passage in which Papias applies the expression, "sayings of the Lord," to Mark's Gospel, about which he has said earlier explicitly that it is about Jesus' "speaking or working." Thus, the only historical evidence the Source Q defenders have ever referred to is based on an unwarranted interpretation of a passage from the work of Papias.

16 These words are, "His winnowing fan is in his hand. He will clear his threshing floor and gather his wheat into his barn, but the chaff he will burn with unquenchable fire." (This is the version found in Matthew; the version found in Luke is very slightly different.)

The Beatitudes can be found in Matthew 5.3–11 and Luke 6.20–26.[17] According to the 2SH, these pericopes contain material which Matthew and Luke have taken from the Source Q.

On the basis of comparing the Matthew and Luke pericopes, it becomes more than unlikely, though (understatement!), that we are concerned with two passages even only vaguely based on the same source, let alone copied from it.

First, in Matthew's version, there are eight (or nine) Beatitudes,[18] in Luke, there are only four; the other four (or five) are "dropped." Second, the four that can be found in Luke are similar, but also different (in some cases, even significantly different) from the corresponding ones in Matthew. Here are the chief differences (in each case, the Matthew version is stated first): "Blessed are the poor in spirit" vs. "Blessed are the poor"; "Blessed are those who hunger and thirst for justice" vs. "Blessed are the hungry": "Blessed are those who mourn" vs. "Blessed are those who weep"; "Blessed are those who are persecuted" vs. "Blessed are you if you are hated, driven out, abused, denounced …"[19]

Third, Luke's pericope includes four "Woes," the opposite of his four "Beatitudes"; the Matthew pericope does not contain these "Woes."

Thus, if Source Q contained Luke's version, Matthew would have been sloppy and dishonest—sloppy by altering the four Beatitudes that he used and by omitting the "Woes";[20] dishonest by making up four (or five) additional Beatitudes and placing them into Jesus' mouth. If Source Q contained Matthew's version, then Luke would have been sloppy and dishonest—sloppy again by changing the content of the four Beatitudes he took from his source, and omitting the remaining four (or five); dishonest by making up the four "Woes" and placing them into Jesus' mouth.[21] There is, of course, a third possibility: That Source Q was different from both of what we find in Matthew and Luke, and that both Matthew and Luke were sloppy and dishonest. Many secularists would say, "That's the possibility we love—you bet that both of them were sloppy, dishonest, and some other things." Someone like me, going by the Fox principle, must state, "Maybe—not for me to say."

Fairness demands, though, to point out that there is a possibility that does not include sloppiness and dishonesty, a possibility I will initially apply to the Matthew and Luke pericopes on the Beatitudes, then, to the entire material allegedly coming from Source Q, and then, to the entire 2SH, which brings me to …

---

17 The Luke passage referred to also contains the so-called Woes. Usually, the 2SH defenders do not consider them a part of the Source Q.

18 The traditional "Eight Beatitudes" are those which begin with the words, "Blessed are they …"; they are followed by a statement beginning with the words, "Blessed are you …" If this statement, addressed to a different group of people, is added, the count of the Beatitudes is nine.

19 One could make a case that Luke's Fourth Beatitude combines Matthew's eighth and ninth, although even so, differences remain.

20 As mentioned in a previous footnote, most 2SH defenders do not think that the "Woes" were included in the Source Q; thus, maybe Matthew can be absolved of the second part of the "sloppiness accusation."

21 Again, as mentioned in a previous footnote, the "Woes" are usually not considered as a part of the Source Q. This raises the question, "Where did Luke get them from?" One can, of course, take recourse to the ad hoc hypothesis that he used a different source from which he got them. Putting to the side the unsatisfactory nature of introducing ad hoc hypotheses whenever a difficulty arises for one's theory (incidentally, 2SH folks are in love with the ad hoc hypotheses procedure), this raises a different question: "By what right did Luke make the 'Woes' coming from a different source into a part of the 'Beatitudes' speech if the source he was using did not contain them as a part of it?" Needless to say, even I would have several ad hoc hypotheses ready to answer that question—but as mentioned, shooting off ad hoc hypotheses is an unsatisfactory method to extricate oneself from a difficulty.

7. Fritz's "modest proposal" concerning the synoptic problem (the hobbyhorse is still with us)

(1) The two "Beatitudes" speeches

What if Matthew's and Luke's accounts of the "Beatitudes" speech are records of two separate presentations that Jesus gave at different times? The significant differences between the Matthew version and the Luke version tends to support (understatement!!!) this possibility. There are, however, additional observations lending credence to it.

The first relates to the events preceding Jesus' presentation(s) and the identification of the surroundings. In Matthew, Jesus sees a crowd of people; he walks up a mountain and sits down; his disciples come to him, and he begins to teach them. Since this teaching occurs on a mountain, it is aptly called, "Sermon on the Mount," and the eight (or nine) Beatitudes are the introduction to an extensive "speech." In Luke, Jesus walks up a mountain, calls his disciples, selects from them a group of 12 whom he calls "apostles," then comes down from the mountain, stands on level ground; there is a huge crowd of people, and "looking at his disciples," he begins to teach. Since his presentation occurs on level ground, it is appropriately called, "Sermon on the Plain." The four Beatitudes and four Woes are the introduction to a much shorter speech than the one Matthew presents, although both speeches also are similar in a number of respects.

Next, the speech Luke presents—the one beginning with the four Beatitudes and the four Woes—occurs, as just stated, immediately after the selection of the 12 Apostles (the Apostle Matthew being one of them), while the speech presented by Matthew appears to be given prior to that selection. Matthew does not record the selection itself; he mentions the names of the Apostles, together with the first instance in which they are sent out on a mission (Mt 10.1–7); it seems that they had been selected by then. One of them, however, the tax collector Matthew, appears to have been called to follow Jesus (the call is reported in Mt 9.9) only after the Sermon of the Mount. Thus, it seems that Matthew's Sermon on the Mount is based on a presentation Jesus gave prior to his selection of the 12 Apostles, while Luke's "Sermon on the Plain" is based on a similar presentation which Jesus gave a little later, immediately after the selection of the Apostles. In addition to being similar to the earlier presentation, that later one also was significantly different in several respects.

(2) The significance of oral traditions based on memorization

Further, we must try to appreciate a communication device that in our time is hardly used at all: Oral traditions based on careful memorization. That's how the Mishna, for example—commentaries on the Jewish law in the Torah[22]—has been transmitted. In the case of the Mishna, its being wedded to oral transmission was so strong that "for centuries, Judaism's leading rabbis had resisted writing down the Oral Law. Teaching the law orally, the rabbis knew, compelled students to maintain close relationships with their teachers, and they considered teachers, not books, to be the best conveyors of the Jewish tradition."[23] This attitude persisted up until the end of the second/beginning of the third century; it was

---

22 See the appropriate segment in the Judaism section.
23 Telushkin, *Literacy*, p. 151.

only then that Rabbi Judah wrote the oral traditions down, fearing that, "with the death of so many teachers in the failed revolts … the Oral Law would be forgotten."[24]

Jesus lived more than 150 years prior to Rabbi Judah; he lived in a Jewish environment. It is not farfetched to hold that the contemporary emphasis on oral traditions based on careful memorization was important in his circles, as it was in those of other rabbis (Jesus is frequently referred to as "rabbi" in the Gospels). Oral tradition based on careful memorization is a learning technique which is, unfortunately, underappreciated today—more correctly: it is totally unappreciated. Whenever I want my students to memorize content, I am likely to be asked in a contemptuous tone of voice, "Do you want us to regurgitate your words?" Whoever looks at ancient times with an attitude even only vaguely similar to the one that student comment expresses misunderstands them.[25]

(3) Explanation of the similarities between the synoptic Gospels

Thus, might there not have been oral traditions going back to Jesus and transmitting, on the basis of careful memorization, the precise content of his words, as well as accounts of what he did? It certainly does not stretch credulity to assume that it was so.[26] If one assumes that the synoptic Gospels were based on these traditions (Matthew may even have been chiefly responsible for one of them), one encounters a plausible explanation of the similarities—except that one point must be added: Jesus spoke in Aramaic, but the language commonly spoken around the Mediterranean Sea was Greek, and that's the language in which the Gospels were written (with the possible exception of Matthew, as remarked earlier). One must, therefore, add that the original Aramaic oral traditions were translated into Greek, and that there were early Greek versions of these traditions, just as authoritative as the Aramaic ones.

(4) Explanation of the differences between the synoptic Gospels

Thus, there is an alternative explanation of the similarities between the synoptic Gospels—an alternative to the 2SH, that is. How about the differences, however, some of which are minor, some of which are significant—even very significant? Are they due to changes either the Gospel authors or the persons responsible for transmitting the early oral traditions made?

Not necessarily.

We read in the Gospels time and again that Jesus went from town to town proclaiming the Good News.[27] We do not know how many towns he went to; but clearly, there were many, many, *many* towns. It obviously stands to reason that whenever he came to a new town, he started out with giving something like a "standard presentation." Since he did not speak from a prepared script (there is no evidence that he ever wrote even a single letter), these presentations might have been similar, but not

---

24 Ibid.

25 In the wake of the damage John Dewey inflicted on the American system of education, this attitude is prevalent not only among American students, but also among American educators.

26 Surely, it does not stretch credulity to the same extent as to having to assume that Matthew and Luke happened to make, independently of each other and by chance, almost 500 of the exact same changes—additions and omissions—to Mark's text from which they allegedly were copying.

27 In the first three chapters of Mark's Gospel alone, there are five instances in which it is stated that Jesus was teaching without any specifics of what he said being mentioned; one of these instances (Mk 1.38–39) specifically states that he went to "nearby villages" (plural) "into their synagogues."

identical. It is quite possible that different oral traditions developed, which went back to different versions of a basic presentation Jesus gave.

All of this is in keeping with the words of Farnell who says that the Gospels rest on "stable traditions from apostolic eyewitnesses," standardized with the help of the "memorization techniques of ancient times."[28] If this is how it was, one would be provided with an explanation of the similarities between the Gospels, up to and including the same language (or almost the same language) being used; one would also be provided with an explanation of the differences. Moreover, the explanation is in keeping with the unanimous second-century tradition about the authorship of the synoptic Gospels.

---

28 F. David Farnell, "Independence Response to Chapter 1" in Robert L. Thomas, ed., *Three Views on the Origins of the Synoptic Gospels* (Grand Rapids, MI: Kregel, 2002), pp. 115–116.

CHAPTER TEN

The Life of Jesus According to the New Testament

(I) JESUS PRIOR TO HIS PUBLIC MINISTRY

According to the New Testament, Jesus was a descendant of David, the second king of the united kingdom of the Israelites. The New Testament calls him "Son of David," using the word "son" as jumping generations, in the sense in which we use the word descendant. The mother of Jesus was Mary. His birth supposedly was announced to her by an angel and occurred as a virgin birth, without the intervention of a human male:[1] As the angel told Mary, "The Holy Spirit will come upon you, and the power of the Most High will overshadow you." (Lk 1.35) Christians interpret the following passage from Isaiah as predicting Jesus' virgin birth: "The Lord himself will give you this sign: the virgin shall be with child, and bear a son, and shall name him Immanuel." (Is 7.14) The name "Immanuel" means "God is with us." According to the Christian understanding, Jesus literally is "Immanuel." Needless to say, when Joseph, Mary's husband-to-be, found out that she was pregnant, he was upset and intended to break the engagement off. Supposedly, however, an angel informed him in a dream about the circumstances of Mary's pregnancy, and he took her into his home. When Jesus' birth had been announced to Mary, she was living in Nazareth; but his birth occurred in Bethlehem, a town about five miles south of Jerusalem. Mary and Joseph had to travel there to comply with the requirements of an official census which made people go to the town they were from. Joseph was a descendant of David who had been born in Bethlehem. After Jesus' birth, they moved back to Nazareth, according to Matthew's gospel, only after having spent quite some time as fugitives in Egypt, because King Herod intended to kill the child: A group of wise men (magi) had

---

1 At times, this virgin birth is mistakenly called "Immaculate Conception." This term applies, however, to the belief that Mary was, from the moment of her conception on, kept free from original sin, in contrast to other humans, who are subject to original sin. The belief in Mary's Immaculate Conception is accepted by Roman Catholics, not by Protestants, however. In contrast, that Jesus was born of a virgin is accepted by all traditional Christians.

come to Herod and asked where the "newborn king of the Jews" could be found, whose star they had seen in the East. Herod considered this as a threat to the continuous rule of his dynasty.

The Gospels report only one event falling between Jesus' early childhood and his appearance in public: When he was 12 years old, his parents took him on a pilgrimage to Jerusalem, and they left the town without him, thinking that he was with their travel companions who had gone ahead of them; but they were to find out that he had stayed behind in Jerusalem. They hurried back to Jerusalem and found him three days later in the Temple, where he had amazed everyone with his understanding and with his answers.

Joseph, the foster father of Jesus, worked as a carpenter. In Mark's Gospel, Jesus also is called "carpenter" by the townspeople of Nazareth. Likely, his father had taught him that craft, and he practiced it.

(II) THE PUBLIC MINISTRY OF JESUS

When Jesus was around 30 years of age, he began to appear in public. A little prior to that, his relative (perhaps cousin) John, known as the Baptist, had begun urging people to repent, and as a sign of their repentance, they allowed him to cleanse ("baptize") them in the Jordan River. At one point, Jesus came and requested to be baptized. John was taken aback and said, "I need to be baptized by you, and yet you are coming to me?" (Mt 3.14) He baptized Jesus only when the latter insisted.

After his baptism, Jesus withdrew into the desert for 40 days to fast and to pray. Then, he went from town to town, teaching the people, curing those who were ill, and performing many other amazing deeds. His main theme can be summarized with his own words, "The Kingdom of God is near. Repent and believe in the Good News." (Mk 1.15)

His insistence on the importance of committing oneself with one's heart to what is right and his rejection of a merely outward observance of the law brought him into conflict with an influential group within Judaism, known as the Pharisees. They followed the law with a single-minded devotion, but often, at least as depicted in the Gospels, at the expense of charity. His severe criticism of them motivated them to develop plans, together with the chief priests, to take his life.

(III) JESUS ENTERS JERUSALEM, IS HAILED AS KING ON THE WAY IN, AND OFFENDS THE JEWISH AUTHORITIES

After Jesus had proclaimed the Good News for the most part in Galilee, he made his way to Jerusalem. He entered town coming from the Mount of Olives, sitting on a donkey, accompanied by a large crowd of people who shouted, "Blessed is the King who comes in the name of the Lord." (Lk 19.38) Evidently, many of the people accompanying him believed that he would become the leader of a revolutionary movement which would begin an uprising against the Roman occupation. Thus, had the Roman authorities gotten wind of the fact that a large crowd was entering Jerusalem hailing their leader as king, they might have believed that once again, a revolution against them was in progress, and they might have started "clamping down" on the people in Jerusalem. For this reason, some of the Pharisees in the crowd urged Jesus to "rebuke his disciples." (Lk 19.39) Rather than telling his disciples to be quiet, as has been requested of him, Jesus replied, "I tell you, if they keep silent, the very stones will cry out." (Lk 19.40)

Next, he went to the Temple and threw a group of money changers and other business people out who had, as he put it, made his Father's house into a den of thieves. For the next several days, he came daily to the Temple to continue proclaiming the Good News. Also, he denounced the Scribes and Pharisees, calling them (among other things) hypocrites, blind guides, whitewashed tombs, beautiful to look at from the outside, but inside full of filth and dean men's bones, serpents, brood of vipers, murderers of the prophets. (See Mt 23 for his denunciation of the Scribes and Pharisees.) This further enraged them about him. (The Scribes, by the way, were the ones able to read and write at the time, only a small percentage of people. They had firsthand knowledge of the Scriptures, because they were able to read them on their own. The Pharisees were a group of people intent on keeping the smallest details of the law.)

From the perspective of the Jewish leadership, there were two strikes against Jesus: First, he undermined their authority; second, he posed a danger by possibly making the Romans believe that a revolution was underfoot, which might have motivated them to restrict the freedom of the Jews even further.

(IV) JESUS IS ARRESTED AND FOUND GUILTY BY THE SANHEDRIN, THE HIGH COURT OF THE JEWS

Thus, the elders of the people and the chief priests met in the palace of the High Priest Caiaphas, and plotted to arrest Jesus. Although he came daily to the Temple to speak to the people there, it appears that the leaders were afraid to arrest him at that place: A riot might break out, since many people still supported him; and the Jewish authorities did not know where he spent the night. Unexpected help arrived for them, though, in the person of one of the 12 Apostles, Judas Iscariot, who promised that for 30 pieces of silver, he would lead the Temple guards to Jesus so that they would be able to arrest him secretly during the night.

It was Passover, and Jesus celebrated this feast with his disciples in a house in Jerusalem—that celebration is known as the Last Supper. Then, he went with his followers to the Mount of Olives. There, the Temple guards, led by Judas, arrested him. All his followers left him and fled.

Jesus was immediately brought before the High Court of the Jews. That court, known as the Sanhedrin, appears to have been convened for a special session. The Roman occupation forces had restricted the authority of the court; it did, for example, not have the power to hand a death sentence down. A person could lawfully be executed only after having been condemned to die by a Roman judge.

During the court proceedings, witnesses were called to testify against Jesus. They gave each other the lie, though, which made their testimony useless. At one point, the presiding officer, the High Priest Caiaphas, asked Jesus whether he was the Messiah, the Son of God. Jesus replied, "It is you who say it. But I tell you this: Soon, you will see the Son of Man [me[2]] seated at the right hand of the Power [God] and coming on the clouds of heaven." (Mt 26.64) In the mind of the people listening to Jesus, his words, through which he placed himself at the right hand of God and claimed that he would be coming on the clouds of heaven, that is, exercise heavenly authority, constituted language offensive to God. The official term for this is "blasphemy." According to the Law of Moses, blasphemy was a capital

---

2 Later, we will examine why Jesus calls himself the "Son of Man."

offense (see Lv 24.10–16). Consequently, Caiaphas said in effect (his words paraphrased here), "Never mind what he supposedly did in the past. You all have heard what he just said right here in front of us. What is your verdict?" They stated that Jesus deserved to die. (For Caiaphas's actual words and the response, see Mt 26.65–66.)

There was, of course, the problem mentioned earlier: The restriction of the Sanhedrin's power. Even if the members of the Sanhedrin were convinced that Jesus had committed a capital offense, they would have to persuade the Roman authorities—the governor Pontius Pilate, in particular—that Jesus deserved to die. It was clear to them that an accusation, "He has offended our God," would not persuade Pilate. Another accusation had to be found, which the governor would take seriously. It came in handy now that Jesus had not stopped the crowds a couple of days earlier when they had hailed him as king. Could not a case have been made on the basis that Jesus was a revolutionary, an insurrectionist? And was that not something the governor would consider a serious offense—in fact, a capital crime?

Jesus was, therefore, dragged to Pontius Pilate—by now, it had become morning. Pilate happened to be in Jerusalem because the Jews were about to celebrate a great feast and he wanted to make sure that things would not get out of hand (his regular residence was in Caesarea on the Mediterranean coast).

(V) PONTIUS PILATE SENTENCES JESUS TO DEATH; HE IS EXECUTED, BURIED, BUT SAID TO HAVE RISEN FROM THE DEAD

Pilate listened to the accusation against Jesus—that he had claimed to be the king of the Jews. He then asked Jesus privately about the matter. In reply to the question whether he was the king of the Jews, Jesus replied, "My kingdom does not belong to this world" (Jn 18.36). Responding to Pilate's question, "Then, you are a king," Jesus said, among other things, that that he had been born "to testify to the truth" (Jn 18.37), a statement in response to which Pilate asked, demonstrating an early version of the "What's true for you is true for you and what's true for me is true for me" attitude, probably nothing but contempt in his voice, "What is truth?" (Jn 18.38)

If one reads between the lines, he probably thought, "Well, he claims to be a king; but he says that his kingdom is not of this world—he does not seem to pose a danger to the Roman authorities. Besides, he is into that 'truth thing'; a strange character, but not guilty as charged." At any rate, he was convinced that he was not dealing with a revolutionary and told Jesus' accusers so. When in response, a near-riot broke out before his palace, he ordered that Jesus be executed to quell the disorder, although convinced of the innocence of the man whom he sentenced to death by crucifixion.[3]

As was common, a sign was placed on top of the cross onto which Jesus had been nailed, to indicate the reason why he had been executed. Pilate ordered the sign to be written in Aramaic, Greek, and

---

3 Commanding the execution of a person one believes to be innocent is pretty much the worst miscarriage of justice a judge can become guilty of. Pilate is presented in the Gospels precisely as such a judge. This makes the view held by many that the Gospels present Pilate in a sympathetic way rather odd, to put it mildly. Even Joseph Telushkin, whose work I greatly admire (and quoted numerous times in my presentation of Judaism) falls for that fiction when he speaks of the "gentle, kind-hearted Pilate of the New Testament." (Telushkin, *Literacy*, p. 127.)

Latin. The Latin version is "Iesus Nazarenus Rex Iudaeorum" (acronym: INRI), meaning Jesus of Nazareth, King of the Jews." This wording was chosen by Pilate to mock the Jews, to get back at them for having made him order the execution of an innocent man: "Just look—here is your king, on a cross." The Jewish leadership went to Pilate to request that the inscription be changed to, "He claimed to be King of the Jews." Pilate, who had had absolutely no backbone when it counted, suddenly became firm and said, "What I have written, I have written" (Jn 19.22).

About three hours after Jesus had been nailed to the cross, he died.

With Pilate's permission, his followers took Jesus' body down from the cross and placed him in a nearby tomb. With a high holy day beginning at dusk, however, on which it was not permitted to handle a corpse, there was not enough time to prepare the body appropriately. Thus, the corpse lay in the tomb on Friday, beginning just before dusk, all day Saturday, and on the following Sunday, early in the morning, a group of women came to prepare the body properly for burial—but the tomb was empty. They did not find Jesus.

The Gospels say that Jesus had risen from the death.

Subsequently, Jesus is said to have appeared to his disciples several times over a 40-day period and to have kept instructing them; at the end of that period, he ordered his disciples to go into the entire world and teach people what he had taught; then, he was taken up into heaven, with a promise that he was going to come again.

CHAPTER ELEVEN

What Does Christianity Teach About God?

(I) INTRODUCTORY REMARKS: CHRISTIANS BELIEVE IN ONE GOD, LIKE JEWS AND MUSLIMS

Originally, I had written a more complex title—something like, "Fundamentals of Christian theological teachings"; but then, I decided to go with the simpler version, "What does Christianity teach about God?" Nevertheless, I must explain what the word "theology" means. It is derived from two Greek words. One of them is *theos*, meaning "God"; the other is *logos*, literally meaning "word." Thus, "theology," literally translated, is "word about God"; a bit more freely rendered, it is "teaching about God." Thus, the theology of a religion is that religion's teaching about God and related matters.

Back to the question in the main title: What does Christianity teach about God? ("What is the theology of Christianity?")

Way, way back, I made you think (at least I hope that I made you think) about the cause of the universe according to Jews, Christians, and Muslims. They consider God as that cause. Subsequently, I explained the nature of God as Jews, Christians, and Muslims understand it to be. With this, I explained the core belief of the three religions mentioned in the title of this course, which also is the core belief of Christianity: Christians hold that there is one—and only one—God who created the universe and everything in it (including space and time); he must keep each and every individual thing in existence, including each and every human being; this God created humans out of love and wishes them to love him back; every single one of us has been created for the purpose of becoming happy through an intimate love relationship with God.

Historically speaking, the understanding of God just explained comes from the Jewish religion. Whatever Jews (and also Muslims) positively say about God, Christians agree with. Why do I say, "Positively"? Because there is, within Christianity, an important addition to the Jewish monotheism with which Jews do not agree (neither do Muslims), which they deny; but that's not a positive statement; rather, it is a negative one.

(II) THE TRINITY: ONE GOD IN THREE PERSONS

1. The "bare-bones" statement; a passage from Matthew's Gospel; what makes the three divine persons different from each other?

What is this addition? The teaching on the Trinity, a word literally translated as "three-ness". In its most basic formulation—I call it the "bare-bones statement"—that teaching is, "There is one God in three persons, the Father, the Son, and the Holy Spirit."

In this context, Christians point at the following passage from Matthew's Gospel: At the end of that Gospel, when Jesus tells his followers to spread his message, he says: "All power in heaven and on earth has been given to me. Go, therefore, and make disciples of all the nations, baptizing them **in the name of the Father, and of the Son, and of the Holy Spirit**, teaching them to observe all that I have commanded you. And behold, I am with you always, until the end of the age." (Mt 28.18–20.) The part printed in bold—known as the Trinitarian Formula—overlaps with the teaching on the Trinity, as stated in what I have called the "bare-bones" statement.

It is important to note that the quotation from Matthew uses the singular form of "name," although three persons (the Father, the Son, and the Holy Spirit) are mentioned, which would make one expect the plural form, "names." Christians see this as an indication that, although there are three persons, there is only one "name," one "entity," one God.

Christians hold that the three persons have the same nature—they are identical in each and every respect; but nevertheless, they are three persons. If you ask a Christian as to how one can "get at" the difference between these three persons, you are told that one must consider how they "relate" to each other, and that there is an ancient document, known as the Nicene Creed, which contains statements about these relations. I am going to call these statements "an ancient formulation of the doctrine of the Trinity," to distinguish them from the simpler "bare-bones statement," and because they stem from that ancient document, about which I am going to say a couple of words next: The Nicene Creed.

2. The Nicene Creed: An ancient formulation of the teaching on the Trinity

(1) History and text of the Nicene Creed

Remember what a creed is? If you say, "A concise, official summary of the beliefs of a religion," go to the head of the class (said with deference to Walter Williams).

The Nicene Creed has its name because it was compiled in a town called Nicaea, located in what is today Turkey, a little southeast of Constantinople (today's Istanbul). Nicaea's contemporary name is Iznik. In the year 325, a little over a decade after the Roman emperor Constantine had decreed that Christianity was henceforth to be tolerated in the Roman Empire, bishops from around the then known world met in Nicaea to clarify the Christian faith. Such meetings are called Ecumenical Councils, and the A.D. 325 meeting is known as the Council of Nicaea.[1] During that meeting, the bishops compiled a creed known as the Nicene Creed. Actually, some of the parts of the creed as used by Christians today were added at a later council, the Council of Constantinople,[2] which met in 381. Sticklers for detail insist, therefore, on calling the Creed the "Nicene-Constantinople Creed"; we are not sticklers for detail here, though—at least not for this detail; so I will continue calling it the Nicene Creed. Here it is—passages in bold print have a bearing on the subsequent explanation of the teaching on the Trinity:

[1] **"I believe in one God, the Father Almighty,** creator of heaven and earth, of all things visible and invisible.

[2] **"And in one Lord Jesus Christ, the only Son of God, eternally begotten of the Father, God from God, Light from Light, true God from true God, begotten, not made, of one substance with the Father,** through whom all things were made; for us men and for our salvation, he came down from heaven: by the power of the Holy Spirit he was born of the Virgin Mary, and became man. For our sake, he was crucified under Pontius Pilate; he suffered and was buried, and on the third day he rose again, in fulfillment of the Scriptures, and ascended into heaven, and sits at the right hand of the Father. He will come again in glory to judge the living and the dead, and his kingdom will have no end.

[3] **"I believe in the Holy Spirit, the Lord, the Giver of Life, who proceeds from the Father (and the Son);[3] with the Father and the Son, he is worshipped and glorified;** he has spoken through the prophets.

[4] "I believe in one holy catholic and apostolic Church; I acknowledge one baptism for the forgiveness of sins; I look for the resurrection of the dead, and the life of the world to come. Amen."

As you see, I have numbered the parts [1]–[4]. This should help one get a handle on the Creed's content: The first part affirms the existence of only one God and deals with God the Father; the second part deals with God the Son; the third part deals with God the Holy Spirit; and the fourth part deals with the following four miscellaneous items: (1) The church; (2) baptism; (3) resurrection; and (4) the life to come.

(2) An imaginary theologian says a few words about the "processions" in the Trinity

Before speaking about that creed myself, I am inviting an imaginary Christian theologian for a short presentation. He might remind you that the differences between the three divine persons in the Trinity consist in the relations between these persons, and that they are related by way of processions.

---

1 More precisely, the First Council of Nicaea, because there was another such meeting in the same town, known as the Second Council of Nicaea. It met in 787.

2 Again, more precisely, the First Council of Constantinople, because there were other such meetings in that town.

3 See next footnote.

Maybe this makes you ask, "What do you mean? By way of a parade?" The theologian would reply, "That's not what 'procession' means in this context. Here, it means, 'the coming forth from.'" Before giving you a chance to ask another question, he adds, "There are two processions in the Trinity. The Son comes forth from the Father, and the Holy Spirit comes forth from the Father and the Son.[4] Did you get it?"

Maybe you reply, "The word 'forth' throws me off a bit; but are you saying that the Son comes from the Father, and that the Holy Spirit comes from the Father and the Son?" A stern theologian would now say, "Don't omit the word 'forth!'" The theologian I invited is on the mild side, though; consequently, he replies. "If this were a course in a Christian seminary, I would not let you get away with skipping 'forth'; but maybe for a 100-level religious studies course at a secular university, it's OK."

So you repeat, "I get it—I think, at least: According to Christianity, the Son comes from the Father, and the Holy Spirit comes from the Father and the Son. Is that what the Nicene Creed says?"

"Well, back to the Nicene Creed," the theologian says. "It begins with affirming a belief 'in one God, the Father almighty, the creator of Heaven and of Earth.' It also affirms a belief 'in one Lord …[5] the only son of God, eternally begotten of the Father, God from God, light from light, true God from true God, begotten, not made, one in substance with the Father.'[6] Twice, you heard the word 'begotten.' That's the first procession in the Trinity: The Son is begotten by the Father." You interject: "So the Son comes from the Father through being begotten by the father?" The theologian replies, "Yes—if I continue compromising on the word 'forth,' that is. Do you follow me?" You complain, "The word 'begotten' throws me off— the problems I do have with the word 'forth' are like nothing compared to it." The theologian states, "We will get to it. But first, the second procession. The creed states, 'I believe in the Holy Spirit, the Lord, the giver of life, who proceeds from the Father and the Son.' There you have it." You ask, "So the Holy Spirit comes from the Father and the Son through proceeding from them?" "Yes."

Here is, therefore, the result of this conversation: There are two processions in the Trinity. First, the Son is begotten by the Father; second, the Holy Spirit proceeds from the Father and the Son.

(3) The significance of the "begetting" language: An affirmation of the equality between Father and Son

Now, let the theologian excuse himself; I am going to continue speaking instead of him. Allow me to return to that troubling word "begotten"—remember, he promised that he would come back to it—but he is gone.

"Begotten" is the passive form (i.e., the form indicating what is done to someone) corresponding to the active form "beget." Instead of "the Son is begotten by the Father," we might as well say, "The Father begets the Son." "Begetting" is an old-fashioned expression indicating a father's "bringing forth" a son. In its literal sense, the word "begetting" applies only to human fathers and sons: There is, of course, no literal begetting in the case of a divine person; literal begetting demands, after all, also a mother,

---

4 My apologies to those Christians—about 30% of the total number—according to whom the Holy Spirit comes forth only from the Father.

5 Jesus Christ (details on that point will be covered later in the text).

6 An often used alternative translation has "one in being" rather than "one in substance."

and that's missing in the case of the divine Father who begets a Son.[7] So why is the word "begotten" used at all? Why is it insisted upon? To get at it, one must pay attention to what it is that the Creed differentiates "begetting" from. It says, "Begotten, not made." This is to provide the clue.

Let us, therefore, think first about the "making" relationship. A computer programmer makes a computer program; a pastry chef makes pastries; a cabinetmaker makes cabinets; and so on. What ranks higher, the maker or the thing made? Why, the maker, of course.

Now, let's think about the begetting relationship. Who ranks higher, the father or the son? Why, they are equal in dignity.[8] Thus, when the Creed says that the Son is begotten by the Father, it does not wish to imply that the Father had some kind of mate[9] with whom he produced the Son; rather, the intent is to highlight the equality between God the Father and God the Son. They are understood to be equal in dignity, power, authority, and everything else: They share the same nature.

3. An "update" of an old speculation about the Trinity

(1) Reminder of the significance of "being in God's image"

And now for something really complicated ("What do you mean? Are you implying that the previous segment was not 'really complicated'? We tend to disagree."). I call it an "update" of an old specula-tion of the Trinity. The speculation goes back to St. Augustine (354–430) and St. Thomas Aquinas (1225–1274). Why "update"? Because I do not dare ascribe to them what I am going to explain—they might not be happy with my presentation.[10] I must acknowledge, though, that what I am going to say is influenced by them.

Prior to going into the speculation itself, I must remind you of a thought which I included in my explanation of the nature of God as believed in by Jews and Christians: Humans are in the image of God, which means that in spite of all the differences, there must be similarities between humans and God. For this reason, considering human nature gives us at least one or another clue about what God is like. Remember the "God is somehow like that" phrase. This thought is to be used in the speculation about the Trinity.

(2) Intermediate step #1: "It is not your nature to exist"

Next, two "intermediate steps" are important. The first one is to acquaint you with a thought my philosopher colleagues[11] are practically in love with, because it has to do with what they call essence and existence. Maybe I should avoid these words, at least the first one, and use "nature" instead of it.

---

7 Qur'an passage 6.101, critical of the idea of God's having a son, seems to understand it in the literal sense: "Wonderful originator of the heavens and the earth! How could He have a son when He has no consort?" (Based on Ali.) Christians would consider this as a fundamental misunderstanding of their view.

8 If a son would have less dignity than the father, humanity would, in view of the many generations for which it exists by now, have "run out" of dignity already.

9 Or "consort," as the Qur'an passage quoted two footnotes ago states.

10 They might consider it as a "down-date."

11 Remember that, in spite of what my dean and my department chair think about my day job, I am not a philosopher, but only a philosophy teacher.

Without a doubt, you *are*, you exist. You would not exist if your parents never had met, if your parents' parents never had met, if your parents' parents' parents never had met, and so on; you get the drift. If we go back only 500 years, the number of things that had to happen precisely at the right time for you to come about (and the right people meeting at the right time is only a small fraction of what was required) is staggering. This also means that 500 years ago (which actually is only a small fraction of the period of time for which humans exist), the odds against your ever coming into existence were overwhelming. Thus, while it is no doubt true that you exist, things could easily have developed such that saying, "You exist," would be false. That you exist is true; but you do not exist necessarily (philosophers would say that your existence is not necessary, but a contingent—a very, very contingent [highbrow for "iffy"] thing). It is your nature to have two eyes, two ears, maybe dark hair—but IT IS NOT YOUR NATURE TO EXIST; existence is not a part of your nature (keep this in mind; the "speculation" being summarized here claims that God is different from you in precisely this respect).

(3) Intermediate step #2: The "What had to happen …" question is meaningful with regard to contingent (not necessary) matters, but meaningless with regard to necessary matters

Now for a second "intermediate step": "What had to happen for you to come about, for you to have brown eyes (assuming that you are a brown-eyed person), for you to have a high IQ (I hope you do)?" All of these are meaningful questions (even if we might not know the answers or not all the answers), and answering them would provide the reasons for its being as it is. If these reasons are assumed to have been absent, matters might be different—it might then be that you would not exist, not have brown eyes, not have a high IQ: None of these things are necessary; they could have turned out differently.

Suppose now that someone were to ask, "What are the things that had to happen for two plus two to equal four, rather than resulting in another sum?" That's a silly question, because under no circumstances could it have been different. In contrast to your having a high IQ, which might be different if there had been some brain disease on your part while your mother was pregnant with you, "Two plus two equals four" is necessary. It could not possibly be otherwise. It is necessarily the nature of two plus two to equal four.

Why "intermediate step?" Well, it was to familiarize you with the concept of some things being absolutely necessary, like "two plus two equaling four," in contrast to your having a high IQ and your existence, which are not necessary.

(4) "What had to happen for God to exist?" Come again? Existence is a part of God's nature

Now, ask someone who believes in the God of Christianity (or Judaism or Islam): "What had to happen for God to exist?" The answer you would get is, "That is a question just as silly as asking, 'What had to happen for two plus two to equal four?' Nothing had to happen. God simply exists necessarily—he could not possibly be nonexistent. God's existence is not like yours—contingent, dependent on so many other things, so unbelievably 'iffy.' God's existence does not depend on anything; it is necessary; it is God's nature to exist; existence necessarily belongs to God's nature or is a part of his nature."

Your nature—that you are a person, a human person, a man or woman with many traits—can be described in detail (your best friend could probably go on and on describing it); but if anyone would add, "And existence also is a part of his or her nature," that would be false. It would suggest that your existence is necessary, when we saw before clearly that it isn't necessary at all, since so many things had to happen for you to come about.[12]

In contrast, not only can God's nature be described (He is a person, omnipotent, omniscient, perfectly good, etc.), but it is true to say about him, "It is his nature to exist"; since he exists necessarily, existence is a part of his nature.[13]

(5) The Son is begotten (generated) through the Father's perfect self-knowledge

Following this detour over my day job, back to the speculation (actually, the day job detour is an important part of the speculation):

Remember: We are in the image of God. We are personal beings—God also is a personal being. Now a "key feature" of persons (a key part of their nature) is awareness of things different from themselves and self-awareness.

Awareness of things different from oneself makes one's mind, as it were, into a mirror of these things.

For our purpose, self-awareness is of particular importance. Knowing oneself is a bit like looking into a mirror. Just as looking into a mirror causes a literal mirror image of oneself, self-knowledge causes, as it were, a mental mirror image of oneself (not a literal one, of course, but a "figurative" one).

If God is a person, he also knows himself.

There are, however, two important differences between human and divine self-knowledge:

First, an obvious one: All human knowledge is incomplete, deficient; it is also shot through with what is incorrect. This applies also to human self-knowledge: The figurative mental mirror image it generates is in many respects incomplete and distorted. There is no human being knowing him- or herself completely and accurately. Think of coming across a mirror in a dimly lit hallway. Imagine that mirror not made of glass, but of a rather dull metal, and parts of it are missing, parts of it are bent out of shape. What you would see of yourself in such a mirror is an analogy for the (figurative) mirror image human self-knowledge generates in the human mind. There are many aspects (parts) of my nature that I do not even know about, that are missing from my own self-image; and many parts of that self-image do not correspond to how I really am—they are incorrect.

In contrast, since God is all-knowing, divine self-knowledge is totally accurate and complete. This means that each and every feature (part) of God's nature must be reflected in his "self-image" precisely as it is in the "original." Remember now one of the features which is a part of God's nature, but not of the nature of humans: Remember that it is God's nature to exist, that existence is a part of God's nature (but not of any human being's nature).

---

12 Besides your existence, the individual traits of your nature are not necessarily either, by the way. The only manner in which necessity enters the picture in the case of a human being's nature is that in some cases, if one feature becomes a part of a human's nature, another feature necessarily also must be present. Suppose someone becomes a murderer ("being a murderer" enters his or her nature). Then, this person will, on the basis of this, necessarily become guilty (a state of guilt enters his or her nature).

13 This thought is involved in a famed attempt to prove God's existence. That attempt has come to be known as the "ontological argument."

Well, if each and every aspect (part) of God's nature must be contained in his self-image generated by his self-knowledge, then God's existence also must be represented in his self-knowledge—and it must be represented there exactly as it is in the original. Thus, God's self-image turns out to have exactly the same features as God (himself) plus existence exactly as God himself does have it. Do you see, then, that the mirror image God's self-knowledge generates is just like God and just as real—real in exactly the same way, shape, and form as God? Thus, God's (the Father's) self-knowledge inevitably generates a second person just like him, just as real as he, a second divine person, called "the Son" by Christian theologians.

Thus, what is it through which the Son is "begotten" (as the Nicene Creed has it)? It is the Father's perfect self-knowledge: The Father's perfect self-knowledge generates (or begets) the Son.

The Father knows himself perfectly since eternity—it is not that only slowly over time did he "find out" how he was (remember that he is not even temporal, but created time); thus, the Son is just as eternal as the father.

In line with this, Christians say: The first divine person (called the Father) necessarily gives rise to a second person (called the Son), in every respect like the first.[14]

(6) The Holy Spirit is generated through the self-donation involved in the love between the Father and the Son

How about the third person called the Holy Spirit?[15]

Remember once again that Christians hold humans to be in the image of God and that, therefore, thinking about human nature gives us some clues about what God is like.

Looking at two human persons, we realize that they can relate to one another in many different ways. In many cases, they are indifferent to each other; they might resent one another; they might envy each other, maybe even hate each other. All of this is regrettable. Try now to find an answer to the following question: "What is the deepest, the most profound, the most desirable way for two human persons to relate to each other?" Why, they should appreciate each other for what each of them is in him- or herself; each should recognize the other's dignity, and joyfully affirm—not only with the

---

14 Anselm of Canterbury (1033–1109) raises the following objection to this train of thoughts: If God the Father knows himself perfectly and if the Son is like him, does having perfect self-knowledge not also apply to the Son? And if that perfect self-knowledge generates a divine person in the case of the Father, would it not have to do so also in the case of the Son? And aren't the two persons generated by the Father's and by the Son's self-knowledge also like the Father and the Son, including with regard to perfect and person-generating self-knowledge so that they also would have to generate additional persons who in turn also would have to generate additional persons and so on, ad infinitum (forever and ever)? In responding to this objection, Thomas Aquinas "puts human reason in its place," as it were. His reply amounts to saying that our awareness of a person-generating self-knowledge in the case of God the Father is based on revelation only, and that revelation also tells us that this person-generating self-knowledge is limited to the Father. Maybe the following thought can be added—not that anyone should dare to improve on Aquinas in a footnote to a religion text for a 100-level course taught at a secular school: "If in the Son, there would be self-knowledge entirely independent of the Father's self-knowledge, there would have to be an 'infinite progression' of divine persons. With regard to self-knowledge, however, what is 'mirrored' in the Son is the Father's knowing himself. The Son 'knows himself' in the Father's self-knowledge; that is, in the very self-knowledge that generates the Son. This is why the 'person-generating self-knowledge' terminates in the Son."

15 Those Christians—a minority, including the Eastern Orthodox—who hold that the Holy Spirit proceeds from the Father only will not be all that happy with this part of the old speculation.

mind, but with the heart—that the other's existence enriches the world. In short, they should love one another.[16]

Is it difficult to see that something similar applies also to the two divine persons—the Father and the Son who is begotten through the Father's perfect self-knowledge? I hope not. If these two persons are perfect (as Christians hold they are), they love one another.

Now back to human love: If two human persons truly love one another, one tells the other, "I belong to you—I am yours," and the other says the same. Thus, human love involves an element of self-donation, in a manner of speaking at least.

The "in a manner of speaking at least" supposedly goes by the wayside in the case of the love between God the Father and God the Son—but not the self-donation: In loving each other, the Father gives himself to the Son and the Son returns that gift. This mutual self-giving is characterized by such a force or intensity that it (or he) is itself (or himself) a person between the Father and the Son, a person known as the Holy Spirit. Since two persons who are entirely alike give themselves to each other, that third person also is in every respect like them.

Thus, there are three divine persons, alike in each and every respect, except for the relationships they have to each other. The Son is begotten by the Father through the latter's perfect self-knowledge; and the Holy Spirit proceeds from the Father and the Son—he proceeds from them as the fruit of their mutual self-donation in love.

4. Why "one God" rather than three?

One "little thing" is to be added. It concerns the question, "If Christians believe in three divine persons, shouldn't they be logical and discontinue their belief in one and only one God? Shouldn't they 'swallow hard' and say, 'Since we hold that there are three divine persons, we admit that we must wind up saying that we believe in three gods?' Aren't Muslims and Jews right when they say that Christianity as it exists today is not truly a monotheistic religion?"

Christians would reply, "We believe that there is only one God because the three divine persons are only one being."

What is that supposed to mean?

Randomly pick three humans—three people sitting in this classroom, for example. They are three persons. How do they relate to each other? Had one of them never been born, the other two could still exist—more likely than not, they would not even know the difference. When one of them will die—one of them will die first (unless they die together, say in a car crash or in an earthquake destroying this classroom)—the others will continue to exist; and, unless that one person dies soon, before the semester is over or before all three graduate, presumably, again, those others will not even know the difference. Thus, they are not only three persons, but they are three beings, which means that the existence of one is not dependent on that of the other(s); they are capable of existing independently of one another. That last statement precisely does not hold true of the three divine persons.

Let us first consider the Holy Spirit in relation to the Father and the Son. Looking at it from the perspective of the Holy Spirit, we recall that he proceeds from the Father and the Son through their

---

16 "Love" is a word frequently misused. "I love you" is one of the most often repeated lies. Often, what is really meant is, "I need you—I want you." What I am talking about is not the Hollywood-type fake love, but *true love*.

mutual self-donation in love: In a manner of speaking, he is the love between Father and Son. Consider now two human persons loving each other. How much sense does it make to say of them, "Even if they would not exist, their love for each other would still be there?" If you say, "None at all," go to the head of the class (said once again with deference to Walter Williams). Nothing is more obvious than saying, "For love to exist, it is absolutely necessary for the two persons loving each other to exist. Love cannot possibly exist independently or apart of the persons loving each other. Assuming the contrary is logical nonsense."

Remember that the Holy Spirit is the love between Father and Son. Thus, in line with what I just explained about human love (an "image" of divine love), considering the Holy Spirit as existing without the Father and the Son is logical nonsense.

It is similar the other way around: From the Father and the Son to the Holy Spirit. Since Father and Son are perfect, they MUST love one another. This means: Thinking of the Father and the Son WITHOUT the Holy Spirit—the love between them—also is logical nonsense.

Next, we turn to the Son in relation to the Father, and vice versa. Remember that the Son is begotten through the Father's perfect self-knowledge—in a sense, the Son IS the Father's perfect self-knowledge. Does it make any sense to think about someone's self-knowledge being there in the absence of that "someone"? Or isn't assuming this to be possible another case of plain logical nonsense? These seem to be rhetorical questions: Of course it is logical nonsense to think that someone's self-knowledge can exist in the absence of that "someone." This makes clear that the Son cannot exist apart of the Father.

Turning matters around, an omniscient being—the Father—necessarily always knows himself completely and perfectly. It is not possible for him ever to exist without perfect self-knowledge. Consequently, wherever the Father is, there also is the Son. Unlike with two human persons, the Father and the Son cannot exist independently of each other, or apart of each other.

The upshot of these considerations for Christians is, "We believe in three divine persons who cannot possibly exist apart of each other. It makes no sense to 'break' one of them 'out' of the unity they constitute, and have him exist by himself. Calling them 'three beings' or 'three gods' would convey the idea that they CAN exist independently of each other. That is impossible, however. Consequently, it is more correct to say that the three divine persons are one being, which is the same as saying that they are one God."[17]

---

17 Polytheists believing in Zeus, Hera, and Apollo, for example, call them not only three persons, but also three beings and three gods.

CHAPTER TWELVE

Who Do Christians Say That Jesus Is?

W ho is Jesus, according to Christianity?[1]
To find an answer to this question, we begin with looking at the New Testament record: What does Jesus say there about himself? What do his followers say about him? How does he react to their words?

Subsequently, I will summarize what Christians believe about Jesus.

(I) THE NEW TESTAMENT ABOUT JESUS

1. The "Son of Man": Two ideas to be conveyed

I have pointed out already that Jesus often refers to himself as the "son of man."[2] Whenever Jesus uses these words, he is speaking about himself. One can replace it by "I" or "me." When he says, for example, "The Son of Man is to be handed over to men, and they will kill him, and he will be raised on the third day" (Mt 17.22–23), he intends to affirm, "I will be handed over to men, and they will kill me, and I will be raised on the third day." His words, "Who do people say that the son of man is?" (Mt 16.13) mean, "Who do people say that I am?"

---

1 As with the entire Christianity presentation, the explanations given here concern traditional Christianity. The vast majority of contemporary Christians are traditional Christians. Some nontraditional Christians, such as the Unitarian Universalists, the Jehovah's Witnesses, the Mormons, or the Christian Scientists, disagree with the beliefs concerning the person of Jesus as they are held by traditional Christianity. (Unitarian Universalists probably do not appreciate being mentioned in the same breath as Jehovah's Witnesses and Mormons; this does not alter the fact, though, that all three groups share a rejection of what traditional Christians hold about Jesus.)

2 "Man" is intended to mean here "human being"; consequently, a more accurate (although a bit awkward) translation would be "son of human beings."

Why does he refer to himself as the "son of man"? It is to convey at least two different ideas.

The first one sounds harmless enough, initially at least. A "son of man" in the sense of "son of humans" is himself human; thus, by calling himself "son of man," Jesus wants to emphasize that he is truly human, genuinely a member of the human community: He is really and truly one of us.[3]

This is not all, though: He also wants his listeners to think of a vision the Prophet Daniel describes. As many such visions, it is presented in the past tense, although Christians understand it as referring to the future: "As the visions during the night continued, I saw one *like a son of man* coming on the clouds of heaven; when he reached the Ancient One [God] and was presented before him, he received dominion, glory, and kingship; nations and peoples of every language serve him. His dominion is an everlasting dominion that shall not be taken away, his kingship shall not be destroyed." (Dn 7.13–14)

Thus, whenever Jesus applies the phrase, "son of man" to himself, he intends to convey, in addition to the "harmless" idea that he is truly human: "I am the one who will be presented before God's throne; I am the one who will receive kingship; I am the one whose rule will never be destroyed."

Someone might now ask, "What makes Christians think that Jesus actually intends to convey these additional ideas? Maybe he is using the expression, 'son of man,' the way it is used in the work of Ezekiel, who also is often called 'son of man,' without any controversial implications.[4] Maybe Jesus does not intend to allude to the Prophet Daniel." In response, Christians would point out that Jesus himself makes the connection to Daniel quite obvious in the answer he gives to the High Priest Caiaphas during the trial before the Sanhedrin. Caiaphas requested, "I order you to tell us under oath before the living God whether you are the Messiah, the Son of God." Jesus replied, "You have said so. But I tell you: Soon, you will see the Son of Man seated at the right hand of the Power and 'coming on the clouds of heaven'" (Mt 26.63–64). The words between single quotation marks are from the Daniel passage.

2. Jesus claims to be king

As was explained, Jesus claims that the Daniel passage about "someone like a son of man" applies to him. This passage states that the son of man will receive kingship. Thus, by applying this passage to himself, Jesus claims to be king.

There are other New Testament passages conveying the idea of Jesus' kingship.

When Jesus entered Jerusalem riding on a donkey, his followers hailed him as king. The Pharisees, fearing that the Roman governor Pontius Pilate might get wind of it and cause trouble for the Jews, told Jesus to "rebuke" the people. Rather than telling them to be quiet, Jesus said, "I tell you, if they keep silent, the very stones will cry out." (Lk 19.40) Thus, he accepts the title, although he did not think of himself as a king in the sense in which many of his followers presumably understood the title: That he would start a revolutionary movement, throw the Romans out, and turn the Roman province Judaea into an independent monarchy ruled by him.

---

3 Christians say that his having emphasized this was important, as is made evident by the fact that it was overlooked by an early Christian sect called "docetism," according to which Jesus was not truly human, but only appeared or seemed to have a human nature.

4 See, for example, Ez 18.1, 19.1, and many other passages in the same book.

In his description of Judgment Day, which starts out with the words, "When the son of man [I] will come in his [my] glory" (Mt 25.31), he also calls himself "the king": "Then, the king will say to those on his right ..." (See Mt 25.34).

In his conversation with Pontius Pilate, he implies that he is a king, although he says that his "kingdom does not belong to this world" (Jn 18.36): There is no earthly capital where he is going to have his palace; no identifiable stretch of land he will have power over.

Still, Christians consider him as the "king of kings," the "king of the universe."[5]

3. Jesus, the "judge of the world"?

The passage about the last judgment referred to in the previous segment is the basis of another role which Christians ascribe to Jesus: He is going to be the judge of the world.

On that fateful day on which "the son of man will come in his glory," all humans will be judged. Those who have helped others in need will be rewarded; those who ignored others when they needed help will be punished.

Thus, Christians say, looking at the title I have given to this segment ("3. Jesus, 'the judge of the world'?"), "Remove the question mark."

4. Jesus, the Messiah?

Does the New Testament say that Jesus is the Messiah?

In support of an affirmative answer to this question, Christians refer, among other things, to the following exchange between Jesus and his disciples: In answer to Jesus' question, "Who do you say that I am?" Peter replies, "You are the Messiah, the son of the living God" (see Mt 16.15–17), and Jesus calls Peter "blessed" for having answered in this way; that is, he accepts the answer as correct.

Another passage Christians would appeal to records a conversation Jesus had with a Samaritan woman at a well near the town of Sychar. During the exchange, he astounds her by knowing that she had had five husbands and that the man she was living with at the time was not her husband, although Jesus had never met her before. At one point, she says, "I know that the Messiah is coming ...; when he comes, he will tell us everything." Jesus replies, "I am he, the one who is speaking to you" (See Jn 4.25–26).

5. Christianity considers Jesus as God

(1) Introductory remarks, including a reminder on what the neutrality requirement imposed on me does not refer to

From what has been explained, it becomes clear that Christians consider Jesus as the "son of man" whom the Prophet Daniel speaks about, that they also consider him as king of the universe, as the judge of the world, and as the Messiah.

---

5 Some Christians even hold that the time will come in which Jesus will rule also in a literal sense for a thousand years, basing this view on a literal interpretation of some passages contained in the Book of Revelation.

If you say, "That's quite a bit," they would reply, "In a sense, you 'haven't seen nothing yet.' Jesus is God."

"Come again?"

"We are not making things up," they would affirm; "that's what the New Testament says."

So for us, the question is, "Does the New Testament actually say that Jesus is God?"

An affirmative answer to this question is controversial today in many quarters. According to a popular view (think Dan Brown), the belief that Jesus is God came about only several centuries after the New Testament had been written.

Prior to me stirring around the hornet's nest of that controversy, however, it is important for you to remember: Whether or not the New Testament affirms that Jesus is God is not a question to be decided by an appeal to revelation (although it is a question important for Christianity); rather, it is to be decided by a careful reading of the text. Consequently, I am allowed to state and defend my position on it even at a secular school, just as I am with respect to the questions, "Does the Bible say that God exists?" or "Does the Bible say that there are angels?" An appeal to revelation would come into the picture only with regard to an attempt to support an affirmative answer to the question, "Is Jesus, in fact, God?"

So "here goes," as they say.

(2) Does the New Testament say that Jesus is God?

First, I turn to the beginning of the introduction of John's Gospel.[6] The language used there strikes us 20th-century people as strange: Jesus is called "the Word." Isn't your reaction "calling him the 'son of man' is nothing compared to that"?

Why is he called "the Word"? I am skipping the reason of particular interest for my day job colleagues;[7] I am only stating the reason which can be gathered from the beginning of another New Testament book, the *Letter to the Hebrews*. Here it is: "In times past, God spoke in partial and various ways to our ancestors through the prophets; in these last days, he spoke to us through a son" (Hb 1.1–2)—the son is Jesus. If God spoke through him, then he is, in a manner of speaking, like a word that God addresses to us. This is among the reasons why John calls Jesus "the Word."

Now, that it is clear what John has in mind when using the expression "word," let us consider the opening sentence of his Gospel: "In the beginning was the Word, and the Word was with God, and **the Word was God**." (Jn 1.1) "The word was God." Christians would ask, "Clear enough?"

Incidentally, those who ask, in spite of my earlier explanation, "How do you know that 'the Word' is Jesus?" might wish to read a passage also occurring in the opening chapter of John's Gospel, several verses after the one just quoted: "And the Word became flesh and made his dwelling among us, and we saw his glory, the glory of the Father's only son, full of grace and truth" (Jn 1.14). Here, John speaks about Jesus' becoming human and clearly identifies "the Word" with the Father's "only son."

---

6 The official designation for that introduction is "prologue."

7 The expression John uses is *logos*. In ancient times among the Greeks, there was a philosophic current which can be referred to as "logos philosophy," with the logos representing something like thought or mind, playing a pivotal role. One of the implications of John's using that word for Jesus is that according to the understanding of Christians, Jesus is, in contrast to the views contained in alternative logos speculations, the true logos.

Among the many other passages Christians would appeal to when asked, "Where does the New Testament say that Jesus is God?" let me refer to the following—also from John's Gospel: After his resurrection, Jesus supposedly appeared to his disciples on the very evening of the day on which he had risen from the dead. One of the apostles, Thomas, was not present when Jesus appeared. When the others told him about it, he did not believe a word. A week later, though, Jesus appeared again, and this time, Thomas was present. Jesus urged him "to believe." John's Gospel continues the account with the words, "Thomas answered and said to him, 'My Lord and my God.'" (Jn 20.28) Stop and think: What did Thomas call Jesus? "God!" And how did Jesus react? With dismay, telling Thomas to stop using language that amounted to blasphemy, calling someone who is a mere human "God"? No! Here is Jesus' actual reaction: "Have you come to believe because you have seen me? Blessed are those who have not seen and have believed" (Jn 20.29). Does Jesus accept being called "God"? Obviously.

Does the New Testament say that Jesus is God? Equally obviously. When Dan Brown, author of *The Da Vinci Code*, denies that it is so, he simply does not know what he is talking about; neither does the semipopular ("semi" compared to Dan Brown) theologian Karen Armstrong, who also argues, in her book *A History of God*, that the belief in the divinity of Jesus is a post–New Testament theological development. Saying that both of them are "all wet" is putting it mildly.

Closely connected with the "not purely religious" question, "Does the New Testament affirm the divinity of Jesus?" is, of course, the question, "Is Jesus God?" Since this is a purely religious question and since this course is taught at a secular university, all this religion teacher can say is, "Well, Christians think so." If you insist, "But is it true?" the Fox principle needs to be activated once again.

That the New Testament teaches the divinity of Jesus is beyond doubt, though.

"But does the New Testament not also teach that Jesus is human?" Yes; remember, for example, the first of the two thoughts to be conveyed by Jesus' calling himself the "son of man."

"But how can Jesus be human and God? Isn't this a contradiction if there ever was one?"

This question brings us to a summary of the Christian teaching of who Jesus was.

(II) SUMMARY OF THE CHRISTIAN UNDERSTANDING OF WHO JESUS WAS

As for who Jesus was according to Christianity, the bottom line is that they consider him as truly human, and at the same time as truly divine—as true man and true God.

To understand what this is supposed to mean, the following questions may be useful: In what way is Jesus like other humans? In what way is he different from other humans?

Prior to asking the two questions just formulated, we must consider another question: How does Christianity understand human nature?

1. How does Christianity understand human nature?

What are humans like, according to Christianity? In answer, Christians observe:

Humans do have a physical body, that complicated, involved, living structure that starts out as one cell, called fertilized ovum, with a distinctly human arrangement of genes and chromosomes, which grows in its mother's womb, is delivered at birth, grows further, matures, becomes old, ill, and then dies.

But Christians think that the physical body, that "part" that fills space, is not all there is to a human. It is not even the "key thing." The key thing is that part of the human being in which consciousness—awareness—resides, the spiritual part, the "ego," the "I." Christianity—calling this "part" the "soul"—is emphatic about stating that the "I-part" of the human being cannot be reduced to the physical body, is totally different from it, although intimately united with it. In statements such as, "I am sad," "I am happy," "I decided to come to class today," the word "I" refers to the spiritual part of the human being. Nothing in your body is sad, happy, or decision-making; these things apply only to your spiritual person. In contrast, in the statement, "I fell down the stairs," or "I am still in bed," the word "I" refers to the totality of your spiritual person and your physical body: You do not wish to tell me that only your spiritual person and not your body fell down the stairs or is still in bed. Similarly, it is impossible for your spiritual person to come to class while your physical body stays behind in your bed. The decision to get out of bed and come to class was made only by your spiritual person, and it was that decision that set your physical body (which has the spiritual person "residing within it") in motion; but "coming to class" involves both your physical body and your spiritual person.

Thus, for Christians, each human being is a physical body joined with a spiritual person.

2. What does Jesus have in common with other humans according to Christianity?

This allows us to highlight what Jesus supposedly does have in common with other humans: He does have a genuinely human physical body, a body in each and every respect like that of other humans. If genetics would have been known at his time, it would have been possible to determine that he had 46 chromosomes with an arrangement of genes characteristic for humans; had the genetic codes of his ancestors been available, one would have been able to determine that one of them was David, another Abraham. He may very well have had facial features making him resemble his mother Mary or some of his other ancestors. As far as the physical side of his existence is concerned, he was like other humans. He had a genuine human nature; that's why Christians insist on calling him "truly human."

3. In what respect does Christianity see Jesus as different from other humans?

In what respect was he different from other humans, though? This requires me to formulate a statement, the first part of which will strike you as deserving a "duh!" response: In your case and my case, the spiritual person joined together with the physical body is a *human* person (DUH!!!!) called into existence and joined to our bodies by God at the moment our mothers conceived us in their wombs. In contrast, in the case of Jesus, the spiritual person joined to his human body growing in his mother Mary's womb is a divine person, the second person of the Trinity. Thus, unlike in the case of other humans, the person of Jesus did not come into existence at the moment of his conception; rather, that person exists independently of his conception as a human, and from our perspective at least, prior to it.[8] In other words, had the man Jesus never been born, had he never been wrapped in swaddling

---

8 I qualified the expression, "prior to it," with "from our perspective at least," because Christians consider God as existing outside of time.

clothes, had he never been placed in a manger, his person would still exist. Had God not bothered to create a universe, the person of Jesus would still exist—as the second person of the Trinity; for had God decided not to create anything, there would be (nothing but) the one God in three persons whom Christians call the Father, the Son, and the Holy Spirit. There would then, of course, have been no one to call them that way, for the three persons in the Trinity do not need words to convey their thoughts to each other (actually no "conveying of thoughts" is necessary, for each of them knows what the other[s] is [are] thinking).

Christians see Jesus himself emphasizing his existence independently of his being conceived in Mary's womb and born in Bethlehem when he says in response to the objection, "You are not yet fifty years old, and you claim to have seen Abraham," "Before Abraham came to be, I AM." (See Jn 8.57–58.)

4. "Before Abraham came to be, I AM"—why on earth "I AM"?

Why does he say, "I AM," though? Isn't the grammatically correct way of formulating this "I was," or something similar? Christians would remind you that God is outside of time and that consequently, there is no past or future for him, only what is called an "eternal NOW." We humans are so "tied up" with time that our language makes it next to impossible for us to speak in a nontemporal manner; but human language is the only ordinary means available to us for communicating thoughts to each other. In the absence of a convenient way of speaking in a nontemporal sense, Jesus must do something that initially strikes us like a mutilation of language; but he does it to ascribe nontemporal existence to himself in his divine person.

As an aside, the "I AM" statement is another passage that can be used to show that the New Testament teaches the divinity of Jesus: He ascribes an existence outside of time to himself, and God is the only being to whom such an existence applies. As a further side point, it might also bear mentioning that "I AM" is God's reply when Moses asked him for his name: "I am who am—tell the Israelites I AM sent me to you." (Ex 3.14) The name God gave to himself at this point was considered to be so sacred by the Jews that it was not even supposed to be uttered; but now, Jesus did not only utter it, but even applies it to himself. This explains the reaction of those who were listening to him. For them, he had committed blasphemy, to be punished by stoning according to the Law of Moses. (See Lv 24.10–16.) That's exactly what they intended to do: "They picked up stones to throw at him; but Jesus hid and went out of the temple area." (Jn 8.59)

5. Summation of the summary

To return from these "tangents" briefly to the main point: Christians consider Jesus as truly human, because they believe him to have a true human body, a genuine human nature, a nature exactly like yours or mine. They also consider him as truly divine, because person-wise, he is the second person of the Trinity, having joined to himself a human nature. As Paul writes in his Letter to the Philippians, "Have among yourself the same attitude that is also yours in Christ Jesus, who, though he was in the form of God, did not regard equality with God something to be grasped. Rather, he emptied himself, taking the form of a slave, coming in human likeness, and found human in appearance." (Phil 2.6–7)

CHAPTER THIRTEEN

Christianity's Explanation of the Suffering and Death of Jesus

(I) THE NON-CHRISTIAN: "GOD DIED? ARE YOU SERIOUS?"

1. The non-Christian's argument

A non-Christian might say at this point, "Permit me to continue having doubts (to put it mildly) about the identity Christians ascribe to Jesus. Let me put this problem to the side, however; let me concentrate only on what looks to me like a glaring inconsistency between two beliefs that Christians hold: On the one hand, they consider Jesus as the second person of the Trinity, they affirm that he is divine; on the other hand, they assert that he suffered and died, that he was executed like a criminal, that he was killed unjustly. 'A person who is God being executed!' If you do not see the contradiction involved in this idea, I cannot help you."

Is this a sound argument against Christianity? The Fox principle stands in the way for me to try to answer this question. All I can do is try my best to explain how Christians respond to the objection just presented. In the course of this explanation, we will come across some additional key teachings of Christianity.

2. A preliminary response: Christianity claims that its understanding of the nature of dying resolves the contradiction allegedly contained in the statement, "Jesus, the Second Person of the Trinity, died"

A preliminary point concerns the Christian understanding of what it means to die: "Our understanding of death is different from the atheist's (and from that of many agnostics). The latter sees death as a total and permanent extinction of a person's consciousness; as an absolute end of the existence of a human person. If that's what dying is, then the idea of a 'dying God' would indeed involve an inconsistency at least as serious as the one involved in the assertion, 'two plus two equals seven'; it would involve an absolute impossibility: If Jesus is person-wise assumed to be like the God Jews, we Christians, and Muslims believe in, and if dying is assumed to involve the extinction of the dying person, then our belief that Jesus—who supposedly is God—died would indeed be the kind of contradiction that would make it impossible for Christianity to be true. According to our understanding, though, death does not involve the extinction of the spiritual person of the one dying, but a separation of this spiritual person from the physical body. If God, the second person of the Trinity who does not have a physical body to begin with, freely decides to adopt a human nature, including a human physical body, what should be so strange about the idea that he should agree to a temporary (or even permanent) separation from that body which is part of the nature he freely adopted? His (divine) person would keep on existing during this separation."

3. The non-Christian (atheist) focuses on what he sees as the "real problem"

In the interest of the Fox principle, I must leave it to you to judge the quality of that response. The Christian claims, though, that at least a part of the contradiction has been resolved. Surely, though, the atheist will remain skeptical, to put it mildly. He might continue, "The contradiction I really had in mind has not even been addressed yet. Remember what you say about the way in which Jesus died (excuse me: 'The way in which his spiritual person got separated from his body' [don't say that I am not giving you the benefit of the doubt]): Through a process involving agonizing suffering. 'God suffering.' Does this make any sense? Not to me. I see in it another contradiction—actually, that's the real problem I had in mind when presenting my earlier argument."

(II) CHRISTIANITY'S RESPONSE TO THE NON-CHRISTIAN

To understand the response Christianity would give, a little "tangent" must be gone over first, having to do with punishment. How does that fit here? Be patient, and you will find out.

1. Four functions of punishment; details on the retributive function; a limitation of the state's punishing authority

There are several functions of punishment. One is the protective function: Dangerous individuals are to be separated from society. Another is the deterrent function: When people who are tempted to do wrong see what might happen to them if they get caught, that might motivate them to refrain from the misdeed they are contemplating. A third one is the corrective function: Punishment is to help a wrongdoer learn to avoid similar wrongdoings. Humane punishment always is to involve an appeal to wrongdoers to change, to improve, to behave better in the future.

Important as these functions of punishment may be, there is a fourth one, considered by many—religious and nonreligious persons alike—as the most important one. This is the retributive function of punishment. A person who does wrong *deserves* to be punished; punishment is *due* to him or her. The expression, "Punishment as retribution" recognizes the "due character" of punishment.

Think of the case of Adolf Eichmann, the head of the Gestapo's Jewish Section in Nazi Germany. He oversaw the Nazi program aimed at exterminating Jews from the face of the earth, and was responsible for unspeakable cruelties committed against them. At the end of World War II, he was captured by the Allies, but escaped and fled to Argentina. There, Eichmann adopted a new identity, and lived the life of a harmless civilian. Suppose he had succeeded to live out his life there without ever being "bothered" by anyone about his horrendous misdeeds, without ever being found out. Would this not have been a crying injustice? Did not justice demand that he would be forced to face up to his misdeeds? Does this not show that doing wrong causes something like a "deformity" in the universe which can be "straightened out," to a certain extent at least, only by appropriate punishment being inflicted? Fortunately, that happened in the case of Eichmann: Israeli agents discovered his whereabouts, captured him, "smuggled" him out of Argentina, and brought him to Israel, where he was tried for crimes against the Jewish people and against humanity, and executed (in 1962). If your reaction is "Served him right," you demonstrate that you do have an appreciation for the retributive function of punishment. The absence of retribution is itself something like an injustice; that "justice is done" means that there is retribution for wrongdoing.

Any wrongdoing deserves punishment.[1] Incidentally, I do not view this a (purely) religious statement, but a statement of what I consider a sound philosophy; consequently, in arguing in support of it (without appealing to revelation, of course), I do not violate the neutrality imposed on me regarding statements that can be supported only through taking recourse to revelation.

It is important to recognize, however, that the punishment authority of the state is limited to instances of wrongdoing which involve the breaking of laws. In the case of minor children, parents do have the right to punish conduct that the state has no authority over. If the world is to be ultimately just, there would have to be retribution for each and every wrongdoing, including instances of wrongdoing which do not fall under the state's punishing authority. This is one of the reasons why to an atheist, the world as it is must ultimately appear unjust: Countless misdeeds go unpunished during a person's earthly existence (which is all there is for the atheist); those who try hard to lead good lives often suffer greatly. Jews, Christians, and Muslims say, of course, that "matters are going to be set right" in the world to come, and that the divine authority will make sure that there be the kind of retribution that is deserved and just.

2. The proportionality principle to be joined with retributive punishment

Punishment as retribution must now be connected with a "rule" called the "proportionality principle." Even if punishment is deserved, two contrary instances of injustice are to be avoided by the ones who have the authority to determine the appropriate punishment (courts in the case of lawbreakers; parents in the case of minor children). One consists of inflicting punishment that is too lenient; the other consists in inflicting punishment that is too severe.

An example of the first would be punishing a rapist with nothing but a $150 fine; an example of the second would be sentencing someone who maliciously damaged another person's car to life in prison without the possibility of parole.

---

1 If you let the meaning of these words sink in and consider your past life, you might have to feel rather unsettled.

3. One additional point concerning punishment: Targets of human wrongdoing; these targets as co-determinants of the seriousness of wrongdoing

What does all this have to do with the "suffering God"?

Christians would say, "Be patient once more—one more point will be added. That point will make you see that the proportionality principle, which must be combined with the retributive function of punishment, seems to place us humans into a totally hopeless situation."

To understand what this is supposed to mean, we must reflect on what the targets of human wrongdoings are—that is, against whom human wrongdoing is directed. We also need to understand that these targets co-determine the seriousness of wrongdoing.

Take the action of torturing. I do hope you agree that it is wrong. But what is worse: torturing an animal, or torturing a baby? Both are serious; but obviously, all other things being equal, torturing a baby is much, much worse than torturing an animal. In accordance with the proportionality principle, torturing a baby deserves a punishment much more severe than torturing an animal.

All of us have been guilty of wrongs that do have other humans as their target. Consider now the example of someone mistreating your child. The direct target of the other's wrongdoing is your child. But you, as the child's parent, will consider your child's being mistreated also as an affront against yourself. You also are a target of the perpetrator's wrongdoing. We can say in general: Whenever wrong is done to a human being, wrong also is done to all those who love that human being.

"Stop and think—what did you just hear?" the Christian will ask, "'... to all those who love him or her.' According to what we Christians believe, who is the one who loves each and every human being more than any one of us can even imagine? If you just said, 'God,' go to the head of the class." (I do not bother anymore with expressing deference to Walter Williams.) When you do wrong to another human being, God says, as it were, "How dare you mistreat that person, whom I love more intensely than you can imagine?"

Let me "rub this thought in," as they say: According to Christianity, against whom is each instance of doing wrong to other humans directed, in addition to these other humans? If again you said "God," go even further than the head of the class—if that is possible. (If I ever should bump into Walter Williams, I will ask.) Thus, any wrongdoing against other humans also is an affront against God.[2]

And now, remember that the seriousness of wrongdoing depends on the status of the one the wrongdoing is directed against. Just as an instance of wrongdoing against a child is, because of the child's higher status, more serious than an instance of wrongdoing against a squirrel, so is wrongdoing against God more serious than wrongdoing against any human.

---

2 For the purpose of what I am explaining here, I am limiting the discussion to instances of affronts against God connected with wrongdoings against other humans. Christianity maintains, though, that there are other ways of acting against God, including more direct ones, such as blasphemy and expressing hatred of God.

4. The truly unsettling thought: A component of infinite seriousness creeps into human wrongdoing

At this point, a really unsettling thought begins to enter the picture—unsettling on the basis of the presuppositions of Christianity, at least: Although we humans are above the animals,[3] we are only finite beings. Consequently, inasmuch as an offense is directed against another human, it is only of finite magnitude, great as it might be.[4] Remember, however, that according to Christianity, any wrongdoing against another human also involves an offense against the one who loves that human being more than anyone else—God. God is infinite; thus, wronging another human also involves wrongdoing against someone who is infinite. Doesn't that mean that an infinite component of seriousness creeps into each wrongdoing? Christianity, at least, suggests that it is so.

Thus, inasmuch as wrongdoing is directed against another human being, its magnitude is finite; inasmuch as wrongdoing is directed against God, its magnitude is infinite. In consequence, the "totality" of the seriousness of wrongdoing is the "sum" of a finite and an infinite component. Even if you are not a mathematics genius, you probably can figure out that finite plus infinite equals infinite.

5. "How can anything humans do be that serious?"

"How can anything that humans do be that serious?"

Well, remember the Fox principle. I am only reporting; it's up to you to decide. Consider, however, the following example showing that something which on first sight did not appear that serious turned out to be a very, very serious wrong:

Betsy is walking home from school with two friends. At one point, they catch up with Holly, a girl who is being teased a lot. Betsy and her friends start making fun of Holly. She does not seem to be too upset; rather, she even laughs herself about some of the jokes the others make at her expense, although an unbiased observer would have noticed that her laughing sounded forced.

They come to the intersection with Douglas Street; Holly walks left, the others continue straight.

If someone were to ask Betsy whether her conduct had been appropriate, she likely would admit, "It was not nice." She would probably add in her own defense, "But it was no big deal. Holly did not mind too much. Even she thought our jokes funny."

Actually, Betsy does not give any further thought to the matter—until the next morning, that is. For when she arrives at school, the principal is waiting for her already—waiting in front of the building. In a somber tone of voice, he orders her to follow him. Her two friends are already in his office. And now, Betsy finds out: Holly did not go home when they had separated at Douglas Street. Rather, she had made her way to the roof of the abandoned six-story office building at Plains Drive and jumped into the courtyard. A hastily scribbled suicide note found with her said that she just could not take the constant bullying anymore. The note identifies Betsy and her friends as the chief offenders.

Now, what Betsy would earlier have thought of as "maybe not that nice but relatively harmless fun" certainly will appear to her in a totally different light. …

---

3 Some PETA people might not like this; but this does not convince me that it is false.
4 "Finite" can be unbelievably large. Just think of the U.S. public debt, which is, in spite of its enormous size, infinitely removed from actually being infinite (these words are not intended as a consolation for President Obama!).

Christianity asserts—rightly or wrongly, not for me to say—that something like the "Betsy/Holly story" applies to each and every instance of wrongdoing. (Instead of "something like," I should probably have said, "something much more serious.")

6. Doesn't the proportionality principle give rise to a situation hopeless for us humans?

At this point, it is time to remember the proportionality principle: "The severity of punishment must correspond to the seriousness of the wrong done"—otherwise, there would be no justice.

As was explained, Christianity holds that each and every wrongdoing contains an infinite component of seriousness. What does that mean for the severity of punishment? By the proportionality principle, it must contain a component of infinite severity.

Where does that leave you and me? It appears that there are only two options left.

One would be for God to inflict on humans the punishment they deserve—an "infinite-component-of-severity-containing" one. That would wipe us off the face of the earth; for how could any one of us possibly withstand such a punishment?[5]

The second option would have been for God to pretend that things are fine in the absence of the appropriate punishment—but seriously thinking about that option shows it to be not a real one, because justice would not be done by it, and God supposedly is just.

This brings us back to the first option. The situation seems rather hopeless, does it not? Contemplating that option, the following analogy comes to mind: As I am standing by the seashore, suddenly, I see that terribly high tsunami-like wave rushing toward me. There is not enough time for me to run away, and it is clear that I cannot possibly withstand that wave: I am a goner. But even if the wave is 30 feet high, it is still infinitely removed from being infinite. How on earth could I possibly withstand an infinite-component-containing punishment?

7. How God resolved the seemingly hopeless situation, according to Christianity

What if there were an option in addition to the one that would wipe us out, and to the one under which justice would not be done, that is, therefore, not a real option? What if there were a member of the human community, someone who is truly one of us, able to withstand a punishment with an infinite component?

Impossible?

Christianity replies, "Not impossible. That's where Jesus comes into the picture."

Remember who he is, according to Christianity: God (the second person of the Trinity) having become human, having assumed a human nature. He is truly one of us, a genuine member of the human community. Thus, he can be our true representative; he is capable to stand in for us and pay the debt humanity incurred through the many wrongdoings of its members. Since in his person—a divine

---

5 Many Christians would hold that, had God intended something along these lines, he would not even have bothered creating us humans and, since we do not have a "right" to exist or a claim to existence, since existence is a free, undeserved gift, we would have no right to complain (besides, we would not even be able to complain because we would not be around to do so).

person—he is infinite, he can withstand the punishment humanity deserves. Although it contains an infinite component of seriousness, he is not wiped out through it. It is as if he were to stand in front of humankind as humanity's representative and deflect the force of the punishment from individual members, although humanity as a whole receives what it deserves.

Going back to the previous example of the huge wave coming at me, it is as if there is a huge rock behind which I can hide as the wave breaks over me, a rock that deflects the force of the wave from me.

In this way, justice is done according to Christianity, and humanity is preserved. Each and every human can move once again toward the goal for which God "invented" us in the first place: To enter into an intimate love relationship with God.

8. The debtor analogy

Consider the following analogy for what Jesus has done for us, according to Christianity:

After graduating from college, you find an excellent, well-paying job. You get married, buy a house, and have two children. Two expensive cars are in your garage and matters are going very well for you. An acquaintance persuades you, though, to participate in an investment deal questionable in some respects—but if it works out, you stand to make a fortune and would be able to quit your job. Things "go south," however, and not only do you not make a penny, but you wind up with staggering debts which you are unable to pay. You default on all your loans. The repo man comes and takes one of the beautiful cars away. Your electricity is turned off, as is your telephone—at least, the people to whom you owe money cannot call you anymore. Another repo man arrives and takes the second car. Later that day, you walk to the mailbox—and in it, you find a notice that tomorrow, the bank will hold a foreclosure sale of your house. You, your wife, and your children will be out on the street.

After a sleepless night, you decide to go to the bank to ask them to give you another month, although this will only postpone what seems inevitable. You have to walk there—two miles. All the loans you did default on are with that bank; so you have fallen out of their good graces, to put it mildly. You walk into the building, not daring to look up because for the past several times you have entered it, even the guard at the door has let you feel his contempt. You approach a teller, intending to ask whether you can speak to the manager—but instead of the surly "Yes?" you have gotten used to, you hear the most friendly, "Oh, hello there—how can I help you?" You look up, and she is actually smiling at you, as is everyone else in the room. The manager comes out of his office, also all smiles, and asks you to follow him. In his office, he motions to a chair, and as you sit down, he says, "I know that the past couple of months have been terrible for you—I do hope, though, that you will be ready to continue doing business with us." You are totally at a loss. "What do you mean?" you inquire. "Don't you know?" he asks back. When you continue looking at him dumbfounded, he says, "Your next-door neighbor was here about half an hour ago, paid off all your loans, and opened up an account in your name, in which he deposited $100,000 for you." Then, the man begins speaking about investing the money in CDs or a savings account or …

… You hardly listen. You excuse yourself, saying that you will be back, and leave the building to collect your thoughts …

Try to compare how you would feel in that story walking out of that bank compared to how you felt walking in.

Christianity claims: "What the next-door neighbor did for you in that story is a tiny analogy for what Jesus did for each and every member of the human family, including you: He paid all the debts you incurred and opened up an account in your name."

As he said on the cross—his final words before dying according to John's Gospel: "It is finished"; also meaning "It is paid in full."

CHAPTER FOURTEEN

The Christian Way of Life

(I) HOW IS ONE TO AVOID WINDING UP ONCE AGAIN IN THE PREDICAMENT FROM WHICH ONE HAS BEEN LIBERATED?

Remember the story about your debt which has been paid in full (hopefully, not too difficult to remember; the story has just been told, after all). Suppose as you are walking down the street toward the river, you happen to meet the acquaintance who had talked you into the risky business deal. For some reason, he knows about your good fortune and says, "How about trying it again? There are many other excellent investment possibilities."

What will your reaction be? If you are smart, you will tell him off as fast as you can.

Christianity says, "Just as in that story, you must try your best to avoid winding up once again in the predicament from which you have just been rescued, so it is with us: We must avoid sliding back into the condition from which the suffering and death of Jesus has liberated us."

How is this to be done? By adopting the way of life Jesus demands of his followers. The various Christian denominations disagree with one another as to precisely what is involved here—they even disagree with regard to the precise significance of this way of life and how this significance is to be defined.[1] Most groups of traditional Christians, though, agree with the following basics I am going to explain.

---

1 If we were to discuss these disagreements, one of the things we would have to take up is the "faith/works" controversy constituting a core disagreement between many traditional Protestants and Catholics.

(II) CHRISTIANITY AND THE 613 TORAH LAWS

As you hopefully recall from the Judaism segment of this course, the Torah contains 613 laws. From your acquaintance with Christianity, though, you probably know also that there are many laws that Christians do not keep, such as the laws concerning kosher and nonkosher foods.

What, then, is the Christian stand toward the laws stated in the Torah? To appreciate that stand, it is helpful to remember a distinction we came across when considering Reform Judaism: that between the moral and the nonmoral law.

1. The nonmoral law has been fulfilled; it is, therefore, no longer binding for Christians

Concerning the nonmoral law, Christians call attention to the following words of Jesus: "Do not think that I have come to abolish the law or the prophets. I have come not to abolish, but to fulfill." (Mt 5.17) On first sight, this seems like the strongest statement imaginable indicating that the law is going to "stick around" unchanged. How come Christians do not keep kosher anymore, or do not mind starting up their cars on the Lord's Day?

In response, Christians invite us to consider the following two thoughts:

First, think of an example of an order that is carried out: "I have done what you told me," or of a promise kept, "I have fulfilled what I promised you." Neither the order nor the promise is binding any longer. Similar, Christians say, "Jesus has fulfilled the law, so it is no longer binding."

Second, they urge us to consider the precise meaning of the word which is, in Jesus' word about the law that I have quoted, translated as "fulfill." It could also be translated as "complete," "finish," or "bring to an end." Thus, Jesus, after saying that he will not simply do away with the law ("I have not come to abolish"), adds that he will bring it to completion. In line with this, Christians say, "Since Jesus has brought the law to completion, it is no longer binding."[2]

2. Christianity's stand on the moral law

The stand Jesus took toward the moral law becomes clear from the following exchange "Someone approached him [Jesus] and asked, 'Teacher, what good must I do to gain eternal life?' He answered him, '… If you wish to enter into life, keep the commandments.' He asked him, 'Which ones?' And Jesus replied, 'You shall not kill; you shall not commit adultery; you shall not steal; you shall not bear false witness; honor your father and mother; and you shall love your neighbor as yourself' (Mt 19.16–19)."

---

2 If this is so, then why is Jesus saying immediately after the passage I have quoted before, "I say to you, until heaven and earth pass away, not the smallest letter or the smallest part of a letter will pass from the law, until all has taken place" (Mt 5.18)? Christians reply, The words "until heaven and earth pass away," constitute hyperbole (using exaggerated language to make a point); and the "all" will have "taken place" refers to Jesus' dying on the cross; that's when the completion, the "finishing," the final fulfillment of the Torah's (nonmoral) law will occur. In fact (as was mentioned earlier), according to John's Gospel, Jesus' final words on the cross immediately before dying are, "It is finished (fulfilled) (Jn 19.30)." Although the original of John's Gospel uses a word different from the one Matthew uses, the words do have similar meanings. (As indicated earlier, the phrase in John's Gospel also has the meaning, "It is paid in full," thus indicating that the debt humanity has incurred is taken care of.)

The first five items that Jesus mentions are from the Ten Commandments, which constitute a key part of the Torah's moral law; the last item represents the moral law outside of the Ten Commandments. Thus, Christians hold that obeying the moral law of the Torah is mandatory.

3. One more word on the nonmoral and the moral law

Initially, all persons who became Christians came from Judaism; as "former" Jews, they were accustomed to obey the entire Jewish law, nonmoral and moral. Doing so was second nature to them. Abandoning the nonmoral law was contrary to what they were used to. For this reason, in spite of what Jesus had said about the law (the nonmoral law is finished, completed, fulfilled; the moral law must be observed to gain eternal life), some "nudging" was necessary even after Jesus' resurrection for them to get the point that the nonmoral law was no longer binding for them. This occurred in an episode told in the Acts of the Apostles and involving the Apostle Peter.[3] He had come to a town named Joppa, and was staying in the house of a certain Simon, a tanner.[4] At noontime, Peter went up to the roof terrace while a meal was prepared for him because he was hungry. There, he supposedly had a vision: A large sheet was lowered from the sky by its four corners. That sheet contained many animals, including some which Jews consider as nonkosher. "A voice said to him, 'Get up, Peter. Slaughter and eat.' But Peter said, 'Certainly not, sir. For never have I eaten anything profane and unclean.' The voice spoke to him again, a second time, 'What God has made clean, you are not to call profane' (Acts 10.13–15)." This was repeated three times.

Peter got the message. He applied this "new" (actually, at that point, no longer entirely new, for it confirmed what Jesus had said) understanding of the nonmoral law immediately to another nonmoral prescription: Whose houses to stay out from. Jews were barred from associating with gentiles through entering their houses. A little after Peter's "vision," he was asked by several men sent by a certain Cornelius, a gentile, to visit him and speak to him. Peter said in response to that request, "You know that it is unlawful for a Jewish man to associate with, or visit, a Gentile, but God has shown me that I should not call any person profane or unclean (Acts 10.28)." He went with the men and visited Cornelius in the latter's house.

Based on this, the nonmoral part of the law is "out" for Christians. In contrast, the moral law continues to be "in." The latter comprises those ethical prescriptions which can be understood as obligatory apart from what the Torah says. Since they can be known as obligatory apart from the Bible, Paul says about the Gentiles—those for whom the Bible is of no authority, "The demands of the law are written in their hearts (Rom 2.15)." This cannot possibly refer to the nonmoral laws, such as the Jewish dietary prescriptions. How should one know apart from the Torah that one is not to eat lobster or shrimp? In contrast, one can know apart from the Torah that one is not to steal, or lie, or to be unfaithful to one's spouse; and the same applies to many of the other moral prescriptions of the Torah.

What is demanded of a Christian can, therefore, be summed up as follows: live in accordance with the moral law of the Torah, as interpreted and amplified by Jesus.

---

3 Roman Catholic Christians consider him as the first pope.
4 That person's occupation had nothing in common with "tanning booths"; rather, he turned animal skin into leather.

(III) DETAILS ON THE CHRISTIAN WAY OF LIFE

1. The two greatest commandments

Next, allow me to mention at least some details about the way of life demanded of Christians. I must begin with two of the moral laws that Jesus considers as the foundation of all other obligations which humans do have:

One of the Pharisees asked Jesus which one of the commandments is the greatest. In response, Jesus mentions two: First, "You shall love the Lord your God with all your heart, with all your soul, and with all your mind (Mt 22.37)" (here, Jesus is quoting Dt 6.5—maybe you recall that this is a quotation from the Shema Israel); second, "You shall love your neighbor as yourself." (Mt 22.39; Jesus is quoting Lv 19.18.) He continues, "The whole law and the prophets depend on these two commandments (Mt 22.40)."

Love God with all your heart; love your neighbor as yourself: that's what is required of a Christian.

As you hopefully remember, I have spoken about the love of God in the monotheism segment of this course. Jews, Christians, and Muslims tell us to love God.

2. Love of neighbor

Allow me, therefore, to turn immediately to the second of the greatest commandments: "Love your neighbor as yourself."

Who is the person whom I must love as myself? Who is my neighbor?

First, let's look at the word that is used in the Gospel for what is translated as "neighbor." A more literal translation is, "the one near you." Thus, the "love your neighbor (the one near you)" commandment involves everyone you meet. You must love everyone you meet as yourself.

Second, Jesus is specifically asked, "And who is my neighbor?" In response, he tells what has come to be known as the story of the Good Samaritan. A man fell victim to robbers who beat him and left him half-dead by the side of the road. A priest came by; a Levite came by; both ignored the injured man and walked by on the other side of the road. Then, a Samaritan walked down the road (maybe if Jesus were to tell the story today, he would have made the man into an "illegal alien") and was moved with pity, bandaged the man's wounds, put him on his animal, and took him to an inn where he cared for him. When he left, the Samaritan gave the innkeeper money to care for the injured man and promised to give him what had to be spent in addition upon returning. Then, Jesus asked, "Which of these three, in your judgment, was neighbor to the robbers' victim?" The Pharisee answered, "The one who treated him with mercy." Jesus told him, "Go and do likewise." (See Lk 10.29–37)

Whom must you love as yourself according to Christianity? Everyone you meet. How do you show that you love yourself? By making sure that you have enough food, warm clothes, enough money, a place to live, a functioning car, etc. It is important to you to have those things. What is involved in loving your neighbor as yourself? It must be as important to you that the people you meet have these things as it is to you that you yourself have them. Quite a way to go, isn't it—if you are a Christian, that is (if you are not a Christian, you can take the "easy way out" and ignore these matters). In line with all of this, Jesus formulates a statement which has come to be known as the Golden Rule: "Do to others whatever you would have them do to you." (Mt 7.12)

3. How about our enemies?

If by now, you think that living up to the norms Jesus formulates is difficult, "you ain't seen nothing yet," as the saying goes.

In the so-called Sermon on the Mount, Jesus says, "You have heard that it was said, 'You shall love your neighbor and hate your enemy.'" Thinking about Jesus' listeners, one can easily imagine that many of them thought, "Great. That's precisely how I feel. When he's right, he's right." Jesus, however, continues, "But I say to you, love your enemies and pray for those who persecute you." (See Mt 5.43–44.) In other words, the "Love your neighbor as yourself" rule is to be extended even to your enemies, which means that as far as you are concerned, you are not to have any enemies. If others have feelings of hostility toward you, there may be nothing you can do about it; but you are not to respond in kind.[5]

(IV) WHAT LEGACY TO LEAVE BEHIND?

1. The criterion for judgment

It is important to humans to leave a legacy behind, an accomplishment by which they will be remembered after their death.

Christianity would comment, "Much more important than any achievements by which people will remember you is what God thinks about your life—whether his judgment is negative or positive."

What does that judgment depend on? According to Christians, Jesus spells this out in his account of the last judgment. Here it is—a passage from Matthew's Gospel (Mt 25.31–46, NIV):

> When the Son of Man comes in his glory, and all the angels with him, he will sit on his glorious throne. All the nations will be gathered before him, and he will separate the people one from another as a shepherd separates the sheep from the goats. He will put the sheep on his right and the goats on his left. Then the King will say to those on his right, "Come, you who are blessed by my Father; take your inheritance, the kingdom prepared for you since the creation of the world. For I was hungry and you gave me something to eat, I was thirsty and you gave me something to drink, I was a stranger and you invited me in, I needed clothes and you clothed me, I was sick and you looked after me, I was in prison and you came to visit me." Then the righteous will answer him, "Lord, when did we see you hungry and feed you, or thirsty and give you something to drink? When did we

---

5 While there is an Old Testament passage commanding love of one's neighbor (Lv 18.18), there is none that commands hatred of one's enemies. Jesus may, however, have referred to the Mishna, the oral commentaries on the Torah formulated by teachers of the law. Interestingly, in expressing disagreement with some of Jesus' teaching, Rabbi Joseph Telushkin says, "Judaism does not demand that one love one's enemies." See Telushkin, *Literacy*, p. 129.

see you a stranger and invite you in, or needing clothes and clothe you? When did we see you sick or in prison and go to visit you?" The King will reply, "Truly I tell you, whatever you did for one of the least of these brothers and sisters of mine, you did for me." Then he will say to those on his left, "Depart from me, you who are cursed, into the eternal fire prepared for the devil and his angels. For I was hungry and you gave me nothing to eat, I was thirsty and you gave me nothing to drink, I was a stranger and you did not invite me in, I needed clothes and you did not clothe me, I was sick and in prison and you did not look after me." They also will answer, "Lord, when did we see you hungry or thirsty or a stranger or needing clothes or sick or in prison, and did not help you?" He will reply, "Truly I tell you, whatever you did not do for one of the least of these, you did not do for me." Then they will go away to eternal punishment, but the righteous to eternal life.

In line with this, a Christian would tell you: "Instead of worrying about leaving a legacy behind by which people will remember you (the vast majority of us will have been totally forgotten anyway only three, or at the most, four generations after our deaths), you should be concerned about the following questions: "(1) Did I feed the hungry? (2) Did I give a drink to those who were thirsty? (3) Did I take the stranger in? (4) Did I clothe the naked? (5) Did I comfort the ill? (6) Did I visit those in prison?" In short, "Did I help others when they needed me?"

Those who will be able to answer these questions with an honest and sincere "Yes" will, upon their death, be invited into God's presence and joyfully follow that invitation: Helping those in need is the most efficient means of preparing one's heart to be ready to accept God's love and requite it.

Those who must say, "I ignored my fellow humans in their need; I was occupied only with my own well-being"—they will wish for nothing more than to be as far away from God as possible: Closing one's heart to the needs of others is the surest way to closing one's heart to God, causing oneself to be put off, terrified, horrified when experiencing the magnitude of the affection he has for each and every human, to react like the person in my analogy whose eyes are hurt by the breathtaking beauty of the sunny morning in the mountains after fresh snow has fallen …

… Which reminds me, of course, that I still owe you that analogy. It illustrates the two ways in which people will respond when, immediately after their death, they will find themselves in the presence of God, experiencing the magnitude of God's love.

It is late fall. A man invites his coworker to spend a weekend with him in his cabin in the mountains. The other accepts, and Friday afternoon, after work, they drive off. They arrive at their destination around 10:00 P.M., when it is pitch-dark already. They go to sleep immediately. Overnight, there is the first snowfall; but even before sunrise, the clouds disappear.

Now I, your old prof, can assure you that there is hardly anything more beautiful than a sunny morning in the mountains after fresh snow has fallen. When the two men look out the window after having woken up, they see the breathtaking beauty. They get dressed quickly and run out, even prior to having a sip of coffee.

One of them is practically blown away by the beauty; he jumps for joy and is made happy by the glorious sight.

The other, though, cannot stand the light. His eyes hurt, the brightness almost blinds him, and he runs back into the cabin to hide there …

As I indicated, these two men represent two possible responses to experiencing the magnitude of God's love when one will find oneself in his presence after death, as Christianity maintains.

One response is like that of the first man, the one who jumps for joy, being made happy by the glory of the morning. That man represents those who will be able to accept God's love joyfully and requite it. They are the ones who have prepared their hearts through doing the will of God; in particular, through helping those in need.

The second response is like that of the man who cannot stand the brilliant brightness of the beautiful morning. That man represents those who will be unable to accept God's love. They will say, as it were, "What do you want of me? Leave me alone—that's altogether too much for me; I cannot stand it."

The chief difference between the person who cannot stand the bright sunlight and the one who is put off by the magnitude of God's love is that the weakness of the former's eyes is not his fault (next time he should bring sunglasses), while the one unable to stand God's love is responsible for his condition. He has brought it about himself through what he has done and failed to do. A chief contributor to his condition was his failure to be there for those who needed him.

What will God do with those unable to stand his love and incapable to respond to it? Imposing itself is incompatible (highbrow for "does not go together") with love. Consequently, God will comply with the desire of those who cannot bear being in his presence; he will remove them from himself, and the "fire" of their selfishness, their anger, their bitterness, their resentment, their greed, and their hatred will keep on "burning" in the depth of their hearts—or so Christianity states.

2. An incident to remember

Remember the following incident—it may have occurred in your life not precisely as it is told here; but I am sure that you will recall something similar:

You receive a letter from the Rhode Island Division of Taxation, claiming you owe a large amount of back taxes. It is obvious, though, that the tax folks are mistaken. You try to call the division to straighten matters out; but for days and days you get only voice mail messages and no one ever bothers calling you back as promised in the outgoing message.

Finally, you decide to drive to Providence to speak to them in person. Parking is notoriously difficult in that town, but you are lucky: You find a spot not too far away from the office you need to visit. You get out of your car and feed the parking meter. Then, you walk into the direction of the office building; and as you are rounding a corner, you see him, about 25 yards ahead: that unkempt guy, holding a plastic cup in his hand, hustling for money. You want to avoid a confrontation; so you cross the street and even walk down a side road to get as far out of his way as possible.

Your meeting with the tax officials goes much better than you had anticipated. The wait is short, the lady you get to speak to is friendly; she admits that the whole matter is their fault, and gives you a written certificate stating that you do not owe them any money. You leave as the proverbial "happy camper" and walk back to your car.

Whom did you entirely forget about? The hustler! You see him again only when it is too late. As you are unlocking your car, he is determinedly walking up to you. He shakes his cup, saying, "I am starving.

Can you please spare some change? Please?" You yell, "Leave me alone—get lost!" "Excuse me, mister," he says as he backs away from you …

Who was that?

Your answer might have been, "A lazy bum who thinks that he can live at other people's expense."

Christians would disagree: "We beg to differ. That was Jesus asking you whether you could help him out, and you told him to go to hell." They do not think, of course, that it was Jesus in the literal sense; but according to them, the solidarity Jesus feels with those in need is so deep that telling them off is as good as telling Jesus off.

Maybe you defend yourself: "Had I given that guy money, he would likely have used it only to buy fortified wine. I did him a favor by not giving anything to him."[6] In reply, Christians would say, "How do you know? Besides, this does not justify yelling at him. Moreover, he told you that he was starving. There was a sandwich shop barely 50 feet away from where your car was parked. Why did you not offer to buy him a sandwich? (Had he declined, that would have confirmed your suspicion.)" You reply, "But I was afraid of him …"

Well, let's put him to the side; nothing can be done about that incident anymore anyhow. Christianity urges you, though: "Ask yourself in light of that incident, 'What have I been doing to help those in need? What am I doing? What will I be doing?' Make helping others one of your first priorities, for otherwise … otherwise you will, at one point, hear the words, 'Depart from me, you who are cursed, into the eternal fire prepared for the devil and his angels.'"

(V) "I'VE BLOWN IT …" "NOT SO FAST!"

1. "No hope for someone as wretched as I …"

The kind of life Jesus expects his followers to lead is demanding—without any doubt. Even putting to the side the expectations I did not even mention (can what has not been mentioned be put to the side?), how on earth can I get myself to love my neighbor as myself? To treat others the way I would like to be treated by them? To love even my enemies? How often did I ignore those who needed my help? How often did I not only "pass by" them, but treat them with contempt—or worse?

Well, as far as the life demanded by Jesus is concerned, I have blown it already. I am done in for. There is nothing that can be done about it anymore: I have flunked the test. It is as if I had gotten zeroes on all my quizzes and the midterm: I cannot get a passing grade anymore; I have failed the course. I might as well ignore those difficult demands of the Christian life which are next-to-impossible to comply with anyhow. I might as well enjoy myself while I still can: "Eat, drink, and be merry, for tomorrow, you may be gone."

---

6 John Stossel's March 25, 2011, special "Freeloaders," broadcast on the Fox News Channel, comes to mind as something you might use to undergird your excuse.

2. It is never too late, as long as you are still breathing ...

Christianity would respond—rightly or wrongly, not for me to say (how often did I state something like that? The situation of religion at secular schools makes me repeat it time and again), "You are mistaken if you think that it is too late. As long as you are still breathing, you do have time to make a commitment to the Christian way of life, provided your commitment is sincere. A more-than-shady past is not an obstacle, no matter how long or how dreadful that past may have been. This is the point Jesus makes in the following parable":

> The kingdom of heaven is like a landowner who went out early in the morning to hire workers for his vineyard. He agreed to pay them a denarius[7] for the day and sent them into his vineyard. About nine in the morning he went out and saw others standing in the marketplace doing nothing. He told them, "You also go and work in my vineyard, and I will pay you whatever is right." So they went. He went out again about noon and about three in the afternoon and did the same thing. About five in the afternoon he went out and found still others standing around. He asked them, "Why have you been standing here all day long doing nothing?" "Because no one has hired us," they answered. He said to them, "You also go and work in my vineyard." When evening came, the owner of the vineyard said to his foreman, "Call the workers and pay them their wages, beginning with the last ones hired and going on to the first." The workers who were hired about five in the afternoon came and each received a denarius. So when those came who were hired first, they expected to receive more. But each one of them also received a denarius. When they received it, they began to grumble against the landowner. "These who were hired last worked only one hour," they said, "and you have made them equal to us who have borne the burden of the work and the heat of the day." But he answered one of them, "I am not being unfair to you, friend. Didn't you agree to work for a denarius? Take your pay and go. I want to give the one who was hired last the same as I gave you. Don't I have the right to do what I want with my own money? Or are you envious because I am generous?" So the last will be first, and the first will be last. (Mt 20.1–16, NIV)

In this story, the landowner represents God; the workers represent the ones who make a commitment to Christianity. Just as it made no difference for the payment the workers received at what time of the day they began working, so does it not make any difference for the final outcome of a person's life when in his or her life the commitment of being a follower of Jesus is made, provided it is sincere.

3. Three conditions for getting out of the "I-have-blown-it" situation

Thus, any moment of a person's life can be the beginning of an attempt to comply with the demands of Jesus (living up to the Torah's moral law as interpreted and amplified by Jesus—especially "being there" for one's fellow humans in need).

---

7 A denarius was a Roman silver coin, the value of which was about equivalent to the pay for a day's work done by a common laborer.

Apart from the sincerity of this commitment, there are three conditions which must be met for such a resolve to be effective, with regard to getting oneself out of the "I-have-blown-it" condition; to be forgiven by God, no matter how terrible one's past has been.

First, one must be sincerely sorry for past wrongs one has done. This is more than just admitting that one has done them, although at least admitting past wrongs is a precondition for being sorry for them. One can, however, admit that one misbehaved without being sorry. Suppose a man used abusive language against an acquaintance and made her cry. When someone says, "Don't you see that what you just did was wrong," he replies, "Sure it was wrong; but I enjoyed every second of it. I will do it again as soon as I get another chance." In this case, there would be an admission of the wrong done, but no "being sorry" for it. The key part of the first condition to be forgiven for past wrongdoing is sorrow, repentance—more than just admission.

Second, one must sincerely resolve to avoid the wrongs one feels sorry for, to attempt one's best not to do them again. This resolve to change may, of course, be connected with a realistic recognition of one's weakness, and that falling again and again will be unavoidable (we all do have our "favorite faults" which seem to be next-to-impossible to overcome); but in this case, looking into the future, the resolve to change must be connected with the intent to make a "fresh start" whenever necessary.

There is a third condition for past wrongs to be forgiven—perhaps the biggest obstacle for many who would like to change. It consists in forgiving those who have wronged us.

That I am required to forgive those who have wronged me becomes clear from the following exchange between Jesus and Peter: "Then Peter came to Jesus and asked, 'Lord, how many times shall I forgive my brother or sister who sins against me? Up to seven times?' Jesus answered, 'I tell you, not seven times, but seventy-seven times.'" (Mt 18.21–22, NIV)

It is impossible to keep track of whether or not one has forgiven another 77 times (some ancient manuscripts of Matthew's Gospel even have "seventy times seven times" instead of "seventy-seven times"), except perhaps for those who are obsessive-compulsive with regard to counting how often they forgave; what Jesus means, therefore, is that one must always be willing to forgive. The consequences of an unforgiving attitude are spelled out by Jesus in the following parable, which he tells immediately after having stated that one must always be willing to forgive:

> The kingdom of heaven is like a king who wanted to settle accounts with his servants. As he began the settlement, a man who owed him ten thousand bags of gold was brought to him. Since he was not able to pay, the master ordered that he and his wife and his children and all that he had be sold to repay the debt. At this the servant fell on his knees before him. "Be patient with me," he begged, "and I will pay back everything." The servant's master took pity on him, canceled the debt and let him go. But when that servant went out, he found one of his fellow servants who owed him a hundred silver coins. He grabbed him and began to choke him. "Pay back what you owe me!" he demanded. His fellow servant fell to his knees and begged him, "Be patient with me, and I will pay it back." But he refused. Instead, he went off and had the man thrown into prison until he could pay the debt. When the other servants saw what had happened, they were outraged and went and told their master everything that had happened. Then the master called the servant in. "You wicked servant," he said, "I canceled all that debt of yours because you begged me

to. Shouldn't you have had mercy on your fellow servant just as I had on you?" In anger his master handed him over to the jailers to be tortured, until he should pay back all he owed. This is how my heavenly Father will treat each of you unless you forgive your brother or sister from your heart. (Mt 18.23–35, NIV)

That forgiving others is a precondition for being forgiven also becomes clear from the following words of Jesus: "If you forgive other people when they sin against you, your heavenly Father will also forgive you. But if you do not forgive others their sins, your Father will not forgive your sins." (Mt 6.14–15)

Moreover, everyone saying the Lord's Prayer promises to forgive others. The promise is included immediately after having asked for forgiveness: "And forgive us our debts, as we also have forgiven our debtors" (Mt 6.12). Actually, it is more than just a promise. It is a statement that one has forgiven already (even though many translations use the present tense—"as we *forgive* our debtors"—the original Greek uses a tense indicating the past,[8] as does the translation I used).

By way of a summary, Christians might say, "There are several reasons for which the words of Jesus are called the 'Good News.' One of them is that your past life does not need to keep you from committing yourself to his demands. No matter what that life has been like, you will be forgiven, provided you get yourself to sincerely repent of past wrongs, resolve to avoid them in the future, and to forgive from the heart all those who have wronged you. Remember, though, that wrong conduct is not confined to actively doing things you are not supposed to do; a chief type of misconduct consists of remaining inactive when one should act, especially when one is to help those in need. The resolve to avoid misconduct in the future also must extend to a resolve to avoid the 'inactivity-wrongs.'"

(VI) A RISK TO BE AVOIDED

1. "Goody-good! I can still have fun for a while ..."

Someone convinced that changing his or her life is required might ask a Christian (just to be on the safe side), "Did you say that it is never too late to be forgiven and to begin leading the kind of life Jesus demands?"

The Christian might reply, "It is never too late as long as you are still breathing."

The other exclaims, "Goody-good; that means I can still have lots of fun."

"What do you mean?" the Christian asks.

The other gives back, "I know that I must change—I must turn my life around. But I am not doing it just yet. I will change maybe after I graduated from college; maybe after I got married; maybe ten years from now; maybe when I am in my forties; or maybe when I am as old as that Fritz Wenisch guy when I will no longer be able to have any fun anymore anyhow—maybe then, I will change. Right now,

---

8 The tense is called *aorist*; it does not exist in the English language.

I am going to continue to enjoy myself. But 'You must change' is on my to-do list, definitely; it is the final entry, though, and written in small letters."

2. The reply to the "goody-good" exclamation

In reply, Christians would point at a parable Jesus told with respect to the "goody-good" attitude:

> The ground of a certain rich man yielded an abundant harvest. He thought to himself, "What shall I do? I have no place to store my crops." Then he said, "This is what I'll do. I will tear down my barns and build bigger ones, and there I will store my surplus grain. And I'll say to myself, You have plenty of grain laid up for many years. Take life easy; eat, drink and be merry." But God said to him, "You fool! This very night your life will be demanded from you. Then who will get what you have prepared for yourself?" This is how it will be with whoever stores up things for themselves but is not rich toward God. (Lk 12.16–21, NIV)

Returning to what the "goody-good" guy or gal said—"I know that I must change, but just not yet …"—Christianity asks, "How do you know that you will still be alive at the time you plan to get around to changing? You do not even know whether you will live to see tomorrow. Moreover, do not many types of wrongdoing have a tendency to become habits that are difficult to break? Might not some of them become like addictions, next-to-impossible to give up, making a change for the better more and more difficult over time the longer you persist in these habits? When saying, 'I know that I must change; but I am not doing it just yet …'—when saying this, aren't you taking a two-fold risk, the first one being that, since one's death may happen at any day, there may not be an opportunity for you to change at the time for which you planned it; the second is that you might make changing much more difficult for yourself, maybe even next to impossible? If a change is necessary, isn't the time to change NOW?"

Incidentally, that last question is answered affirmatively not only by Christians, but also by Jews and Muslims. Many people who do not believe in God also agree with it—"The time to become a better person is NOW"—although, of course, they do not think that such a change has any repercussions for a future life (this is what atheists think—they do not believe the existence of such a life), or although they plead ignorance as to what, if any, these repercussions are (this is the agnostics' attitude).

My hands are tied (or maybe better "my lips are sealed"), of course, once again by the Fox principle. That principle permits me to say, though, the following—one can understand it to be true through one's own thinking regardless of any revelation: If we live in a universe that is ultimately meaningful, leading a moral life is one's chief task.[9]

---

9 If the universe would ultimately be meaningless, there would be no "overarching" task for our lives.

CHAPTER FIFTEEN

A Reality Check for Secular Academicians

Profs at secular universities are generally not very fond of Christianity (understatement). Some of them might have a positive attitude toward liberal Christianity; but traditional Christianity, the type to which the vast majority of Christians worldwide belong, is largely considered unacceptable at contemporary secular universities. It is considered outdated, backward, regressive, to be thrown out.

Interestingly, though, many of the secular academicians who scoff at Christianity (in its traditional form at least) begin "singing a different tune" when the conversation turns to Jesus. They might say things like, "Whatever the so-called followers of Jesus have made of his teachings is to be abandoned; but Jesus himself is a different matter. He belongs into a list of the great moral teachers of humanity, together with Socrates (c. 469–399 B.C.), the ancient Greek philosopher who, like Jesus, also was executed for his convictions; Mahatma Gandhi (1869–1948), the great Hindu religious leader and social reformer; the U.S. civil rights leader Martin Luther King Jr. (1929–1968), or Mother Teresa (1910–1997), the Albanian-born Roman Catholic nun who made it her life's mission to take care of the poorest of the poor on the streets of Calcutta. Just as these other great moral teachers of humanity were mere humans, nothing more, so it is with Jesus. He was a human being, a great human being, one of the greatest—but only human, not more. The greatness of his teaching reverberates through the Gospels—even for us non-Christians. Unfortunately, his followers got carried away and began considering him as more than human. That exaggeration needs to be scaled back, or rather abandoned; but that the Jesus of the Gospels was a truly great human being is beyond question."

An example of a secular academician holding the view of the "great-but-merely-human" Jesus is the agnostic Bertrand Russell, who says in an essay entitled, "What Is an Agnostic?":[1] "Most agnostics admire the life and moral teachings of Jesus as told in the Gospels, but not necessarily more than those of certain other men."

---

1 Available on the Web: https://scepsis.net/eng/articles/id_5.php

I do have news for these people: Given the actual New Testament record, the "great-but-merely-human Jesus" theory is not in the cards. It is based on a selective reading of the Gospels; as soon as one considers them in their entirety, one will see that one must abandon that view.

Jesus says too many things that would make him into a rather miserable man if one assumes that he is merely human, not more. Let me mention three examples:

First, remember the words "Soon, you will see the son of man [me] seated at the right hand of the Power, and coming on the clouds of heaven" (Mt 26.64). Suppose Socrates had said, "Just wait—it won't be long, and you will see me sitting at the right hand of God and coming on the clouds." Who would not begin to doubt his sanity and/or his veracity?

Second, consider Jesus' words, "Before Abraham came to be, I am" (Jn 8.53). Imagine Martin Luther King Jr. saying, "I was around way before George Washington ever lived." "Is he totally off his rocker?" would have been the only appropriate reaction.

Third, Jesus said, "Whoever eats my flesh and drinks my blood has eternal life" (Jn 6.54). Imagine this as something Mother Teresa had said. Wouldn't it strike you as absolutely crazy (understatement)?

People wishing to continue defending the "truly-great-but-merely-human Jesus" theory might respond, "No one is perfect—that's what it means to be merely human. Even great people do have their lapses. What you quoted are such lapses on the part of Jesus."

Here is a three-point response:

First, some lapses are so serious that someone's being involved in only one of them is sufficient to shoot down the idea of his or her greatness. Each of the three examples mentioned is a lapse of such seriousness. Just look back at the three words of Jesus quoted, and realistically picture a mere human saying one of them. Wouldn't your reaction have to be "Forget about him or her"? The only reason some secular academicians might react differently is that they had a Christian upbringing during which they heard these words of Jesus prior to abandoning their Christian faith and got "kind of" used to them, failing to see just how outlandish it would be if a mere human were to say them about him- or herself.

Second, in addition to the three examples mentioned, other sayings of Jesus could be cited that sound just as outlandish if a mere human were to apply them to himself.

Third, remember that Jesus calls himself the "Son of Man," a title through which he intends to convey the idea that he will be presented before God's throne and receive an everlasting kingship. He uses this title for himself not once or twice only, but continuously. If he would be a mere human and nothing more, then using that title only once or twice with the intention indicated would be another lapse going beyond the seriousness threshold of what could coexist with true greatness; but his using it constantly would make a mere human Jesus into a walking picture of total outlandishness, rather than into a great individual.

Thus, "Jesus, the 'great-but-merely-human-and-nothing-more' person," the Jesus image many secular academicians are so fond of, does not square with the Jesus image the Gospels present. If Jesus as depicted in the Gospels is assumed to be merely human, he would not belong into a list of truly great persons; rather, he would have to be considered as insane or untruthful or both. The "truly-great-but-merely-human-Jesus-of-the-Gospels" goes down the drain and out the window.

Approaching the Gospels with the attitude of sound realism leaves only the following three possibilities for who Jesus was/is (the first and the second might, of course, go together): Jesus was either dishonest or insane—or what he claimed to be—The Son of God. The "harmless" middle position—"great, but merely human"—must be abandoned. Following C. S. Lewis, who in his book *Mere Christianity*, calls what I have designated as the harmless middle position "patronizing nonsense,"[2] the choices have been framed as "liar, lunatic, or Lord."

Saying that Jesus as portrayed in the Gospels must be either a liar or a lunatic or Lord results from reading them with an open mind and without being selective; it has nothing to do with relying on revelation. Revelation might, however, have to come into the picture as soon as the question is asked, "Which of these three possibilities applies?" "Is he a liar? Is he crazy? Is he Lord?"

I report, you decide …

---

2 In this respect at least, I am a bit more polite than C. S. Lewis.

CHAPTER SIXTEEN

The Faith of Muslims

Matters of Origin and Background

W hat non-Muslims say about the origin of Islam differs significantly from the Muslim understanding of how their religion originated. I will present both views. Which one is correct? Fox principle …

(I) THE ORIGIN OF ISLAM: TWO PERSPECTIVES

1. A non-Muslim's understanding of the origin of Islam

Here is the non-Muslim's "take": Islam originated in the early 600s (early seventh century) in Mecca on the Arabian Peninsula. The founder of Islam was Muhammad. He was born around 570 into a polytheistic family. The town of his birth was a center of pilgrimage. Pagans from the surrounding areas came together there to worship the gods and goddesses they believed in. A shrine in the center of town, known as the Kaaba, was filled and surrounded with images of deities. The Meccans were said to believe in 360 of them, one for every day of the year, with some to spare. Maybe you state at this point, "With some to spare? They were shy by a few." Well, like Islam afterward, the Meccans had a lunar year, which is a bit shorter than our solar year.[1] Therefore, 360 gods and goddesses are more than enough, so that one for every day of the year "is available."

Given Muhammad's upbringing, one of the religions he was familiar with was pagan polytheism.

As a young man, he traveled outside of the Arabian Peninsula. There, he met Christians and Jews and became familiar with Christianity and Judaism.

Islam is a blend of these three religious traditions.

---

1 The details of the Muslim calendar will be explained later.

The belief in Jinni (these are beings between angels and humans), the ascription of importance to the Kaaba, the veneration of the black stone set into one of the exterior angles of the Kaaba, and considering Mecca as a center of pilgrimage go back to the paganism in which Muhammad had grown up.

Monotheism, in the sense of a belief in one God in one person with an explicit rejection of the idea of the Trinity, goes back to Judaism.

The acknowledgment of Jesus as one of the greatest prophets in human history goes back to Christianity.

The understanding of Judaism as well as of Christianity as found in the Qur'an is flawed, however, deviating from what these two religions really stand for. Jews, for example, are severely criticized for considering Ezra as the son of God.[2] No contemporary Jew has the slightest inkling what this is supposed to refer to, and there is no evidence of this having ever been a Jewish belief.

The Christian doctrine that Jesus is the son of God is misunderstood as implying that, if God was to have a son, he would have needed a consort.[3] As shown in the chapter discussing the Trinity, this is not at all implied by what Christians understand Jesus' sonship to be. A case can even be made that the Qur'an misrepresents the teaching on the Trinity as involving God, Jesus, and Mary rather than the Father, the Son, and the Holy Spirit.[4]

2. A Muslim's understanding of the origin of Islam

That Muslims do not agree with what just has been said is the understatement of the century. Even considering Muhammad as the founder of Islam is mistaken according to them. They hold that Islam existed long before the birth of Muhammad. The word *Islam* means "to submit"—the understanding is, "submitting *to the will of God.*" A Muslim is "one who submits"; again, "to the will of God" is mentally to be added. There have been people prior to Muhammad who faithfully submitted to the one and only God the Qur'an urges us to believe in. They were Muslims; their commitment was that of Islam.

Examples are Adam, Noah, or Abraham. Abraham is especially important, because the group of people from whom Muhammad was born descended from him.

Abraham believed in one and only one God just like Muhammad, as did Moses, as did Jesus. Unfortunately, the followers of Moses (the Jews) and Jesus (the Christians) distorted the teachings they had been given.

The Jews, fortunately, did not give up their monotheism; but they mistakenly assumed that some of the promises that were made to Abraham's descendants applied to them—Abraham's descendants over his son Isaac—when they actually applied to the Arabs, Abraham's descendants over Ishmael.

Christians even gave up the monotheism that Jesus had reemphasized for them; they began considering Jesus as the son of God and as God; then, they adopted the idea of the Trinity.

---

2 "The Jews say: Ezra is the son of Allah; and the Christians say: The Messiah is the son of Allah. These are the words of their mouths. They imitate the sayings of those who disbelieved before. Allah's curse be on them! How they are turned away!" (Surah 9.30, based on Ali.)

3 "How could he [God] have a son when he has no consort?" (Surah 6.101, based on Ali.)

4 "And when Allah will say: O Jesus, son of Mary, did you say to men, 'Take me and my mother for two Gods besides Allah?' He will say, 'Glory be to you! It was not for me to say what I had no right to say. You would indeed have known it. You know what is in my mind.'" (Surah 5.116, based on Ali.)

The people living on the Arabian Peninsula deviated from the original revelation their forefathers had received even more than the Jews and the Christians, sinking deeply into polytheism. Among the inhabitants of Mecca, Muhammad's birthplace, there remained, however, at least an inkling of the ancient monotheism by way of a recognition of "the god," Allah, the final remnant of the God that had been revealed to Abraham (and also to the true believers before him). He was, however, considered as one of many, and not even worshipped anymore.[5]

Muhammad was called by God not to preach a new religion totally unheard of prior to his time, but to restore religion to its original purity, the purity it had had at the time of Abraham, of Moses, and of Jesus. For the Arabs, this meant, of course, motivating them to get rid of the polytheism they had adopted. For the Christians, that meant getting back to the monotheism Jesus had preached to them, getting rid of the idea that Jesus was the son of God and, of course, abandoning the false belief that he was God. For the Jews, it meant an acknowledgment of whom God's promises had been made to, and a purification of the understanding of God that had developed among them.

Since the Jewish and the Christian Scriptures had been intermingled with many portions not revealed by God to an extent that the original revelations could not even be identified anymore in them, it was also necessary that these Scriptures be replaced by a new revelation, the Qur'an.

(II) THE PLACE OF ORIGIN OF ISLAM: GEOGRAPHY AND RELIGIOUS SITUATION

1. Mostly geography (very brief)

Islam as preached by Muhammad originated on the Arabian Peninsula, located in Asia, to the south of today's countries Jordan and Iraq, surrounded by the Red Sea (in the west), by the Persian Gulf (in the east) and by the part of the Indian Ocean known as the Arabian Sea (in the south). Today, the largest country on that peninsula is Saudi Arabia. Muhammad's birthplace Mecca is located in that country.

In the century of Muhammad's birth (sixth century), the majority religion in that region of the world was polytheism. There were, however, also Jewish and Christian minorities.

The polytheism varied from place to place. Each town had its own gods and goddesses. Most people did not live in cities, though, but led a nomadic life, moving from place to place with their animal herds. Each of these tribes had its own gods and goddesses.

2. The religious situation in Mecca around the time of Muhammad's birth

What was the religious situation in Mecca, Muhammad's birthplace, like around the time of his birth?

As was mentioned, the Meccans believed in 360 gods and goddesses, one for every day of their lunar year, with some to spare.

---

5 More will be said about Allah as believed in by the pre-Muhammad Meccan polytheists in the later description of these beliefs.

The chief god was Hubal, with a role similar to that of Zeus among the ancient Greeks or Jupiter among the ancient Romans.

Especially popular were three goddesses believed to be sisters: Al-Lat, the goddess of motherhood, Manat, the goddess of fate, and Al-Uzzah, the goddess of the morning star (Venus, actually not a star, but a planet)[6] and of love.

Since these three were sisters, they had to have the same parents. Nothing was said about their mother; their father was supposed to be Allah. With the popularity of these goddesses, one would surmise that at least some of it would be transferred to their dad; but this was not the case. No one cared about Allah. There were no images of him; no temple was dedicated to him; he was not prayed to; he did not even have a name. If you say, "What do you mean? To me Allah sounds like a name that is good enough," I must tell you what that word means. It is a contraction of *al-ilah*, simply meaning "the god." That's how he was called: "the god." For the consciousness of the Meccans, he was "a vague and distant figure."[7]

As has been mentioned earlier, in the center of Mecca, already at the time of Muhammad's birth, there was a structure built of stone, known as the Kaaba. It is still standing there, and is today the most important Muslim sanctuary. Its dimensions are given by Lammens as "39 feet by 33, with a height of 49.5."[8] At the time of Muhammad's birth, it was a pagan temple, filled and surrounded by images of gods and goddesses. According to Muslims, the Kaaba was built by Abraham and his son Ishmael. Into one of its corners of its outside wall, a black stone is inserted.[9] Pre-Muslim pagans probably worshiped that stone; Muslims venerate it as a gift of God. Near the Kaaba is the famous holy well, Zamzam. Like the Kaaba, it predates Muhammad. According to Muslims, it came into existence miraculously to save Hagar's and her son Ishmael's life. They had been brought to the region by Abraham, Ishmael's father, to live there; when they were almost dying of thirst, the well Zamzam appeared for them.[10]

---

6 The planet's name is derived from that of the Roman goddess, Venus, also the goddess of love; she "evolved" from the corresponding Greek goddess Aphrodite.

7 H. A. R. Gibb, *Mohammedanism—An Historical Survey* (New York: Oxford University Press, 1962), p. 52. Note that Muslims object strongly to their religion being called "Mohammedanism," as the title of Gibb's book does.

8 H. Lammens, *Islam—Belief and Institutions*, translated by Sir E. Denison Ross, (Haarlem: Frank Cass & Co. Ltd., 1968) [henceforth referred to as "Lammens, *Islam*"], p. 17.

9 "The black stone is built into the south-eastern angle [of the Kaaba] 5 feet above the ground." Lammens, *Islam*, p. 17.

10 A similar account, also a miraculous generation of a well, is contained in the Book of Genesis 21.14–19.

CHAPTER SEVENTEEN

The Life of Muhammad (Told from the Muslim Perspective)

(I) MUHAMMAD PRIOR TO BEING CALLED AS A PROPHET

Muhammad—the name means "the praised one" or the "famed one"—was born around 570 into the Meccan tribe of the Quraish, a tribe practicing polytheism. His father's name was Abdullah, his mother was Amina. His father died prior to his birth; his mother died when he was about six years old. Until he was eight years old, he was taken care of by his paternal grandfather, Abdul Mutalib. When Abdul died, Muhammad was taken in by his paternal uncle Abu Talib, who raised him. As a young man, he became involved in the caravan trade and accompanied his uncle on the latter's travels, including into Syria when Muhammad was 12 years old. There, he likely encountered Jews as well as Christians.

Later, he entered the employ of Khadija, a wealthy widow, and took care of her trading. When he was about 25 years old, she became his first wife. She was about 40 years old at the time. By all accounts, the marriage was a happy one. During her lifetime, she was his only wife, although polygamy was common then.[1]

(II) MUHAMMAD'S CALL; LOOKING AHEAD (A BIT AT LEAST)

Muhammad seems to have been a meditative person; he seems to have spent much time by himself in prayer. He loved to go to a cave outside of Mecca to pray there. Once, in the year 610 (he was about

---

1 Polygamy literally is "plural marriage"; in its literal sense, the word is indifferent to whether one husband and several wives are involved, or vice versa. In our neck of the woods, it is used for one husband's having more than one wife because this is the more common form of plural marriage. Sticklers for detail would, however, call the practice of one husband's having more than one wife "polygyny," derived from the Greek *polys*, meaning "many" and *gyne*, meaning "woman" or "wife."

40 years old at the time), he had a frightening experience while praying at that place: A man appeared to him, coming down from the sky, and shouted, "Recite!" Muhammad was scared out of his mind and asked, "What shall I recite?" "Recite!" the man shouted again. This was repeated a third time, with the man saying in a loud voice, "Recite in the name of your Lord who creates—creates man from a clot, recite and your Lord is most generous, who taught by the pen, taught man what he did not know …"[2]

When the man disappeared, Muhammad, filled with fear, thinking that he might be going insane or that an evil spirit might be persecuting him, ran home and told his wife what had happened. She, however, surmised that the experience involved neither insanity nor an evil spirit, but that he had received a message from God. She took Muhammad to one of her relatives named Waraqah, according to some sources a Christian priest of the Ebonite sect.[3] Muhammad told him what had transpired. He listened carefully, and then expressed his view that Muhammad had received a genuine revelation, and that he had been chosen by God as the prophet for the Arab people (Muslims would add, of course, "and for the entire world").

Muhammad's immediate reaction was something like a hesitant "If you say so"; soon, however, his fear was replaced by confidence, especially when the "man from heaven" kept on appearing to him again and again, proclaiming additional messages to him.

Looking ahead, Muhammad kept on receiving messages off and on for the rest of his life. Muslims believe the "man" who visited Muhammad to be the Angel Gabriel, who "revealed it [the messages] to your [Muhammad's] heart by Allah's command" (Surah 2.97, based on Ali). Muhammad himself was not able to read or write; but whatever Gabriel told him imprinted itself deeply on his mind: He was able to repeat it to others. Some of the messages were recorded in writing during his lifetime already; others were committed to memory by his followers. After Muhammad's death, all of the messages were collected and written down as a unified whole. They constitute the Qur'an, the Holy Book of Islam. Thus, according to Muslims, their Holy Scriptures have been dictated to Muhammad word for word by the Angel Gabriel. Incidentally, Gabriel is also called "the Holy Spirit" and "the Faithful Spirit": "The Holy Spirit has revealed it [the Qur'an] from your Lord with truth." (Surah 16.102, based on Ali.) I will say more about the Qur'an when we will consider the chief teachings of Islam.

(III) MUHAMMAD'S EARLY PREACHING

1. The decision to "go public"

Back to Muhammad's life: His fears had been taken away and he had become confident that he was receiving genuine messages from God through an angel. At first, however he told only close friends

---

2 These words can be found at the beginning of Surah 96 (v. 1–5) of the Qur'an. The quotation is based on Ali, who uses, however, "read" instead of "recite."

3 Actually, there are two early Christian groups known as Ebonites. One of them insisted that the Law of Moses be observed in its entirety, including the nonmoral law of the Torah, and denied the divinity of Jesus, as well as his virgin birth. If Waraqah actually was an Ebonite, it is more likely that he belonged to the group just described rather than to the other group, which had heavily been influenced by Gnosticism.

and members of his immediate family about it. Khadija, who had become convinced that the messages he received were genuine even before he did, is venerated by Muslims as the first one to believe in him.

At one point, though, he felt the urge to go public. He did so with fear and trembling, in the year 613.

From Qur'an chapters that likely were revealed early in his career, one can easily guess what his message might have been. It consisted in three chief points, the third one to be broken down into four sub-points.

2. The basics of Muhammad's message to the Meccans

(1) One, and only one, God

First, there is one—and only one God—Allah. Remember that the Meccans at the time had a vague idea of a God they called "Allah—the god." Muhammad could therefore, tell them. "Even you, being seduced into believing in many false gods, did not manage to forget the one, true God completely; but you did 'push' him into the background, 'hiding' him behind the fog of the unreal gods and goddesses your forefathers did invent. Get rid of these deities; focus on Allah, the one and only God, **the** God (rather than "the god"). All of the other gods and goddesses must be thrown out."

Even Al-Lat, Manat, and Al-Uzzah, the popular sister-goddesses, had to go: "Have you then considered Lat and Uzzah, and another, the third, Manat? Are the males for you and for him the females? This indeed is an unjust division! They are nothing but names which you have named, you and your fathers—Allah has sent no authority for them" (Surah 53.23, based on Ali).

I cannot resist the temptation of throwing in a side remark here on the Qur'an passage just quoted. In its attempt to show the absurdity of assuming that Allah would have daughters, it uses as a premise a view commonly accepted at the time: That having sons is much better than having daughters. The implication is, "Allah does not have any children, neither male nor female ones; but if one were to assume his having children, it is doubly absurd to think that he would have daughters instead of sons."

Back to the first point of Muhammad's initial message to the Meccans, though, and to summarize it: He taught a strict monotheism.

(2) Judgment day

A second chief point which Muhammad likely emphasized during his early preaching concerned a judgment day, also known as the last day. A day will come on which the dead will be resurrected, and all humans will be assembled before God who will judge them. Those who have obeyed God will be rewarded; those who did evil will be punished. An example of a Qur'an passage about judgment day is

> When the sun is folded up, and when the stars are dust-colored, and when the mountains are made to pass away, and when the camels are abandoned, and when the wild animals are gathered together, and when the cities are made to swell, and when men are united, and when the one buried alive is asked for what sin she was killed, and when the books are spread, and when the heaven has its covering removed and when hell is kindled, and

when the Garden is brought near—every soul will know what it has prepared (Surah 81.1–14, based on Ali).

Allow me to examine two parts of that passage in detail, that about the camels and that about "one buried alive."

Owning camels was a sure sign of wealth, like owning a fancy Mercedes or a Cadillac today. For many rich people, caring for one's camels was, therefore, among their highest priorities. The arrival of judgment day leads, however, to a total reversal of their priorities. Suddenly, they realize that being wealthy has no bearing on one's reaching the goal for which one has been created, as becomes clear from their abandonment of their camels.

How about the "burying alive" passage? Among Muhammad's contemporaries before they accepted Islam, not only was having sons preferable to having daughters, but when daughters instead of sons were born again and again in a family, people grew so sick and tired of having another daughter that they threw the newborn baby girl into a ditch and buried her alive. This horrendous crime is criticized in the passage, with God being depicted as asking the resurrected girl, "What wrong did you do to deserve to be treated in that way?" She will respond, "All I did wrong was being a girl" (she might as well add "The way you made me"). Then, God is going to punish those who did the terrible deed of killing her. When Muhammad became the leader of most of Arabia, he made sure that the brutal practice of killing infant girls ceased.[4]

(3) Four basic duties

The third chief point of Muhammad's early message concerns four duties that humans have:

The first one consists in leading lives of prayer. People must condition themselves to be conscious of always being in the presence of God. As we will see in the discussion of the Five Pillars of Islam, this developed later into a duty to participate in five daily prayers. Also between these "official" prayers, though, a person must make sure to be continuously aware of God's presence.

Second, one must submit to God's will, similarly as Christians say as a part of the Lord's Prayer, "Your will be done." The significance of this duty is driven home by the fact that it gave the religion discussed right now, as well as its adherents, its name. As was stated, "Islam" means "to submit" (add: "to the will of God"); a "Muslim" is "one who submits" (again, add: "to the will of God").

Third, one is to resist the temptation to sin. Observe yourself during a given day: There are constant inducements to do wrong. Often, you succumb—maybe only in minor matters; at times, though, even in serious ones. Muhammad said, "Resist—do not give in."

Finally, he urged his contemporaries to take care of those who were, as we often say euphemistically today, "less fortunate"; more accurately, they are to be called "poor"; maybe even "dirt poor." At Muhammad's time, most widows and orphans beloved into this group;[5] so the fourth duty can be formulated as, "Take care of the poor, of widows, and of orphans."

---

4 Earlier, a Qur'an passage was quoted, implying that it is better to have boys than girls. In spite of protestations of some Western Muslims, that earlier passage makes it questionable that the Qur'an does away with the view of it being better to have sons than daughters, although fortunately, killing of infant girls is eliminated.

5 Muhammad's first wife Khadija was an exception to this rule.

(IV) REJECTION BY THE MECCANS

After this "detour" into Muhammad's early message, I return to his life. How did the Meccans react to what he told them? The "fear and trembling" he had entertained about going public proved to be justified. He was rejected, hated for his message, despised because of it, and persecuted. In part, economic considerations were behind this reaction. As I have mentioned earlier, Mecca was a place of pilgrimage for the polytheists living in surrounding areas. When they visited the town, they needed places to stay and food; one could sell them amulets, all kinds of trinkets, etc. What would happen to those pilgrims if Muhammad's message would catch on, and a belief in the many gods and goddesses whose images adorned the Kaaba would disappear? Would the Kaaba then not become a rather lonely place?[6] The Meccans had no idea at the time that the pilgrimage would continue, even significantly grow with respect to the number of pilgrims that would be involved. When Muhammad began preaching, they feared that a significant economic boon would disappear if Muhammad would be taken seriously. This was one of the reasons for his being rejected.

Fortunately for him, though, he had a powerful supporter: His uncle Abu Talib. Even though the latter did not believe a word of what Muhammad was preaching, for reasons of family loyalty, he stood by him and protected him from the hostilities of the townspeople.

This changed, however, in the year 619, a difficult year for Muhammad. First, Khadija, his beloved wife, passed away; then, Abu Talib died. With the latter's death, Muhammad had lost his protector, and matters came to be almost unbearably difficult for him.

(V) MOVE TO MEDINA—THE HIJRAH

In 622, however, he received an invitation from "up north": About 250 miles north of Mecca, there is the town Medina (at the time called Yathrib). Earlier, a group of pilgrims from there had listened to Muhammad's preaching, and had been impressed by it. They sent a delegation and asked Muhammad to come to live in their town.

To make the famous long story short, Muhammad accepted the offer, and after some from his small band of Meccan followers had left town to move north, Muhammad himself did so.

Soon, he became the leader of Medina and the surrounding area.

His 622 move from Mecca to Medina, known as the Hijrah (literally, "migration"), led to a complete reversal of fortunes for him personally, and for the faith that he was preaching. Thus, the year of the Hijrah is of immense significance for Muslims; in fact, so significant that it marks the beginning of their count of years. They count years as "Before the Hijrah" and "After the Hijrah."

Since I have told you the year of the Hijrah according to our count—622—I am sure that there will be one or the other among you who considers him- or herself as mathematically sufficiently gifted and bold enough to tell us what year 2014 is for Muslims. Did I hear, "1392"? Sorry, that's wrong. How do I dare criticize your math? I don't. My question was "kind of" a trick question. The trick was not

---

6 The Carmodys write, "The livelihoods of the merchants who sold amulets, the soothsayers who sold fortunes, and the semiecstatic poets who lyricized the old gods where all imperiled." Denise and John Carmody, *Ways to the Center—An Introduction to World Religions*, 4th Edition. (Belmont, CA: Wadsworth, 1993), p. 361.

reminding you that Muslims do have a lunar calendar, and that the Muslim year is a little shorter than our solar year. Determining what the current year is for Muslims is, therefore, not as easy as simply subtracting 622 from 2014.

(VI) CALENDAR "DETOUR"

Let me use the occasion for another "detour," however—a "walk" through the Muslim calendar in comparison to our civil calendar.

1. The basics of the Muslim calendar

As with all (or at least most[7]) purely lunar calendars, the Muslim year consists of 12 lunar months. A lunar month is approximately equal to the length of time it takes the moon to pass through its various phases once. This is about 29.5 days (the precise average time is 29 days, 12 hours, and 44 minutes—an average time because its exact length depends on the moon's closeness to the earth in any given month). Accordingly, the Muslim months alternate in length between 29 and 30 days. One of these moths, the "month of the Pilgrimage," may have either 29 or 30 days, for occasional leap days are necessary to keep the months in step with the phases of the moon because of the 44 minutes in addition to half a day it takes the moon to go through its phases once. Each 30-year period has 11 leap years and 19 regular years. The Muslim year has either 354 or 355 days. There are approximately 33 Muslim years to every 32 of our years.

2. Our secular calendar in contrast to the Muslim calendar

As with all solar calendars, the goal of the calendar we use is to keep the parts of the year in step with the seasons. The seasons are determined by the position of the earth on its path around the sun. Thus, the length of the solar year is to come as close as possible to the time it takes the earth to travel around the sun once, which is approximately 365 days.

The calendar used by us is called Gregorian calendar, named after Pope Gregory XIII, who in 1582 ordered a small modification to the Julian calendar, which had been introduced under Julius Caesar in 46 B.C. The reason for this modification is as follows:

The precise amount of time it takes the earth to complete its orbit around the sun once is 365 days, 5 hours, 48 minutes, and 46 seconds. Thus, the length of the solar year is about 365 days and 6 hours, or 365 and a quarter days. To keep the seasons in step with the calendar year, in the Julian calendar, one day—a leap day—was added once every four years. The rule was that every year, the count of which was divisible by four, was a leap year. The year 1500 was a leap year; 1501 was not. This system would work perfectly if the solar year would be exactly a quarter of a day longer than 365 days. As it is, however, under the Julian calendar, every four years, 24 hours were added to the year, when all that was needed were 23 hours, 15 minutes, and 4 seconds. This was overcompensation by 44 minutes and 56 seconds (4 times 11 minutes and 14 seconds). By 1582 this had accumulated

---

7 I cannot claim familiarity with all lunar calendars.

to more than 14 days, with the vernal equinox (beginning of spring) occurring on March 11. The problem was solved under Pope Gregory by eliminating 10 days from October 1582, which caused the beginning of spring of the year 1583 to fall on March 21;[8] to keep the seasons from slowly shifting around the year once again, the number of leap days was reduced slightly: Years ending in hundreds were considered as leap years only if they were divisible by 400, rather than only by 4. Thus, 2000 was a leap year, 1900 was not.[9]

3. Some additional remarks on the Muslim calendar

In a purely lunar calendar, there is no relationship between months and seasons. According to the Muslim calendar, in each year, a given season starts 10 or 11 days later than in the previous year.

The first month of the Muslim year is called "Muharram"; "Muharram 1" corresponds to our January 1. Relating Muslim dates to our calendar, in 2014, Muharram 1 falls on October 25 and marks the beginning of the Muslim year 1436; in 2015, Muharram 1 occurs on October 14 and begins 1437, and in 2016, Muharram 1 occurs on October 2 and begins 1438.

Here are the names of the 12 months of the Muslim year: (1) Muharram; (2) Safar; (3) Rabi' al-awwal (Rabi' I); (4) Rabi' al-thani (Rabi' II); (5) Jumada al-awwal (Jumada I); (6) Jumada al-thani (Jumada II); (7) Rajab; (8) Sha'ban; (9) Ramadan; (10) Shawwal; (11) Dhu al-Qi'dah; (12) Dhu al-Hijjah. Beginning with Muharram, which has 30 days, the months alternate between 30 and 29 days. The 12th month has 29 or 30 days, the latter in leap years.

(VII) BACK TO MUHAMMAD'S LIFE: MUHAMMAD IN MEDINA

It did not take long for Muhammad to become the leader of Medina and the area surrounding it. During the first year following his arrival, he established a mosque with a learning center, and more and more of the people living there adopted the faith of which he claimed to be the prophet. There were, however, also several communities of Jews in the area. Many of them did not agree with his religious views, although he claimed that an examination of their own scriptures would show them the truthfulness of his teaching.[10]

---

8 The reason 10 days instead of 14 days—the number that had accumulated since the Julian calendar had been established—were eliminated was to make the beginning of spring revert to the date on which it occurred in A.D. 325, the year in which the Council of Nicaea took place.

9 The year 1500, used as an example before, was a leap year, because the Gregorian calendar had not been introduced by that time—the man to become Pope Gregory XIII had not even been born yet (he was born in 1502). It would, however, not have been a leap year under the Gregorian calendar.

10 See, for example, Surah 2.40-41 (the person represented as speaking is God): "O Children of Israel, call to mind My favor which I bestowed on you and be faithful to your covenant with Me, I shall fulfill My covenant with you; and Me, Me alone, should you fear. And believe in that which I have revealed, verifying that which is with you." (Based on Ali. The words "That which is with you" are interpreted to refer to the Holy Scriptures of the Jews.)

1. Battle of Badr; banishment of the Jewish tribe of the Bani Qaynuqa

Concerning the town of Muhammad's birth, caravan trade was an important source of wealth for the Meccans, and caravans traveling from Mecca into Syria had to pass near Medina. Muhammad instigated attacks on them.

Following several minor skirmishes, in 624, a large Meccan caravan, led by Abu Sufyan, was returning from Syria to Mecca. As an attack on this caravan was feared, a group of warriors was sent north from Mecca to protect it. Muhammad led a group of a little over 300 people from Medina, planning to attack the caravan. His group met up with the Meccan protective forces at Badr, a location about 80 miles southwest of Medina, and won a decisive victory over the much larger Meccan group. That victory was important with respect to buttressing Muhammad's authority over the Medinans. Historians refer to the armed clash leading to that victory as the Battle of Badr.

One of the Jewish groups in Medina, known as the Bani Qaynuqa, was economically influential and resented the growth of Muhammad's prestige and spread messages critical of him. In response, first, individual Jews were killed by Muslims with Muhammad's approval; in some cases, he even had suggested that this be done.[11] Subsequently, he ordered the Qaynuqa area besieged; after some time, his forces occupied it and most of the members of the tribe were banished. Their property (houses and land) was divided among Muhammad's followers.[12]

2. Battle of Uhud; banishment of the Jewish tribe of the Banu 'n-Nazir

In 625, the Meccans, enraged by the defeat of their forces sent to protect the caravan Abu Sufyan had led, moved against Medina with an army of 3,000 warriors. They encamped at Uhud, about three miles northeast of Medina. Muhammad led a force of 1,000 men against them. This time, his smaller army was no match against the Meccan warriors. Muhammad's group was defeated and had to retreat. Muhammad had been wounded in the fight, so the retreat was led by Abu Bakr, one of Muhammad's fathers-in-law. Although the Meccans had won the battle, they had incurred serious losses. Thus, they decided to return to Mecca instead of attempting to occupy Medina. The 625 fight is known as the Battle of Uhud.

A Jewish tribe living in Medina's vicinity, known as the Banu 'n-Nazir, had accepted Muhammad's leadership following the victory at Badr. In consequence of the defeat of the Muslim forces at Uhud, however, they turned against him. Muhammad sent a group of fighters against them; they were defeated and exiled.

3. Battle of the Trench; elimination of the Jewish tribe of the Banu Quraizah and subjugation of additional tribes

In 627, the Meccans, aided by several non-Meccan tribes, moved once again against Medina. Their army consisted of 12,000 men. Medina had been warned, and Muhammad had ordered a defensive

---

11 See Serge Trifkovic, *The Sword of the Prophet—Islam—History, Theology, Impact on the World* (Boston: Regina Orthodox Press, 2002), pp. 40–41.

12 See Thomas Patrick Hughes, *Dictionary of Islam* [henceforth referred to as "Hughes, *Dictionary*"] (Chicago: KAZI Publications, 1994; originally published in 1886), p. 377.

trench to be dug to protect the town's most densely settled area. He also had made sure that there was enough food available in the town to last through a siege. The trench was defended by 3,000 Muslim warriors. The Meccan forces besieged Medina for almost a month; then, they abandoned their attempt to take the town and left. Because of the trench involved in Medina's defense, that 627 siege is known as the Battle of the Trench.

One of the groups that had assisted the Meccans in their siege of Medina was the Jewish tribe of the Banu Quraizah. After the Meccan forces had withdrawn, Muhammad ordered an attack on that tribe. Its area was besieged for about twenty-five days; finally, the tribe surrendered. The men were killed—several hundred of them (700 according to Patrick Hughes[13] and Alvin Smith,[14] 900 according to Trifkovic,[15] but only 300 according to the Muslim apologist Maulana Muhammad Ali[16]), the women were raped and most of them, together with the children, were made captives or sold into slavery.[17]

Continuing an account of Muhammad's dealing with the Jews, in 629, he moved against a Jewish tribe living to the north of Medina, in the area of Khaibar, about 95 miles from his town, in the northwestern part of the Arabian Peninsula. The area was "subjugated to Islam. ... The subjugation of [three additional] ... Jewish districts ..., on the confines of Syria, followed."[18]

4. Treaty with the Meccans; move against Mecca and surrender of the town

Subsequently, Muhammad decided to make a pilgrimage to Mecca and visit the Kaaba, which was, of course, at that time still used (the Muslims would say "abused") by the pagans as a sanctuary. When he and his people were about two day trips away from the city, his advance was stopped by a group coming from Mecca. Although they prevented him from completing the pilgrimage, they entered, on behalf of the Meccans, into a treaty with him.[19] The terms of the treaty included that there would be no hostility between Mecca and Medina for ten years, and that during the so-called sacred months—the time of the year when the pagans traditionally made their pilgrimage to Mecca—the Medinans also would be allowed to participate unmolested in the pilgrimage. At the next pilgrimage time, Muhammad actually took part in the pilgrimage, accompanied by about 2,000 people. He engaged in the usual activities, including circulating the Kaaba seven times.

A short time later, Muhammad referred to quarrels that had broken out among tribes around Mecca as a breach of the agreement between Mecca and Medina; he considered the event as justification to move against the town of his birth. This occurred at the beginning of the year 630. He arrived

---

13 See Hughes, Dictionary, p. 378.

14 See Alvin J. Schmidt, *The Great Divide* [henceforth referred to as "Schmidt, *Divide*"] (Boston: Regina Orthodox Press, 2004), p. 17.

15 See Trifkovic, *Sword*, p. 44.

16 *The Holy Qur'an, Arabic Text with English Translation and Commentary*, Translated by Maulana Muhammad Ali, comment on Surah 33.26, p. 831.

17 Muslims give as the reason for the extremely harsh treatment of that tribe—much harsher than that of the other Jewish tribes—that its members had actively assisted in a hostile attack on Medina although they were bound by an earlier agreement to help in the defense of the town. I let you be the judge whether or not this argument justifies what was done to them, with Muhammad's approval and in his presence.

18 Hughes, *Dictionary*, p. 380. Hughes identifies the three additional districts as that of Fadak, Wadi l-Qura, and Tannah.

19 It is known as the treaty of al-Hudaibiyah, named after the area in which Muhammad's party was staying at the time the treaty was entered into.

with 10,000 men. Mecca was unprepared and surrendered. Muhammad entered the town, made his way to the Kaaba, and ordered the 360 images of gods and goddesses there destroyed. The inhabitants of Mecca, swayed by his overwhelming strength, submitted to him. From Mecca, Muhammad sent armed groups into the surrounding area to enforce the submission of several tribes living there. Thus, he had become the leader of Mecca and Medina and the sizeable area surrounding these towns. Soon, most of the tribes living on the Arabian Peninsula swore allegiance to him.

5. Return to Medina; a remark on the Byzantine Empire; the last two years of Muhammad's life

After some time, still in 630, Muhammad returned to Medina. Later that same year, rumors reached Medina that the Byzantine Emperor Heraclius had sent armed forces towards the northern part of the Arabian Peninsula. Muhammad sent his own army, consisting of 30,000 men, up north, intending to attack the hostile armed forces at Tabuk, situated in the northwestern part of the Arabian Peninsula. No Byzantine armed forces were to be found, however: The accounts of them moving against the Muslims turned out to be unfounded rumors.[20] Having won the submission of several groups of people living in the area, Muhammad's forces withdrew to Medina.

At this point, it may be appropriate to include a few remarks on the Byzantine Empire, also called the East Roman Empire—we will encounter it several times in the account of the history of Islam after Muhammad. That empire is a successor state of the Roman Empire. After Constantine had become Roman emperor, he moved the empire's capital to a town called Byzantium. It was renamed Constantinople, literally, "The Town of Constantine." (Today, it is called Istanbul.) In the year 395, the Roman Empire split into the West Roman Empire[21] and the East Roman Empire or Byzantine Empire (the designation "Byzantine Empire" goes back to the original name of the town that became the capital).

Back to Muhammad: The following year—631—he decreed that henceforth, the pilgrimage to Mecca would be a Muslim-only event; in fact, non-Muslims were forbidden to enter the town. Since then, Mecca is closed to non-Muslims.

In 632, Muhammad made the pilgrimage to Mecca for the last time in his life. A huge throng of people (40,000 according to some reports) accompanied him. Outside of Mecca, speaking on a hill named 'Arafah, he gave a rousing address, now known as his farewell speech. A short time after his return to Medina, he fell ill and died, still in 632.

---

20 As will be recounted in the chapter on the history of Islam after Muhammad, the Byzantines sent armed forces against the Muslims only six years later. This army was defeated at the Battle of Yarmouk.

21 According to a conventional view, the West Roman Empire ended in 476, when Emperor Romulus Augustus (nicknamed "Augustulus," meaning "little Augustus"), about sixteen years old at the time, was deposed by Odoacer, a West-Roman army officer of Germanic descent.

CHAPTER EIGHTEEN

Five Basic Duties

The Five Pillars of Islam

As I have stated earlier and as many of you probably know anyway, a religion is not only (not even chiefly) a matter of the mind, a set of convictions, but also a matter of the will and of the heart. As far as the will is concerned, a religion involves "doing." This applies also to Islam. Someone converting to Islam becomes subject to five duties which are so important that they are known as the "five pillars of Islam." They are (1) the Creed; (2) prayer; (3) fasting; (4) almsgiving; and (5) a pilgrimage to Mecca.

(I) PILLAR ONE: THE CREED

Considering these five duties one by one, we turn first to the Creed, called Shahada. As you hopefully recall, the word "creed," derived from the Latin *credo* which means "I believe," designates a concise and official summary of the beliefs of a particular religion. One can hardly get any more concise than the Muslim Creed does; it is one of the shortest—if not *the* shortest—creed of any religion: "La ilaha il-Allah, Muhammad-ar Rasul Allah." Even if I would make you memorize it in Arabic, you would have no reason to complain. Here is its English version: "There is no God but Allah, and Muhammad is the messenger of God."

There are two important functions connected with this creed.

The first one relates to the question, "How does one become a Muslim?" As many of you know, in most Christian denominations, becoming a Christian is connected with the rite of baptism. There is no Muslim baptism. One becomes a member of the Muslim religion through saying the Muslim Creed, such that one understands it and agrees with it—that's it. A person capable of doing so and actually doing so has the right to call him- or herself a Muslim from that moment on.

The Creed has a second function. It is to become an aid to remember that one's life is always in God's presence. Suppose a monotheist asks himself, "When is God thinking of me?" The answer is, of course, "Always—at each and every moment of the day." The monotheist would, of course, say, "There is another question to ask: 'How is God thinking of me?'" To this, the answer is, "Lovingly." So, according to the monotheist, God is always lovingly thinking of me. How often do I return the favor? Many monotheists—Jews, Christians, and Muslims—must say if they are honest, "Hardly ever." That's where the Muslim Creed comes into the picture again. "You are to repeat it often during the day as a help to remember that your life is always before God who loves you."

Think about a beautiful piece of music that you hear for the first time. Then, you hear it again—and again—and again. At one point, the time will come at which it is constantly in the back of your mind; maybe even when you wake up during the night, it is there. That's how an awareness of God must become for you; and repeating the Creed often during the day is the means for conditioning yourself that it might become so.

(II) PILLAR TWO: PRAYER

The creed is, of course, a short prayer. There is, however, a different, additional prayer requirement, involving prayers that are longer and more "organized." It constitutes the second pillar of Islam.

Actually, five daily prayers are required of Muslims at specified times: In the morning, at noon, in the middle of the afternoon, in the evening, and during the night. For each prayer, there are ideal times at which it should begin; but one is given a "window of opportunity" for these prayers. The morning prayer is to be said between dawn and sunrise; the noon prayer between noon and the middle of the afternoon; the afternoon prayer between the middle of the afternoon and sunset; the evening prayer between sunset and dusk; and the night prayer during the night hours.

Today, and in our part of the world, it is easy to determine the ideal prayer time—we carry all kinds of devices around that tell us what time it is. That was not always so, however, and even today, there are many parts of the world in which it is not so. Thus, to inform people that it is time to pray, there is an announcer of the prayer, called a muezzin. He calls out from the minaret, a slender tower at the mosque, that it is time to pray. He chants (in Arabic, of course), "Allah is most great. Allah is most great. I bear witness that there is no God but Allah, the one, and that Muhammad is his messenger. Come to prayer. Come to the good. Allah is most great. Allah is most great. There is no God but Allah, the one." When announcing the morning prayer, he adds, "Prayer is better than sleep," to provide additional motivation to get out of bed and pray.

Prayer is to be preceded by ritual washing: One must wash one's face, one's hands, and one's feet. This is to symbolize the state of purity in which one's soul is to be when praying, which is defined as "speaking to God."

The actual prayer involves reciting parts of the Qur'an. Also, prayers are to be said facing the direction of Mecca; in Mecca itself, they are to be said facing the direction of the Kaaba.

How long does each prayer last? The pamphlet, *An Employer's Guide to Islamic Religious Practices*, recommends that employers allow their Muslim employees fifteen minutes of time for the prayers, including the washing.

The Friday noon prayer is meant to be said together with a community, which gathers in the nearest mosque. Many attend a mosque also for other prayers, though. The Friday prayer is also connected with a sermon or homily by the leader of a local Muslim congregation. If both men and women are present in a mosque, they are often separated by being in different rooms set apart by curtains. If there is no such separation, the men are lined up in the front, the women in the back. I am sure that you have seen Muslims pray on television; so you know that the prayer involves kneeling down and prostrating oneself to the ground.

(III) PILLAR THREE: ALMSGIVING

Muslims do have a religious duty to give alms. Almsgiving is called "Zakat," literally meaning "purity," because one purifies one's soul by taking care of the poor. Unless one is poor oneself, one must give each year 2.5 percent of what one owns: The alms tax is not an income tax, but a tax on one's property. One must consider what one has to one's name at the end of the year; that amount is what the alms tax is calculated from. A person owning the equivalent of $10,000 (in bank accounts, gold, silver, jewelry, etc.) is obliged to give $250; a person owning the equivalent of $100,000 is obliged to give $2,500. The duty to give alms does not apply to those who own, when the alms tax is due, less than the equivalent of the value of three ounces of gold. The value of three ounces of gold is called "Nisab." Naturally, its dollar value changes constantly. Here is a link to a website providing current Nisab information: htpp://www.e-nisab.com/current.

According to the Qur'an, the money collected in this way is to be used for "the poor and the needy, and those employed to administer it … and to (free the) captives, [for] those in debt … and the wayfarers" (Surah 9.60, based on Ali).

(IV) PILLAR FOUR: FASTING

Muslims are required to fast during the month of Ramadan, the ninth month of the year.

"What? Fasting for an entire month? Who can survive that?" Well, it is a serious fast, but not as bad as it might have sounded to you: The fasting is limited to the daytime hours, more specifically, from the point of time on from which "the whiteness of the day becomes distinct from the blackness of the night" (Surah 2.187, based on Ali), that is, from dawn to sunset.[1] According to Surah 2.184, those who are traveling, as well as those who are ill, are exempt from the fast, although they must make up the days they missed after the month of fasting has ended. Another group of people exempt are "those who find it extremely hard" (Surah 2.184, based on Ali). Ali includes women who are nursing or pregnant in this group,[2] as well as those who cannot fast because of old age, except that old and healthy persons are not exempt. Those, however, who are exempt from the fast because of hardship must "effect redemption by feeding a poor man" (Surah 2.184, based on Ali); that is, they must make up for not fasting by another good work. The duty to fast begins with the onset of puberty.

Ramadan is believed to be the month during which the revelation of the Qur'an started; so the fast is to commemorate the revelation of the Qur'an.

---

1 That's at any rate how Maulana Muhammad Ali interprets the passage in his edition of the Qur'an.
2 See Maulana Muhammad Ali's commentary to Surah 2.184 in his edition of the Qur'an.

(V) PILLAR FIVE: PILGRIMAGE TO MECCA

Finally, Muslims are obliged to make a pilgrimage to Mecca at least once during their lives unless doing so is impossible, because of poverty, for example. The pilgrimage duty is spelled out in the following Qur'an passage: "Pilgrimage to the house [Kaaba] is a duty which men [humans] owe to Allah" (Surah 3.97, based on Ali).

CHAPTER NINETEEN

The Basic Teachings of Islam

(I) THE QUR'AN

1. The Qur'an's nature; reason for its name

The chief source of the teachings of Islam is the Qur'an. It is to Muslims what the Jewish Holy Scriptures are to Judaism, and what the Old and New Testaments are to Christianity: The Qur'an is the Holy Book of Islam.

The word Qur'an is an Arabic noun meaning "recitation" or "reading." The book is given this name for two reasons: First, the name harks back to the very first word that the Angel Gabriel supposedly revealed to Muhammad by Gabriel. Remember what Muhammad is said to have experienced in the cave outside of Mecca. A man came down from heaven, calling out in a loud voice, "Read ...." (or "recite ..."). Second, the Qur'an is seen as a book not to remain a "dead letter," but actually to be read or recited.

2. The Qur'an's origin according to Muslims

Where does the Qur'an come from in its present form? What I am going to say about the origin of the Qur'an corresponds to the Muslim perspective.

As was stated in the segment on Muhammad's life, during the last 22 years of his life, he kept on being visited off and on by the Angel Gabriel, who brought him messages. Whenever the angel had stated a new revelation, Muhammad, who according to Muslim tradition could not read or write, dictated the message to a scribe for it to be written down, a short time after the angel had left. Much of this secretarial work was supposedly done by a certain Zayd ibn Thabit. Muhammad also saw to it that there would be a sufficient number of people to commit the revelations to memory, so that the messages could be recited also in situations in which written versions were not available or by groups of people, none of whom were able to read (not unusual in those days).

Many of the longer Qur'an chapters and some of the shorter ones were not revealed at once, but in various parts. According to Maulana Muhammad Ali, however, not only the content of the Qur'an as a whole, but also the organization of the material into chapters and the sequence the chapters were to have in the final edition of the Qur'an goes back to Muhammad.

At the time of Muhammad's death, many people were alive who were able to recite the entire Qur'an from memory. At the occasion of several battles that took place during the year 633, however, many Muslims lost their lives, including many who knew the Qur'an by heart. Consequently, the first "successor" of Muhammad, the caliph[1] Abu Bakr, ordered a written copy of the Qur'an to be made, done from the originals written down during Muhammad's life and under the latter's direction. The person to whom this task was entrusted was Zayd, mentioned before.

It did not take long, however, for different versions of the Qur'an to appear, though. This was the case, especially in areas outside of Arabia to which Islam spread. Maulana Muhammad Ali claims, while acknowledging the impossibility of establishing what the precise differences were between these versions and between them and the one done by Zayd, that the discrepancies concerned only the manner of the pronunciation of words, rather than to the work's substantive content. However that may be, the differences were sufficient for Othman, the third caliph, to order all existing versions of the Qur'an to be collected and burnt, and a new edition to be made, reportedly using as a model the copy that Zayd had made which is said to have been in the safekeeping of a certain Hafsah, a daughter of Omar (second caliph) and a widow of Muhammad. Copies of that new version reportedly were distributed to strategic locations in the area across which Islam had spread by that time. Current versions of the Qur'an are said to be based on the ones done during Othman's rule, whose versions are said to be based on the one Abu Bakr had ordered to be made, whose version was based on the originals—or so the Muslim account goes.

3. What is the Qur'an's (and Muslims') stand on previous Scriptures?

While the Qur'an is claimed by Muslims to be the final revelation humans will ever receive from God, it is not considered to be the first such revelation. Muhammad is thought to be the last one in a long list of prophets, many of whom are mentioned by name in the Qur'an; but the Qur'an also implies that there were more than the ones mentioned.

The names of many of the persons mentioned as prophets are familiar to Jews and Christians. This applies especially to the persons listed in the Qur'an as chief prophets: Adam, Noah, Abraham, Moses, Jesus, and Muhammad.

The Qur'an designates Jews and Christians as "people of the book" (see, for example, Surah 5.15). This is an explicit recognition that both Jews and Christians were given holy books, just as the Qur'an was given to Muslims.

Muslims contend, however, that the Jewish and Christian Holy Scriptures have been tampered with. When these books were copied again and again, changes were made to the text, parts were

---

1 "Caliph," literally meaning "successor," is the title Sunni Muslims gave to the early leaders of Islam after Muhammad had died.

omitted, and other parts were added that were not in the originals. The originals of the Jewish and the Christian Holy Scriptures contained nothing but true revelations just as the Qur'an, and many revelations are still preserved in the Jewish and the Christian Scriptures; the genuine revelations are mixed, however, with matters not revealed, and it is impossible to recognize from these Scriptures alone what is genuine and what is not. They need to be corrected by the Qur'an.

4. An example of what many Muslims consider a falsification of the Christian Scriptures: Elimination of a prediction that Muhammad is to come

Muslims claim that one alteration that was made to the New Testament is the obscuring (or rather even deletion) of a clear prediction of the coming of Muhammad and of the revelation of the Qur'an by the Angel Gabriel. The passage was not completely eliminated, but changed to an extent that its significance is lost.

The passage is contained in John's Gospel. During the Last Supper, Jesus told his disciples, "The Advocate, the Holy Spirit, whom the Father will send in my name, will teach you everything and remind you of all that I told you" (Jn 14.26). Christians take this passage as predicting the coming of the Holy Spirit at Pentecost.

(1) The Muslim argument, culminating in an assertion of an anti-Muslim conspiracy among Christian Scripture copyists

Muslims argue as follows:

First, we must understand that the passage speaks about two different persons sent by God (called "Father" in the passage from John's Gospel). We do this by placing an "and" at the appropriate spot, so that the passage becomes, "The Advocate *and* the Holy Spirit the Father will send in my name will teach you everything and remind you of all that I taught you." This makes clear that two persons are spoken about. Remember that for us Muslims, the Holy Spirit is the Angel Gabriel, through whom the Qur'an was revealed.

Next, we "zero in" on the word "Advocate" in the version of John's Gospel Christians use today. The Greek word in the current version is *paracletos*; it actually means "advocate." There is, however, a similar Greek word—only three letters are different. This word is *periclytos*. This word means, "The praised one." And now, it is time to remember what "Muhammad" means. Do you? If you said, "The praised one," go to the head of the class (as your teacher told you earlier at times, imitating Walter Williams). This is the word that the original of John's Gospel contained; copyists took it out and replaced it by a similar word, meaning "the advocate."

Do you understand now what Jesus really said? "The praised one (Muhammad) and the Holy Spirit whom my Father[2] will send in my name will teach you everything and remind you of all that I told you." Is there any clearer way to predict that Muhammad will present messages received from the Angel Gabriel? Christians, of course, falsified that passage which their own Holy Scriptures contained. They did so to conceal that Muhammad's coming was clearly and unquestionably predicted by none other than Jesus himself. A Christian conspiracy against Muslims has eliminated that prediction from the Christian Holy Scriptures.

---

2 With regard to the word "Father," Muslims would add, "Christians agree that this refers to God—Allah—although we do not like that the word 'Father' is used; God does not have a son, after all."

A Muslim scholar using this argument is An-Nabawiyah, who states in his commentary on Surah 61.6 of the Qur'an, with reference to Jn 14.26 (which he misidentifies as 14.16—likely, a typo): "Our doctors contend that Paracletos is a corrupt reading of Periclytos." (See note 5438 of his edition of the Qur'an.)

(2) The Christian reply

What has just been stated is the Muslim argument. Christians reply—rightly or wrongly, not for me (a Fox principle person)—to say:

Just as the Qur'an manuscripts written while Muhammad was still alive, or the version written by Zayd, or the versions written when Othman was caliph—just as these versions do no longer exist, so do we not have the original of John's Gospel. Beginning with ancient times, we do, however, have between 5,000 and 6,000 handwritten Greek New Testament manuscripts[3]—remember that copying a written work by hand was the only way to make a duplicate, prior to the invention of printing. Suppose the original really said, "The praised one," and really made the Holy Spirit into a person different from "the praised one." Would then there not likely be several manuscripts among the thousands that exist in which the original version would be preserved? But all of the existing manuscripts correspond to the one on which the currently used translation is based. Not a single one contains the reading Muslims claim to be the original one.

Even more importantly, assuming the existence of a conspiracy aiming at eliminating a reference to Muhammad from the Bible makes sense only from the seventh century on, after Muhammad had begun to present his message—for why could anyone wish to remove reference to him when he had not even been born yet? There are, however, hundreds of handwritten manuscripts of the New Testament containing John's Gospel and produced prior to Muhammad's birth (including the oldest complete ones, the Codex Sinaiticus and the Codex Vaticanus). All of them say "Advocate" instead of "the praised one," and identify the Advocate with the Holy Spirit instead of presenting them as separate persons. Thus, according to the Muslim argument, Christians would have conspired to eliminate a reference to Muhammad from their Holy Scriptures even before the latter was born.[4]

[As an aside, assuming a conspiracy against the Qur'an centuries before Muhammad was even born is rather difficult to swallow, even for a Fox principle person.]

5. How the Qur'an is organized

The Qur'an is divided into 114 chapters called "Surahs" (singular: Surah). One meaning of the word Surah is "step (of a structure)."[5] Thus, "each chapter is, as it were, a distinct step or degree in the whole book, which is thus compared to a structure."[6] The first chapter is a short opening prayer. From then on, the chapters are organized in descending order of length. Thus, the second chapter is the longest, the third one is the second-longest, and so on. In the case of the very short chapters towards the end

---

3 As you hopefully recall, Greek is the original language in which the New Testament was written, with the possible exception of Matthew's Gospel.
4 It may be added that in John's Gospel, there are at least three additional references to the Advocate, identifying him with the Holy Spirit: See Jn 14.16–17, Jn 15.26, and Jn 16.7–13. Under the Muslim assumption, these passages would have had to be "doctored" in a similar way as the one that has just been discussed in detail.
5 *The Holy Qur'an*, edited by Maulana Muhammad Ali, p. I-25.
6 *Ibid.*, p. I-26.

of the Qur'an, the "descending-order-of-length" arrangement is not strictly maintained: The shortest chapter is Surah 108 rather than Surah 114.

(II) MONOTHEISM

1. The "basics"; Muslim monotheism closer to the Jewish than to the Christian one

As I have stated repeatedly, Islam belongs to the monotheistic religions, the religions believing in one and only one God, the creator and sustainer of the universe and everything in it, the one who made humans out of love, for the purpose of loving him back, and to be forever happy through this love. Most of what has been said in the chapter on monotheism applies to the Muslim understanding of God.

Comparing the Jewish, the Christian, and the Muslim understanding of God shows the Muslim understanding to be more similar to the Jewish understanding than to the Christian. Christians believe in one God in three persons; in contrast, both Jews and Muslims believe in one God in one person. There is one, and only one, God, which means for Jews and Muslims that there is only one divine person; conversely, for Jews and Muslims, there is only one divine person, which means that there is only one God.

In the Jewish Bible, one finds assertions that there is only one God (the Shema Israel being the most important one). There is, however, no critique of the teaching on the Trinity: This idea was formulated only after the Jewish Scriptures had been completed. Expecting such a criticism would be anachronistic.

2. Muslim critique of the teaching on the Trinity

(1) The essentials

In contrast, the Qur'an, written after the teaching on the Trinity had clearly been formulated (the Nicene Creed and even a part of the ancient speculation I explained earlier existed already), does not only assert God's unity, but also seems to include a criticism of the idea of the Trinity. One of the passages appearing to contain such a critique is, "Say not three, desist, it is better for you. Allah is only one God. Far be it from his glory to have a son" (Surah 4.171, based on Ali). Contrary to what this passage commands, Christians say "three": "One God in three persons." Another passage is, "Certainly they disbelieve who say: Allah is the third of the three" (Surah 5.73, based on Ali).

That there is one God in three persons—this is what the two passages just quoted seem to be critical of—is, of course, only one aspect of the teaching on the Trinity. There are three more aspects: "The Father is God, the Son is God, and the Holy Spirit is God." How do they fare in the Qur'an?

(2) Problems with calling Allah "Father"

Concerning the statement that the Father is God, Muslims would object to calling God "Father," because this implies that he has at least one son; but he does not have any. Muslims would say, though, "If you say, 'God is God,' we do not have any difficulties with that."

(3) Jesus is neither God, nor the Son of God

How about the second aspect, Jesus being the son of God and God? Both Jesus' being the son of God and his being God are taken strong exception to by Muslims. Concerning Jesus' sonship, there are several passages rejecting the idea that God has a son or sons. One of them is, "Wonderful originator of the heavens and the earth! How could he have a son when he has no consort?"[7] (Surah 6.101, based on Ali.) Another one is, "Such is Jesus, son of Mary—a statement of truth about which they dispute. It beseems not Allah that he should take to himself a son" (Surah 19.34–35, based on Ali).

The divinity of Jesus is rejected in the following passage: "And when Allah will say: O Jesus, son of Mary, did you say to men, Take me and my mother for two Gods besides Allah? He will say, Glory be to thee; it was not for me to say what I had no right to (say)" (Surah 5.116, based on Ali).

I will come back in a minute or so to the (very problematic, to say the least) statement about Mary contained in that quotation; as far as Jesus is concerned, in the passage just quoted, he is asked whether he told men to take him as God besides Allah, and Jesus replies that he did not. This shows that according to the Qur'an, he is not God.

(4) The Holy Spirit missing from the Muslim representation of the Trinity

Remember now the one remaining aspect of the teaching on the Trinity—that the Holy Spirit is God. What does the Qur'an have to say about this teaching generally acknowledged by Christians at the time the Qur'an supposedly was revealed? Well, not a thing. To non-Muslims, who assume that a human author thought the Qur'an out (a view with which Muslims strenuously disagree, of course), it sounds very much as if the person who wrote the book was ignorant of that very basic fact. True, the Holy Spirit is mentioned in the Qur'an, but identified with the Angel Gabriel. It is never brought up, and therefore not criticized that one of the religions the Qur'an supposedly is to set right considers the Holy Spirit as a part of the Trinity.

(5) A "problematic" critique of the "three-ness" in God

As is made clear by earlier Qur'an quotations, though, the Qur'an is critical of assuming that there is "three-ness" in God. It is wrong to consider Allah "the third of the three." If the son is the second, who is the third? This leads back to the seemingly more-than-problematic part of an earlier Qur'an quotation: To repeat the quotation, "O Jesus, son of Mary, did you say to men, 'Take me and my mother for two Gods besides Allah?'" (Remember: Jesus said that he never said such a thing.)

This comes, as a minimum, close to conveying the notion that according to the Qur'an, Christians consider the three of whom Allah is one as Allah, Jesus, and Mary. Thus, some Christians see a fundamental misunderstanding of the teaching on the Trinity in the Qur'an, inasmuch as it seems to imply that the three persons in God are the Father, the Son, and Mary, rather than the Father, the Son, and the Holy Spirit.

Muslims reject the charge that there is a misunderstanding in the Qur'an, arguing that the rejection of Mary's godhead is to be seen as independent of the rejection of the Trinity. At times, the so-called

---

7 In the segment on the non-Muslim understanding of the origin of Islam, I have briefly remarked on the problem to which the word "consort" gives rise.

Collyridians are referred to, an obscure sect combining ideas of Christianity with a pagan goddess cult; apparently, they worshiped Mary like a goddess. The name of the group is derived from the Greek word "kollyris," designating a type of bread that was offered up to Mary during worship services. Most of what we know about this sect comes from a work *Panarion* (Greek for "Medicine chest," so called because it is meant to be a "medicine" against false teachings), written by Epiphanius of Salamis around A.D. 375 and critical of the group. Although there is no evidence of the group's continued existence in Arabia at the time of Muhammad, it is possible that it was still around. Many defenders of Islam argue that the Qur'an passage critical of worshiping Mary is directed against the Collyridians.

Christianity responds, though: It remains strange that the Qur'an objects to considering God, Jesus, and Mary as persons to be worshiped, but that it does not say anything about the teaching generally accepted by Christians that God is "the Father, the Son (Jesus), and the Holy Spirit"; that nothing critical is said about the teaching on the divinity of the Holy Spirit; that it is passed over in silence (see above, segment (4)).

Some Muslims argue that the prohibition against worshiping Mary is pertinent even today, as according to their understanding, Roman Catholics continue to worship her. Catholicism responds, "This is based on a misunderstanding similar to one that can be found among some Protestants. True, we venerate Mary, as do Eastern Orthodox Christians. Veneration is different, however, from worship, which is due only to God. Veneration is a religious form of admiration, of the kind Muslims have for Muhammad as shown by the attitude which makes them add, 'Peace be upon him,' whenever they say his name. Even those Christians who venerate Mary, however, consider it quite appropriate that she speaks of herself as God's 'lowly handmaid' (Lk 1.48). They consider her as created by God like other humans, having a human father and a human mother; there is no Christian considering her as God: Christians worshiping her as God—or even Christians worshipping her, period (forgive that allusion to President Obama)—are nonexistent."

3. Repeating a point of great significance

Given the Fox principle, I must allow Christians and Muslims to argue that point out on their own, and return to a remark of significant importance: Muslims worship the same one and only God as do Jews and Christians, except that Muslims would insist to amend this statement, to, "As far as our agreement with Christians is concerned, we believe in the same God as long as they limit themselves to what they call God the Father. We must, of course, call to mind once again the reservations (to put it mildly) we have concerning applying the word 'Father' to God."

(III) JESUS IN THE QUR'AN

Who is Jesus, according to Muslims?

1. Agreements between Muslims and Christians with respect to Jesus

It was mentioned already that Muslims consider Jesus as a prophet or messenger of God. They hold him to be one of the six major prophets, but not as the most important one. That role is reserved for Muhammad.

That the Qur'an teaches Jesus to be a messenger of God becomes clear from passages such as, "The Messiah, Jesus, son of Mary, is only[8] a messenger of Allah and His word" (Surah 4.171, based on Ali). This is a point of agreement between Jews and Christianity, although my experience is that it comes as a surprise to many Christians when they hear me say, "According to Christianity, Jesus is a prophet."

True, Christianity considers him as more than only a prophet; but he also is a prophet. In the Old Testament, Moses tells the Israelites, "A prophet like me will the Lord your God raise up from among you" (Dt 18.15). Christianity applies this passage to Jesus, who is, therefore, considered to be a prophet as important as Moses. Further, when Jesus is rejected by the townspeople of Nazareth where he had spent most of his life, he says, "No prophet is accepted in his hometown" (Lk 4.24). With these words, he himself implies that he is a prophet.

Thus, a first important agreement between Muslims and Christians about Jesus is that both consider him as a prophet.

There is a second important and surprising agreement, referring to the manner in which Jesus was conceived in his mother's womb. In the Christianity segment, I pointed out that Christians believe in the virgin birth of Jesus; they hold that his mother Mary became pregnant with him without the cooperation of a human male. There are at least two Qur'an passages also suggesting that it was so:

> Then We sent to her Our angel, and he appeared before her as a man in all respects. She said, "I seek refuge from you to Allah, most gracious: Come not near if you fear Allah." He said, "Nay, I am only a messenger from the Lord to announce to you the gift of a pure son." She said, "How shall I have a son, seeing that no man has touched me, and I am not unchaste?" He said, "So it will be: Your Lord said, That is easy for Me: and We wish to appoint him as a sign for men, and as a mercy from us" (Surah 19.17–21, based on An-Nabawiyah).

The second Qur'an passage making the same point presents the following exchange between Mary and the angel who announced Jesus' birth to her: "'O my Lord, how shall I have a son when no man has touched me?' He said, 'Even so; Allah creates what He wills: When He has decreed a matter, He but says to it, Be, and it is'" (Surah 3.47, based on An-Nabawiyah).[9]

Among further agreements between Muslims and Christians about Jesus, it deserves to be mentioned that according to the Qur'an, just as according to the Bible, Jesus performed miracles, including

---

8 The word "only" is in the passage because the same verse is critical of the view which Christians hold that Jesus is the "son of God": Jesus is only a messenger of God, not his son.

9 The manner in which Maulana Muhammad Ali interprets this (and the previously quoted) passage is contrary to the "standard view" among Muslims. He says in his commentary on the passage, "Mary conceived him [Jesus] in the ordinary way in which women conceive children." This seems to fly in the face of what the passage says. Mushaf Al-Madinah An-Nabawiyah expresses, in its commentary on Jesus' conception, a view contrary to Ali's (see *The Holy Qur'an—English Translation of the Meaning and Commentary*). Nabawiyah's comment refers to the following Qur'an passage comparing Jesus and Adam with respect to neither of them having a human father (Adam lacked, of course, also a human mother): "The similitude of Jesus is that of Adam; He created him from dust, then said to him, 'Be,' and he was" (Surah 3.59). Nabawiyah comments, "If it is said that he [Jesus] was born without a human father, Adam also was so born" (p. 158).

healing the blind, curing people with leprosy, and bringing dead people back to life (see Surah 150.49). Interestingly, the Qur'an does not associate any miracles with Muhammad.

Finally, it is to be mentioned that the Qur'an applies to Jesus the title "Messiah" or "Christ"; thus Muslims agree with Christians that Jesus was the Messiah: "'Behold,' the angel said, 'O Mary, Allah gives you glad tidings of a word from Him: His name will be Christ Jesus'" (Surah 3.45, based on An-Nabawiyah).

2. Disagreements between Muslims and Christians with respect to Jesus

There are also significant disagreements between Muslims and Christians with regard to who Jesus was/is.

Two have been explained already: Christians consider Jesus as the son of God and himself God— the second person of the Trinity. In contrast, for Muslims, Jesus is neither the son of God (Allah has no sons) nor God—there is no Trinity in God.

Another disagreement refers to the reason for Jesus' death and the manner of his dying. As will be recalled, Christians hold that Jesus, being a true representative of the human race, died to bear the punishment due to humanity because of the wrongdoings the human race had committed, is committing, and will commit: He died to pay the debt humans keep on incurring. All of this is rejected by Muslims, in accordance with the following Qur'an passage: "They said (in boast), 'We killed Christ Jesus the son of Mary, the messenger of Allah,'—but they killed him not nor crucified him. Only a likeness of that was shown to them" (Surah 4.157, based on An-Nabawiyah).

3. Isn't the Muslim view about Jesus subject to the "reality check argument"?

As you no doubt recall (am I not the optimist?), at the end of the Christianity presentation, I spoke about those secular academicians who disparage Christianity but admire Jesus as the Gospels describe him. I confronted them with a reality check, arguing that those who consider Jesus as presented in Matthew, Mark, Luke, and John as merely human and nothing more are unrealistic if they consider him as a great person: A merely human Gospel Jesus would either be crazy or a liar or both.

Is not the Muslim view about Jesus subject to the very same reality check? Could it not be turned into a critique of Islam?

Muslims would reply, "Remember that the reality check Fritz presented applies to the Jesus *of the Gospels*. Your teacher even quoted a fellow, the agnostic Bertrand Russell, who specifically said that he admired the life and the moral teachings of Jesus *as told in the Gospels*. If we Muslims were to go along with everything the Gospels say about Jesus, Fritz could beat us over the head with his reality check argument just as effectively as he did Bertrand Russell and company; but we take exception to much of what the Gospels say about Jesus. Thus, the reality check argument does not apply to us. Even your teacher Fritz must acknowledge this."

Yes, I must; whatever arguments people might want to use against Islam, it would be an intellectual mistake to consider the Muslim faith to be subject to the reality check consideration I used against some secular academicians.

(IV) ISLAM AND THE "LAST THINGS"

1. Eschatology (don't worry about that big word)

Among many of the highbrow words being used in the field of religious studies is "eschatology." It is derived from two Greek terms, one being *eschatos*, meaning "last," the other being *logos*. Hopefully, you recall that this second term literally means "word," more freely, "teaching about." Thus, "eschatology" means "teaching about the last (things)"—death, the end of the world, and the eternal destiny of humans. (The title preceding this paragraph tells you not to worry—you will not have to know the word "eschatology" at quizzes and exams. You might wish to remember it anyway, though.)

2. Death and judgment

Concerning death, Islam teaches that dying is not the end of a human being's existence; that there is a hereafter.

Also, as was mentioned earlier—in the context of the summary of Muhammad's message, a judgment day is to come on which Allah will judge people. (An important Qur'an passage has been quoted when judgment day was taken up as one of the points included in the initial message Muhammad presented to the Meccans.)

On that day, there will be a resurrection of the dead:

> I do swear by the resurrection day; and I do swear by the self-reproaching soul. Does man think that we cannot assemble his bones? Nay, we are able to put together in perfect order the very tips of his fingers (Surah 75.1–4, based on An-Nabawiyah).

Following the resurrection, the judgment will take place.

What will people be judged by? The following Qur'an passage spells it out: "As for those who believe and work righteousness, Allah will pay them in full their reward" (Surah 3.57, based on An-Nabawiyah).

One can, therefore expect to be asked two questions. One is, "Did you have faith?" The other is, "Did you live in accordance with your faith, did you practice it—did you perform good works?"

Those who will be able to answer "Yes" to both questions will be rewarded with paradise; those who will have to say "No" to one or both of these questions will be punished with hell.

3. Hell and paradise

There are vivid descriptions of both hell and paradise in the Qur'an.

Concerning hell, we read,

> Surely the tree of Zaqqum[10] is the food of the sinful. Like molten brass; it seethes in their bellies like boiling water. Seize him and drag him into the midst of hell; then pour on his head of the torment of boiling water. Taste this! Truly you are mighty, full of honor! Surely this is what you doubted (Surah 44.43–50; based on Ali).

Another passage is,

> And those on the left hand; how wretched are those on the left hand! In hot wind and boiling water, and in shadow of black smoke, neither cool nor refreshing … Eat of the tree of Zaqqum, and fill your bellies with it; then drink after it of boiling water; and drink of it as drinks the thirsty camel (Surah 56.42–44, 52–55; based on Ali).

About paradise, we read, "Surely for those who keep their duty there is achievement, gardens and vineyards, and youthful companions equal in age; and a pure cup" (Surah 78.31–34; based on Ali).

Another passage about paradise is,

> These [the people in paradise] are drawn near to Allah in gardens of bliss … on thrones inwrought, reclining on them, facing each other. Round about them will go youths never altering in age, with goblets and ewers and a pure drink—they are not affected by head-aches thereby, nor are they intoxicated, and fruits that they choose, and flesh of fowl that they desire, and pure beautiful ones, like hidden pearls—a reward for what they did (Surah 56.11–24; based on Ali).

---

10 The "tree of Zaqqum" grows only in Hell, according to Muslims.

CHAPTER TWENTY

Remarks on the History of Islam after Muhammad

I slam is split into several groups. By far the largest of them, comprising more than 85%, are the Sunnis. Second in line are the Shiites, themselves divided into numerous subgroups, the largest of them being that of the Twelvers. This chapter, concerning the history of Islam after Muhammad, deals mostly, actually almost exclusively, with the Sunnis. The chapter after this will explain some basic facts of Shiite history and some respects in which the Shiites differ from the Sunnis.

(I) FROM MUHAMMAD'S DEATH TO THE END OF THE CALIPHATE OF ALI (632–661)

After Muhammad had died, the question arose as to who should succeed him as the leader of Islam. Abu Bakr, mentioned earlier at the occasion of the Battle of Uhud, was designated for that position, bearing the title "caliph" (= "successor"[1]). He had been among Muhammad's very first followers; moreover, as the father of Muhammad's wife Aisha, he also was one of his fathers-in-law. He was caliph from 632 to 634. Upon Muhammad's death, some of the Bedouin[2] tribes who had sworn allegiance to Islam had begun uprisings. Abu Bakr suppressed these revolts and brought all of Arabia under Muslim dominance. As I told you earlier, he also saw to it that a first edition of the Qur'an be made. Further, he sent armies into Syria, at the time under the sway of the Byzantine Empire, but he died prior to them winning any significant victories.

---

1 This is, of course, not to be understood as "successor as prophet," but only as "successor in the sense of being the leader of the Muslim community."

2 "Bedouins" is a designation for nomadic Middle Eastern tribes. Nomads are people without a permanent home who move from place to place.

Abu Bakr's successor was Omar, whom the former had nominated for the caliphate. Omar ruled from 634 to 644. Originally, he had been opposed to Muhammad's preaching, but had accepted Islam in 615; subsequently, he had been one of Muhammad's closest friends and advisors. Muhammad had married one of his daughters;[3] thus, Omar was, like Abu Bakr, a father-in-law of Muhammad. Under Omar's rule, the armies that Abu Bakr had dispatched were victorious: First, in 635, Damascus, Syria's capital, was conquered. Subsequently, the Muslims defeated a force of 50,000 men sent by the Byzantine Emperor Heraclius to expel them from the area. The event is known as the 636 Battle of Yarmouk. Jerusalem capitulated to the Muslims in 638.[4] In 640 Caesarea was taken over and subsequently the whole of Palestine surrendered to Islam. Egypt was taken in a military campaign from 639 to 641; the Muslims were to push on from there to the west and soon held sway over most of North Africa. Like Syria and Palestine, Egypt and the rest of North Africa had been dominated by the Byzantine Empire when the Muslims conquered the area. In the east, Iraq was conquered in 637. Persia,[5] where the Muslims encountered the strongest opposition they had experienced up to this point, was conquered from 640 to 649. (Islam has almost totally eradicated Zoroastrianism, the religion held by the Persians prior to the Muslim invasion.) During a twelve-year campaign (640–652) the Muslims subdued parts of Asia Minor (today's Turkey is located there). This led to a further reduction of the Byzantine Empire's power.

In 644, after Omar had been assassinated by a slave from Persia, Othman became caliph. He had been married to two of Muhammad's daughters[6] and held the caliphate from 644–656. As mentioned in the segment on the Qur'an, he ordered a second edition of the Qur'an to be published. He brought Islam into Europe by conquering the islands of Cyprus (649) and Rhodes (653).[7] He appointed many members of his own family—that of the Umayyads—to high positions. This caused resentment among non-family members, and in 656, a group of people, including a son of Abu Bakr, assassinated him.

His successor was Ali (656–661).[8] As a son of Muhammad's uncle Abu Talib, he was a cousin, that is, a blood relative, of Muhammad. Moreover, like Othman, he was also Muhammad's son-in-law, being married to the latter's daughter Fatima. In 657, he moved the Muslim administrative capital from Medina to Kufa, in present-day Iraq, about 110 miles south of Bagdad. While Ali was caliph, Mu'awiya, the governor of Syria, an Umayyad like Ali's predecessor Othman had been, claimed the caliphate for himself. Ali mobilized an army against him, but agreed to negotiate the issue instead of fighting about it. To many of his followers, this seemed disappointing indecisiveness, and they began doubting that he was the one who should rule them. In 661, an assassin wounded him with a poisoned sword while he was praying in the Mosque at Kufa, and several days later, he died.

---

3 Her name was Hafsah.

4 Toward the end of the seventh century, the "Dome of the Rock" was erected at the site at which the Jewish Temple once stood. That structure, having been restored/rebuilt several times, exists to this day. Muslims believe this site to be connected to an important event in Muhammad's life: During a night a short time prior to his migration from Mecca to Medina, he supposedly was miraculously transported from Mecca to Jerusalem, to the site on which the Dome of the Rock now stands. From there, he was lifted up to heaven, then back down to the Jerusalem site, and from there, he was transported back to Mecca. Surah 7.1 is said to refer to that night journey. The Dome of the Rock is, together with the Al-Aqsa Mosque, also on the Jerusalem Temple Mount, considered to be the third-holiest place for Muslims (the first is the Kaaba itself, the second is Medina as the place where Muhammad had spent most of the final ten years of his life, and where he died and is buried.)

5 Persia is the area of present-day Iran.

6 Their names were Ruqaiyah and Ummu Kulsum.

7 See Schmidt, *Divide*, pp. 43–44.

8 As will be explained later, the Shiites consider him as the first lawful leader of Islam after Muhammad.

(II) THE UMAYYAD CALIPHATE (661–750): EXPANSION OF THE RULE TO INDIA AND SPAIN

Following Ali's death, his older son Hasan became caliph (661). Mu'awiya continued his uprising, though, and about six months later, Hasan abdicated, and Mu'awiya declared himself caliph, holding the position from 661 to 680. He made the caliphate hereditary; thus, with him, the so-called Umayyad Caliphate (i.e., the Caliphate of the Umayyad Clan) began, lasting from 661 to 750. Mu'awiya moved Islam's administrative capital to Damascus. Muslim domination was extended considerably, in the east as well as in the west. In 699, Afghanistan was taken; in 713, the Muslims entered the Indus valley. In the west in 711, the Muslims crossed the Straits of Gibraltar and began occupying the Iberian Peninsula, the part of Europe on which present-day Spain and Portugal are located. At one point, Islam dominated large parts, about three quarters, of that peninsula, except for the northernmost segment where Asturias and the Basque Country are located. (It was from Asturias that the Christian attempts to reconquer the peninsula would later be organized.) The person governing the area had the title "emir," and he ruled in behalf of the caliph. From the Iberian Peninsula, the Muslims pushed eastward, crossing the Pyrenees into what is today France. The Muslim empire's expansion further into Europe was halted in 732, when Charles Martel, leader of the Franks, stopped them at a famous battle at Tours. His decisive victory is interpreted by many as the factor that prevented the Muslims from overrunning all of Europe at that time; had they succeeded, they would likely have virtually eliminated Christianity, or at least reduced it to an insignificant minority religion. This assessment is based on observing what has happened to Christianity in many other parts of the world occupied by Islam, and to Zoroastrianism in Persia. Many of the parts of the world that the Muslims occupied had flourishing Christian communities prior to the arrival of Islam. This holds true, for example, of Palestine, including Jerusalem, of Damascus, and of Antioch (the town in which the word "Christian" was first used to denote the followers of Jesus; see Acts 11.26). In North Africa, Carthage had been an important center of early Christianity, and Hippo, about 100 miles west of Carthage, was the town in which St. Augustine, one of the greatest Christian thinkers, had been bishop.[9]

During the reign of the Umayyads, the sphere of influence of Muslims came to reach from India in the east to North Africa and the Iberian Peninsula in the west. From the time at which Muhammad supposedly received his first revelation, it took only a little over a century for these astounding conquests.

---

9 Prior to the Muslim conquest, the original Christian centers situated in the west of North Africa had been destroyed by the Vandals (Carthage had been taken by them in 439), who were Arian Christians at the time (that is, they believed that Jesus, the Son of God, was created by and therefore lower than God the Father). The Vandal Empire, which they had established in North Africa, had been conquered in 533 by Emperor Justinian I of the East Roman (or Byzantine) Empire, and the sphere of influence of the East Roman Empire had been extended to this region of the world. The Muslim conquest terminated this influence once and for all, and virtually eliminated the presence of Christianity there.

(III) THE ABBASID CALIPHATE: CLASSICAL PERIOD OF EARLY MUSLIM HISTORY AND DECLINE (750–1258)

In 750, the family of the Abbasids took power from the Umayyad Caliphate. The Abbasids traced their descent back to a certain Abbas, a paternal uncle of Muhammad. The period of the Abbasid Caliphate was to last until 1258. The administrative center of Islam was moved from Damascus to Bagdad,[10] which was built into a magnificent town. The best-known ruler of this period was Caliph Harun ar-Rashid (736–809).

A short time after that ruler, the empire governed by the Abbasids suffered the fate of many great empires that have existed in the history of humanity. Political decay began, and the empire separated into various states. The Muslim rulers of Spain extended their sphere of influence to parts of North Africa; in other parts of North Africa, later in Egypt, in Palestine, and in other areas, the Fatimids ruled. They were in power from 909–1171. Their designation is derived from a claim that their leaders were descendants of Muhammad's daughter Fatima. (They conquered Egypt in 969; the city of Cairo was built under them and made into Egypt's capital.) In the 11th century, the Seljuk Turks, coming from Central Asia, seized power in Persia, Iraq, and Syria. In 1096, the European Christians began the Crusades, a campaign against the Muslims. A chief objective of the Crusades was, in the beginning at least, to retake Palestine, the land where Jesus of Nazareth had lived and in which the holiest places of Christianity were situated. The Christian Crusaders captured Jerusalem from the Muslims in 1099. There were, however, Muslim counterattacks. The Muslim leader Saladin retook Jerusalem for the Muslims in 1187. Saladin, who had been born in Mesopotamia[11] around 1137, was of Kurdish descent. From Bagdad, he had participated in a mission against the Fatimids of Egypt. They had been defeated, and in 1169, he had become the ruler of Egypt, beginning a line of rulers known as the Ayyubid Dynasty. He had extended his power into the parts of Palestine and Syria that the Fatimids had governed; then, he had decided to move into the area held by the Crusaders, including Jerusalem, as noted above.

(IV) DESTRUCTION OF THE ABBASID CALIPHATE BY THE MONGOLS (1258); THE LOSS OF SPAIN (1492)

About seventy years later, a new force entered the picture: The Mongols, coming down from the northeast and committing hair-raising atrocities, destroyed the Abbasid Caliphate in 1258. They were finally beaten back by the Mamelukes of Egypt (see below) and withdrew into Iraq and Persia. About hundred years later, they became Muslims. (The Mamelukes had originally been slave soldiers serving under the Fatimid and Ayyubid dynasties. One of them was Aybak. In 1250, the widow of the last Ayyubid ruler claimed to be Sultana of Egypt after her husband's death, married Aybak, and, having occupied the throne for only 80 days, turned it over to Aybak. Thus, the rule of Egypt by the Mamelukes began. It lasted for a period of more than 250 years.)

---

10 863–892, Samarra, like Bagdad in present-day Iraq, was the capital.
11 The word "Mesopotamia," denoting an area situated in today's Iraq, literally means "[the land] between the rivers." The rivers referred to are the Euphrates and the Tigris.

In Western Europe, the Muslims had, as mentioned earlier, controlled about three quarters of the Iberian Peninsula. Originally, the rulers of the Muslim part of Spain (they were called "emirs") governed in behalf of the caliph of Damascus; in 757, however, an independent emirate was established. In the early 11th century, it broke up into various independent emirates. By 1250, the Muslim presence on the Iberian Peninsula had weakened considerably, with only its southern part still being under Muslim control. In 1492—recall that this was the year in which Christopher Columbus came to America—the Muslim rule in Spain was ended by Ferdinand and Isabella, king and queen of Spain, when Granada, the last stronghold of the Muslims in Spain, fell to Spanish military forces.

(V) RISE AND FALL OF THE OTTOMAN EMPIRE (1301–1918)

Following the elimination of the Abbasid Caliphate by the Mongols and after they had moved into Iraq and Persia, several political units evolved in the Muslim world. Only one of them shall be taken up here: the Empire of the Ottomans. The chief reason for discussing it is not that Austria, your humble teacher's home country, had to ward off attacks from them; rather, the Ottoman Empire was, at the peak of its development, by far the most powerful political unit in the part of the world then dominated by Islam. The empire had its beginning with Turkish Muslims who moved west to settle in Asia Minor to escape from the Mongol attacks. One of them, known as Osman I, claimed the title of sultan for himself in 1301. This is seen as the beginning of the Ottoman Empire. Over time, the empire expanded inside of Asia Minor and incorporated many areas outside of it; during the peak of its power in the 15th and 16th centuries, it included, among other areas, all of Asia Minor, Greece, Bulgaria, the Balkan area, Syria, and Egypt. A significant event was the Ottomans' 1453 crossing of the Bosporus and conquest of Constantinople, which subsequently became the capital of the Ottoman Empire. This brought the once powerful Byzantine Empire to an end, which by 1453 had been reduced to Constantinople and a relatively small area around it. Subsequently, the Ottomans tried to take Austria, besieging its capital Vienna twice, once in 1529, the second time as late as 1683, when a huge army led by Kara Mustafa tried to conquer the city. Almost a thousand years earlier, Christianity in Europe had been threatened from the west (Spain); now it was threatened from the east by the Ottomans, whose vast empire at the time stretched in the south over Palestine through North Africa. (Naturally, with other political powers well established in Europe, for example France and England, there was no great likelihood that the Muslims would, as a consequence of a fall of Vienna, have overrun Europe. Thus, the threat to Christianity at this time was much less existential than at the time at which it was threatened from Spain. Also, by this time, Christianity had already spread to America.) The second siege of Vienna was ended, however, when John III, king of Poland, arrived with an army, relieving the Austrians and defeating Kara Mustafa's forces. (Later that same year, after Kara Mustafa had withdrawn to Belgrade, he was—as penalty for his conduct around Vienna, at the order of Sultan Mehmed IV—choked to death with a silk rope; his head was severed and carried to Mehmet's palace to be presented to the sultan.) Kara Mustafa's defeat at Vienna and the subsequent loss of territories occupied by the Ottomans, including Hungary, which they had occupied briefly, marks the beginning of the decline of the Ottoman Empire. It came to an end in

1918, following World War I. The successor state of the empire is Turkey, which was established as a secular republic in 1923.

(VI) "YOU BE THE JUDGE"; MUSLIM PRESENCE IN TODAY'S WORLD

Especially in the Western world, including the United States, one can find many Muslims asserting that Islam is a religion of peace, and that warfare is allowed only as a means to defend against attacks by hostile forces, including, of course, attempting to forestall such attacks if they are imminent.

Given my brief account of Muhammad's activities after the Hijrah and of Islam's history after Muhammad, as well as the common understanding of "defensive war" in the Western world, is this assessment tenable?

I let you be the judge, and turn to another point: Where can Islam be found in today's world?

Instead of giving you a list of all the countries, I will mention areas, with the occasional country "thrown in":

Islam is the principal religion in most of the Middle East and North Africa; it is well represented in Central and East Africa (being very significantly in the majority in Somalia), Turkey is a largely Muslim country; Islam is present in the Balkans, including Bulgaria; it can be found in places like Iran, Afghanistan, Pakistan, Uzbekistan, Turkmenistan, Kirgizstan, Bangladesh, Indonesia, and parts of the Philippines; it also exists in areas of India. This list is incomplete.

In the Western world, there are significant Muslim communities in areas in which Islam was virtually non-existent 25–30 years ago. This includes the United States.

CHAPTER TWENTY ONE

Tradition (Hadith), Sunnis, and Shiites

(I) GENERAL REMARKS; TRADITIONS

As stated earlier, the two chief branches within Islam are the Sunnis (as mentioned, comprising more than 85% of all Muslims) and the Shiites. The split between these groups is due to diverging views on who was supposed to lead Islam after Muhammad's death.

The word "Sunni" is derived from "Sunnah," which literally means "custom"; Sunni Muslims are, therefore, known as "traditionalists" ("those who adhere to customs"). The word "Shiites" is derived from "Shi'ah," the literal meaning of which is "followers." This name is used for the Shiites because, as will be shown, they consider themselves as followers of Ali, taken to be the fourth caliph by the Sunnis.

At this point, some remarks on the Muslim understanding of "traditions" are to be included.

As should be clear by now, the chief source of Muslim teaching is the Qur'an, considered to be an inspired written source of revelations. As Hughes points out, all Muslims, "whether Sunni, Shi'ah, or Wahhabi," hold that Muhammad received, "in addition to the revelations contained in the Qur'an," revelations not written down at his time that made him able to give "authoritative declarations on religious questions, either moral, ceremonial, or doctrinal."[1] These "declarations" were handed down orally. In addition, oral accounts were handed down describing how Muhammad acted in certain situations; Muslims hold that his conduct is to be imitated as an example. At one point, these traditions, known as "Hadith," were collected and written down. Sunni Muslims accept at least six such collections. The two most important of them were compiled by al-Bukhari, completed a little less than 250 years after Muhammad's death, and by a man named Muslim, completed just about 250 years after Muhammad died.[2]

---

1 Hughes, *Dictionary*, p. 639.
2 The remaining four chief collections are by at-Tirmizi, Abu Da'ud as-Sajistani, an-Nasa'i, and Ibn Majah, all of them compiled a little after the ones done by al-Bukhari and Muslim. See Hughes, *Dictionary*, p. 643.

Since "Traditionalists" is one of the connotations of the designation Sunnis use for themselves, among Western writers, "it is often stated that the Shi'ahs reject the Traditions."[3] This is a misunderstanding, though.[4] True, Shiites do not accept the collection of traditions considered authoritative by the Sunnis, but they have their own written collections of what Muhammad is alleged to have said and done.[5] These collections were compiled later than the ones used by the Sunnis—between about 320 and 450 years after Muhammad died.[6]

(II) THE CAUSE OF THE SUNNI–SHIITE SPLIT

The split between the Sunnis and the Shiites was caused by a disagreement concerning the requirements a person had to meet to be a legitimate leader of Islam after Muhammad's death.

As I told you earlier, the de facto (and for Sunnis, legitimate) first leader (called "caliph" by Sunnis) was Abu Bakr. Shiites hold, however, that the leader of Islam has to be a member of Muhammad's family in the sense of being a blood relative of Muhammad. They base this on a passage from the Qur'an and on one of their Traditions containing a saying of Muhammad.

The Qur'an passage is 2.124: "And when the Lord tried Abraham with certain commands he fulfilled them. He [God] said: 'Surely I will make thee a leader [Imam[7]] of men.' (Abraham) said: 'And my offspring?' 'My covenant does not include wrongdoers,' said He." (Based on Ali.)

Shiites take the wrongdoers, who are excluded from being leaders, to be those who are not descendants of Abraham, and argue: One had to be a descendant of Abraham to be a legitimate leader; analogously, one must be a blood relative and through him a descendant of Muhammad to be a legitimate leader of Islam. Ali was a blood relative; his sons with Fatima, the daughter of Muhammad, were grandsons of Muhammad, and their descendants were descendants of Muhammad. Shiites strengthen their argument through appealing to one of their traditions (not accepted as genuine by Sunnis) according to which Muhammad said: "O ye people! I am the Prophet and Ali is my heir, and from us will descend al-Mahdi,[8] the seal [i.e., the last] of the Imams."[9]

Accordingly, for Shiites, Ali is the first legitimate leader of Islam. They consider Abu Bakr, Omar, and Othman as usurpers. Instead of "caliph," they call their leaders "imam," which simply means "leader." (Sunnis use the word "imam" to designate the person leading the prayers in the mosque.) The second imam is Hasan, Ali's son, a grandson of Muhammad. Although he resigned his leadership position in favor of Mu'awiya and withdrew to Medina, as recounted earlier, Shiites think that he actually continued to be imam up to his death in 669, alleging that he was poisoned by one of his wives at Mu'awiya's instigation. They think that at his death, the imamate passed to his younger brother Husain, who gathered, after some hesitation, an army to move against the Umayyads. By that time, Yazid had succeeded his

---

3 Hughes, *Dictionary*, p. 643.
4 Your humble teacher must confess that at one time, he, too, was caught up in that misunderstanding.
5 For a listing of the five chief collections of Traditions the Shi'ahs consider as authoritative, see Hughes, *Dictionary*, p. 643.
6 Hughes gives for each of the five chief collections recognized by the Shiites the precise year of its compilation. See *Dictionary*, p. 643.
7 "Imam," literally, "leader," is the word Shiites use for the leader of Muslims. See below.
8 For an explanation of who the Mahdi is, see below.
9 Quoted in Hughes, *Dictionary*, p. 305.

father Mu'awiya as caliph. Husain and his band of followers were defeated and brutally massacred at Karbala, a town in Iraq. This happened in 680. The anniversary of Husain's death continues to be an important day of remembrance for Shiite Muslims, with an extensive mourning ritual taking place at Karbala. Husain is buried in that town; his tomb is one of the most important shrines for Shiites.

(III) THE TWELVERS

As mentioned earlier, the Shiites are split into various groups. The largest of them is that of the Twelvers, so called because according to them, there have only been twelve legitimate imams. The first three were Ali, Hasan, and Husain. After Husain's murder, the imamate passed to his son, also named Ali, like the first imam. There were seven additional ones; then came number 12, named Muhammad, also known as Imam al-Mahdi or Muhammad al-Muntazar (= "the expected one"). He was last seen in 878. Non-Shiites would say that that's probably when he died. Shiites belonging to the group of the Twelvers, however, contend that he went into hiding and is still kept there by Allah, now for more than 1,135 years. At one point in the future, he will come back as the Mahdi, that is, "the guided one," to restore the true faith (which will include making all Muslims Shiites) and assume the leadership of his people.

(IV) AGREEMENTS AND DISAGREEMENTS BETWEEN SUNNIS AND SHIITES

Both Sunnis and Shiites accept the Qur'an. Both also accept Traditions, that is, accounts of what Muhammad said and did, although they disagree on what the authoritative collections of these traditions are.

The collection of the Sunni Traditions contains the following important saying of Muhammad: "My people will never agree upon an error."[10] This can be interpreted as implying something like a "majority principle" in the following sense: If a teaching or a practice has been accepted by most Muslims over a significant amount of time, it can be considered reliable. Needless to say, the Shiites do not accept this principle (the saying on which Sunnis base it is not contained in any of the Shiite collections of Traditions): Since Shiites are in the minority, the principle would invalidate all the beliefs and practices on which they differ from the Sunnis.

Concerning other teachings and practices of Islam, if there were an opportunity to go into more detail, we would come across other differences between the Sunnis and the Shiites. With regard to the practices and teachings of Islam that were taken up in earlier chapters, the vast majority of Shiites agree with the Sunnis.

It might still be worth mentioning that Iran is a country with a Shiite majority; significant minorities of that branch of Islam can be found, among other places, in Iraq and Syria.

---

10 This saying is contained in the collection compiled by at-Tirmizi as well as in the one compiled by Abu Da'ud as-Sajistani.

CHAPTER TWENTY TWO

Two Controversial Muslim Beliefs

Among Muslim beliefs creating controversy, I will take up polygamy and holy war (Jihad).

(I) POLYGAMY

1. The Qur'an allows polygamy

Polygamy is derived from two Greek words, *polys*, meaning "many," and *gamos*, meaning marriage. Thus, although the word is, in our language, used to designate an arrangement according to which one husband may simultaneously be married to more than one wife, according to the expression's derivation, it might also mean one wife's being married simultaneously to more than one husband. "Polygamy" has, however, acquired the "one husband and several wives" meaning, because when having more than one spouse was permitted, in the majority of cases, one husband was allowed to have several wives rather than the other way around.[1]

The Qur'an allows polygamy, as becomes clear from the following passage:

> If you fear that you cannot do justice to orphans, marry such women as seem good to you, two, or three, or four; but if you fear that you will not do justice, then marry only one, or that which your right hands possess (Surah 4.3; based on Ali).

---

1 "Polygyny"—derived from *polys* and *gyne*, the second word meaning woman or wife, is a more accurate expression, clearly indicating that there is more than one wife. The counterpart is "polyandry," containing an expression derived from the genitive of the Greek *aner*, meaning man (in the sense of male human being). "Polyandry" designates an arrangement according to which one wife may have simultaneously more than one husband.

According to this passage, a husband may marry up to four wives and women who were captured in war—they are referred to by the phrase, "that which your right hand possesses." Prior to discussing the conditions which must be met for several wives being allowed to one husband, it is to be observed that polygamy has actually been practiced by Muslims over the history of Islam, it is currently being practiced, and it was practiced by Muhammad. In fact, Surah 33.50 gives a rule for Muhammad different from the one contained in the passage just quoted: He is not limited to four legal wives, but may marry more than that:

> O Prophet! We have made lawful to you your wives to whom you have given their dowries; and those whom your right hand possesses out of those whom Allah has given you as prisoners of war; and the daughters of your paternal uncle and the daughters of your paternal aunts, and the daughters of your maternal uncle and the daughters of your maternal aunts who fled with you; and a believing woman, if she gives herself to the Prophet, if the Prophet desires to marry her. It is especially for you, not for the believers (Surah 33.50; based on Ali).

There are conflicting traditions about the number of wives Muhammad was married to after Khadija had died. If in the Qur'an passage just quoted, one ignores, "those whom your right hand possesses," and is content with interpreting plural forms as signifying "two" (including phrases which combine two plural forms, such as "the daughters of your paternal aunts"), the passage just quoted seems to allow eleven joint wives to Muhammad. If one includes the ones mentioned prior to the "right hand possesses" phrase among those mentioned after that phrase, the total is nine; thus, whatever the historic record says, nine is the absolute minimum of joint wives the Qur'an allows to Muhammad, which is more than twice the number other Muslim men may be married to.

2. A Muslim's comment on the permission of polygamy: Two conditions for its appropriateness

If Muslims see you shaking your head about this, perhaps thinking, "What a convenient revelation," they would comment as follows:

First, four wives are allowed to ordinary Muslim men not unconditionally, but conditions for having more than one wife are set. The chief condition is that the husband must treat all wives to whom he is married as equals. Some Muslim commentators argue that it is next to impossible for a man to comply with this, very few outstanding individuals exempted; for this reason, they argue, polygamy ought to occur only in rare and extraordinary circumstances. They might add, "Moreover, there is another restriction: The general passage about polygamy begins with the words, 'If you fear that you cannot treat orphans justly, you may marry ...' Not only must this context be paid attention to, but also the wider historic context. Muhammad received the message that allowed four wives to ordinary Muslim men after a military engagement known as the Battle of Uhud, which took place in 625.[2] Many Muslim men had lost their lives in that battle. This meant that there were now many widows and fatherless young women. Given the conditions at the time, these females had no one who would naturally care for them; but given the social justice motive involved in the Qur'an's message, including

---

2 This was a battle between forces from Medina led by Muhammad and Meccan forces.

taking care of the poor, there was an obligation to care for them. It was, however, to be feared that justice would not be done to them because of their great number—it is, after all, difficult to take care of all people in need if there are many of them. It is much easier to take care of members of one's own family. Consequently, allowing these female orphans to become, through marriage, members of a man's household—up to four of them per man—caused it to be more likely that a greater number of them would be cared for. Thus, one of the purposes of the institution of polygamy is to ensure that women are taken care of in situations in which there are more women than men, because many men lost their lives in military engagements. The time after the Battle of Uhud was not exceptional in this respect: Because of the many wars that accompanied the history of Islam, often, similar situations arose, and that second condition justifying polygamy—the first being equity among one's wives—was met."[3]

3. Response to the Muslim considerations

This raises, of course, the following question perhaps troubling to a Western non-Muslim: Why, then, was/is polygamy practiced also among Muslim men in circumstances when warfare had/has not decimated the number of men in comparison to that of women? Why was/is polygamy practiced by many Muslims, not only by those rare and outstanding individuals who are able to treat their wives equally?[4]

There is even a more serious question: As the "imaginary Muslim's" comments on the passage justifying polygamy in principle pointed out, the passage begins with a reference to doing justice to orphans. This sounds—and it is agreed to by Muslim commentators especially in the Western world—as if a precondition for taking a woman as a second wife is that she be an orphan. One might now make a case that many women whose parents had died and whose husbands had been killed in war would meet the definition of "orphan," even if they were older. When Muhammad married Aisha, however,[5] he was, according to some accounts at least, married to Sawada, and Aisha was not an orphan. Her father, Abu Bakr, was to outlive Muhammad by two years, and became Muhammad's first successor, the first caliph.[6]

4. A Muslim reply, concerning the timing of the polygamy revelations

The Muslim interlocutor would reply—in addition to pointing to alternative historic records claiming that Muhammad married Aisha before marrying Sawada: "The Qur'an passage allowing 'regular' Muslim men four wives, together with the conditions limiting polygamy, including the orphan condition, was revealed only after Muhammad had married Sawada, Aisha, and then several other wives. Thus, that new revelation raised the question whether Muhammad had to divorce some of his wives to

---

3 On a "personal" note (not that much of the rest is not "personal"), several semesters ago, a deeply committed Muslim student from Iran attended my class. She gave several presentations to the class, and provided a passionate defense of polygamy along the lines that I have just explained.

4 Muslim commentators could respond, of course, that the breaking of a rule does not abrogate it. A "Fox principle" guy like me can, however, not "decide" between different interpretations of the Qur'an and designate one as "the right one"; all he can say to these commentators is; "Well, there are Muslims who do not go along with your stricter interpretation of the Qur'an."

5 All of this occurred after the death of his first wife, Khadija.

6 The historic record seems to be somewhat "sketchy" in this respect; according to other accounts, Muhammad married Aisha before marrying Sawada. [A side remark: I am passing over the problem caused by Aisha's age when Muhammad married her and when the marriage was consummated.]

comply with the requirements of the 'four-wives' passage. In response to that question, another Qur'an passage was revealed, which exempted Muhammad from the 'only four wives' restriction, making clear to him (and to his wives) that there was no need for him to divorce the wives beyond four he was married to. He was told, however, not to take any additional wives, as becomes clear from the passage, 'It is not allowed to you to take wives after this, nor to change them for other wives'" (Surah 33.52; based on Ali).

5. Another "tough spot" for the non-Muslim ...; referral to an imam

Maybe the Muslim interlocutor should not have mentioned the Qur'an passage, according to which Muhammad was not allowed to take additional wives because it begs the following question:[7] If the "four-wives" passage was revealed after the Battle of Uhud in 625, then it stands to reason that the passage which made an exception for Muhammad would have to be revealed a short time later—or there would have been a lengthy period of time during which Muhammad would seem to have lived in opposition to what God allowed. Remember that the passage contains an order not to take additional wives. Then why did Muhammad marry, in 328; that is, three years after the Battle of Uhud, Maria Al-Qibtiyya?

The Muslim commentator might enlighten me, "He did not marry her as a free woman, but she was given to him as a gift a Muslim emissary brought from Egypt. Remember the 'what your right hand possesses' part of the polygamy passage you quoted before."

This remark tempts me, of course, to say, "Well ..." but I better stop at this point, except for adding, "Do you see, dear interlocutor, that someone looking at Islam from the outside is confronted with some difficulties connected with the teaching on polygamy?"

Maybe the interlocutor replies, "Tell your students to see an imam[8] and ask him about the matter. I am sure that he can explain it much more satisfactorily than you."

As you just heard, I am passing the interlocutor's message on. I am turning to another matter causing difficulties for non-Muslims:

(II) HOLY WAR (AKA JIHAD)—A BRIEF DIALOGUE

Even for the previous segment, I pictured having an interlocutor. Let me become even more extreme in this respect and present the Holy War segment as a conversation between a Muslim friend and myself—it summarizes/amplifies several actual conversations I have had on the topic. I will jump back and forth between the right and left side of this lectern; if I am standing at the left side, it's me talking; if I am standing at the right, it's my Muslim friend. [In the written version, "F" represents Fritz Wenisch; "M" represents the Muslim friend.]

---

7 Because of my day job, I must add that I am not using "begging the question" in the sense in which logicians at times are using it to designate the fallacy of circular reasoning, but in its ordinary, everyday sense.
8 A Muslim religious leader.

F: Many people do have serious problems with Islam and Holy War …

M: Good that you bring it up. Holy War, aka Jihad, is very likely the Muslim belief about which there is more confusion and misunderstanding among non-Muslims than about any other belief Islam stands for. I am glad that I get a chance to straighten matters out.

F: What are the confusions?

M: To begin with, most non-Muslims do not know that two entirely different types of Jihad are to be distinguished. One involves actual warfare, of the type of a defense against an attack. The other is the "war" all humans must fight against themselves. We must get ourselves to resist temptations to do wrong, attempting to become better persons. This second sense is even the primary meaning of the word "Jihad."[9] There is, of course, also literal fighting. [Takes the copy of the Qur'an lying on the lectern, opens it, reads:] "And fight in the way of Allah against those who fight you, but be not aggressive. Surely Allah loves not the aggressor" (Surah 2.190; based on Ali). Clearly, all that is allowed here is defensive warfare; fighting against those who attack one's territory.

F: That sounds encouraging; but how about passages such as [takes the Qur'an, opens it to a different page[10]], "So when the sacred months have passed, slay the idolaters [that is, people worshipping false gods] wherever you find them, and take them captive and besiege them and lie in wait for them in every ambush" (Surah 9.5; based on Ali)? To my ears, this does sound rather aggressive and intolerant.

M: I agree, the way you read it, it sounds terrible. You must, however, not take it out of context. Earlier, the Surah talked about an agreement that was made with the pagan tribes. Some broke the agreement. The passage you read refers to them; it is not to be understood as being about idolaters in general. Moreover, the limited group of idolaters spoken about is not to be killed because of their religion, but because of having broken an agreement. So do not worry—we *are* tolerant.

F: I can imagine a non-Muslim Westerner say, "There would be less worrying on my part if the passage that Fritz read would actually spell out the interpretation his Muslim friend just gave"; but however this may be, let me move to another worrisome Qur'an pass …

M: [Interrupting] I believe that the Surah's other parts, especially its beginning, which you did not read, makes perfectly clear that my interpretation of the passage is correct. Hand me the book! Here, listen: "A declaration of immunity from Allah and His Messenger to those of the idolaters with whom you have made an agreement" (Surah 9.1, based on Ali): That's the introductory statement to the Surah from which you read. That's the group of

---

9 Ali, p. 416.

10 From now on, I will dispense with remarks indicating that the Qur'an is handed back and forth during the conversation—except if it is a part of the actual conversation, of course.

idolaters spoken about; within this group, those who keep the agreement enjoy immunity; the ones to be killed are only those within this group who break the agreement.[11] What's the other so-called worrisome passage, though?

F: First, let's get clear about the meaning of an important expression: "Those who have been given the book" are Jews and Christians, correct?

M: Correct.

F: Now listen to this Qur'an passage: "Fight those who believe not in Allah, nor in the Last Day, nor forbid that which Allah and His Messenger have forbidden, nor follow the Religion of Truth [Islam], out of those who have been given the Book, until they pay the tax in acknowledgement of superiority and they are in a state of subjection" (Surah 9.29; based on Ali). Does this not mean that Christians and Jews are to be fought until they have been reduced to the status of second-class citizens? Is it surprising that many non-Muslims believe the Qur'an to order the killing of pagans and the subjugation of Jews and Christians?

M: No, this is not surprising at all because, as you surely know as a university teacher, people love to take things out of context. For the pagans, I have given an explanation before, and I refer back to it. As far as Jews and Christians are concerned, the passage refers to the Jews in Arabia who had assisted the pagans in their fight against Islam, not to Jews in general; the Christians are mentioned because, as Ali says here in his note to the Qur'an passage you just read,[12] the Roman Empire was mobilizing against the Muslims with view of subjugating them. Muhammad led, in 630, an army north to Tabuk (today in Saudi Arabia); but he met no army, so he returned—the Roman army must have withdrawn.

F: By Roman Empire, Ali must mean the East Roman Empire, aka the Byzantine Empire; what he says is based on later Muslim sources, and there is no contemporary Byzantine account at all stating that the empire planned any military campaigns against the Muslims. Silence is no proof, of course—except that there is not total silence: According to contemporary evidence, Heraclius, the East Roman emperor at the time, was involved in activities other than planning for war. They included a barefoot pilgrimage to Jerusalem. The later Muslim commentators could be right, however, anyway. Even so, though, again, I can imagine a Westerner saying, "Would it not be nice if the Qur'an passage Fritz just read would make clear that it is not about Jews and Christians in general, but only about those Jews who assisted the pagans against the Muslims and those Christians who supposedly planned to attack the Muslims?"

---

11 Fritz's remark (not a part of the conversation): There seems to be an alternative natural way to read Surah 9.5 in the context of the material presented in Surah 9.1–29: That the command to slay the idolaters, take them captive, and besiege them applies to all idolaters outside of the group with which an agreement has been made.
12 Ali, p. 404.

M: What is wrong with … Sorry, I almost said, "with you." What is wrong with making sure that the historic background on which a segment of a text is based is taken into consideration? Don't Christians and Jews—except perhaps for some fundamentalists—do the same with the Bible? I can assure you that Islam is a tolerant religion. As the Qur'an says, "There is no compulsion in religion—the right way is indeed clearly distinct from error" (Surah 2.256; based on Ali), and "Allah forbids you not to respect those who do not fight you for religion, nor drive you away from your homes, that you show them kindness and deal with them justly" (Surah 60.8; based on Ali). See?

F: Does the early history of Islam bear out what you just read?

M: What do you mean?

F: The way I understand you, Islam allows only defensive wars.

M: Correct—you got it.

F: Well, within only about 80 years of Muhammad's death, Islam had expanded to an area including Spain, North Africa, Palestine, part of Asia Minor, Iraq, Iran, and to the east as far as the Indus Valley. This spread was not accomplished through peaceful missionary work, but by armed conflict—countless battles were fought. Do you understand why some have difficulties seeing in Islam a religion of peace? If one considers, for comparison purposes, the early history of Christianity …

M: Good for you to mention Christianity. Just remember the Crusades. Any Christian who accuses another religion of violence better fall silent when they come to mind.

F: No one can justify the cruelties against non-Christians—and even against Christians the Crusaders disagreed with—that were committed during the Crusades. It is, however, important to remember that one cannot excuse bad behavior by pointing at someone else's bad behavior. Moreover, the Crusades began in 1098—surely no longer "early Christianity." I was suggesting, though, that we compare the early spread of Christianity with the early spread of Islam. For more than 250 years from the inception of Christianity on, Christianity was outlawed, persecuted by the Roman Empire; but nevertheless, it spread through the entire region and even to the east, outside of the Roman Empire, almost without exception through peaceful means, by missionaries, many of whom died as martyrs. In contrast, try to show me how I am mistaken when I doubt (to put it mildly) that Islam spread through peaceful means when it expanded within eight decades from Spain to the Indus Valley.

M: Remember the Crusades.

F: As I indicated, no one in his or her right mind can deny that they were terrible in many respects—although some would say that a just view of them is not supposed to neglect that there were fights for areas that once had been centers of Christianity and had been taken over by Muslims, and that among the immediate causes of the Crusades were continuous encroachments of Muslim forces into non-Muslim European territories.[13] Be that as it may, though, to move to the present, is it surprising that the existence of the Taliban and Al Qaeda and other extreme Muslim groups cause worries to non-Muslim Westerners?

M: One is not supposed to represent Islam as a whole in the light of some crazy fringe groups who completely misunderstand the Qur'an. It would be like seeing Christianity as a whole in the light of the crazies at the Westboro Baptist Church who use military funerals for their anti-gay protests and show signs utterly offensive to the people whose loved ones have been killed in the war and are being buried.

F: They are indeed a minuscule percentage of the more than two billion Christians that exist. Can one be as confident about the percentage of extreme Muslims relative to Islam as a whole?

M: The percentage of Muslim extremists is small.

F: Maybe I am permitted a comment on another example …

M: Of course you are permitted. You can say what you want.

F: Remember September 2005, the month of the publication of the Danish newspaper cartoons about Muhammad.

M: Surely, you do not wish to justify making fun of the Prophet, as these despicable cartoons did?

F: I do not approve of offending Muslims. But surely, you do not approve of attempting to assassinate the cartoonist and people cooperating with him at the newspaper?

M: Again, I must repeat that there are only few Muslim extremists.

F: In terms of numbers, I am troubled by the fierce riots in many parts of the Muslim world which followed the publication of the cartoons, including riots during which killings were reported. People lost their lives who had nothing to do with the publication of the material.

M: I must repeat that the images published in Denmark were deeply offensive to us Muslims.

---

13 An excellent commentary on the commonly accepted "politically correct" views on the Crusades can be found in Paul F. Crawford, "Four Myths about the Crusades," in *The Intercollegiate Review*, spring 2011, pp. 13–22.

F: I understand; but what is the justification for taking this as a motive to commit acts of violence, including murder, against people who were entirely uninvolved with the offensive action? Moreover, let's talk numbers—in an area where hard figures are difficult to come by. Suppose the radical Muslims amount to only 1% of the total. With more than 1.5 billion Muslims in the world, this would still be 15,000,000 radicals—more than enough to make the world a horrible place for the rest of humanity.

M: The radical Muslims amount to much less than 1%.

F: Make it a tenth of a percent—1.5 million still is a large number. Maybe it is time for me to come to your assistance, though, instead of giving you a hard time. Listen to this—I am reading from a newspaper column: "A couple of weeks ago, on the occasion of the annual Hajj, in which 2.5 million Muslim pilgrims fulfill their obligation to travel to Mecca, prominent Muslim clerics from Asia, Africa, and Saudi Arabia, along with the leaders of Saudi Arabia, Egypt, Pakistan, Indonesia, Turkey, Afghanistan and Iraq denounced violence in the name of Islam and issued a manifesto signed by all, declaring that 'murder of innocents is never justified and violates the teaching of Islam.'"

M: There you have it! It confirms what I told you. But listen, I must have missed this event—maybe because I was busy preparing for my PhD thesis defense.

F: You have not missed anything. The columnist continues, "If you haven't heard about this, it is because it never happened."[14] Muslims living in the Western world like to assert that Islam is a peaceful religion. Can you see that such assertions would instill more confidence in worried non-Muslims if there would be significantly more unambiguous and forthright Muslim condemnations of acts of violence perpetrated by what you call Islamic fringe groups—condemnations similar to the fictitious example in the column I read from? Some of my non-Muslim Western friends even think that here in the West, the Muslim condemnations of such acts of violence are too infrequent and too muted.

M: I think you are totally mistaken in this respect.

F: Well, if something is a matter of degrees, there can easily be disagreements about whether or not something is present to the "right degree." At any rate, I will take your suggestion that the peaceful groups within Islam will win out in the final analysis …

M: What do you mean "Will win out"? They HAVE won out.

F: So you say. I will take your suggestion into consideration for the final message I will try to convey to my students about the three religions we covered in this course. I truly hope that what I will tell them will not forever remain utopian.

---

14 The column from which the quotations are taken was written by Mona Charen and reprinted on p. 22 of the December 8, 2010, issue of the *Conservative Chronicle*.

CHAPTER TWENTY THREE

Tolerance—Is It Possible?
Does It Suffice?

(I) A PRAYER AND A QUESTION

By now, our joint excursion into the territories of Judaism, Christianity, and Islam has almost come to an end. One matter of great significance is still to be taken care of, though.

What I will say next is based on hope. I do hope that it is not "hope against hope." Many—Robert Spencer, for example[1]—might consider me as caught up in wishful thinking, maybe even as delusional. Here goes anyway, though:

First, permit me to invite you to listen to the following prayer:

"In the name of God, the compassionate, the merciful: Praise be to God, Lord of the Universe, the compassionate, the merciful, King of the Day of Judgment! You alone we worship, and to you alone we turn for help. Guide us to the straight path, the path of those whom you have favored, not of those who have incurred your wrath, nor of those who have gone astray."

In past semesters, I asked my students, "Is this a Jewish or a Christian prayer?" They were to indicate by a show of hands what they thought.

In some semesters, the Jews won the contest—significantly more people declare the prayer Jewish; in other semesters, the Christians won; then again, sometimes, the outcome was about 50/50.

My inquiry had been a trick question, though. The prayer is neither Jewish nor Christian but Muslim. It is the opening prayer of the Qur'an.

---

1 Robert Spencer is the author of *Islam Unveiled—Disturbing Questions about the World's Fastest-Growing Faith*, and other similar books.

(II) TWO SIGNIFICANT POINTS OF AGREEMENT

There was "method" behind my trickery, however: That the Surah with which the Qur'an begins can easily be mistaken for a Jewish or Christian prayer is strong evidence in support of the statement that Muslims believe in the same God to whom Jews and Christians pray. Whatever the differences between these religions may be, all three hold that there is one and only one God, compassionate, merciful, almighty, all-knowing, and forgiving. This one and only God is said to have called the universe into being out of nothing—the universe which we know today to be much larger and vaster than people would have been able to imagine even only some decades ago; the universe with billions of stars in our galaxy which is only one of an unbelievably large number of galaxies—God is said to have called this unimaginably large universe into being and to keep it in existence.

He is said also to have created us humans. Why? Out of love. For what purpose? So that we might love him back and be forever happy through being loved by him and requiting his love.

Whatever the differences between Jews, Christians, and Muslims may be, isn't this a significant belief they share in common?

To me at least it seems so.

There is a second important agreement. Remember Abraham?

Jews, Christians, and Muslims look back to him with great reverence.

Picture asking your Jewish friend Rob, "Who is your father?" He might answer, "Solomon Cohen." You reply, "That's not what I meant." "Oh," he might say, "I get it ... my father is Abraham." Jews consider themselves as sons and daughters of Abraham—"sons" and "daughters" used in the sense of "descendants"; they consider Abraham as their father—the word "father" used in the sense of ancestor. Maybe you ask, "How do those fit into this picture who were not born as Jews but converted to the Jewish faith later in life—maybe because they married a Jewish spouse? They are not descendants of Abraham." Jews would reply, "Didn't you ever hear about adoption? Maybe you know children who have been adopted. Their adoptive parents treat them exactly like they do the other family members. So is it with people who are not Jewish from birth, but did convert later in their lives: They are sons and daughters of Abraham in the spirit of adoption."

As you might recall from what has been said about the early history of Judaism, Jews trace their descent back to Abraham over his younger son Isaac whose mother was Sarah: Abraham—Isaac—Jacob (aka Israel)—his 12 sons—the 12 tribes of Israel. Ten of these 12 tribes were obliterated when the Assyrians destroyed the northern kingdom of Israel. With regard to tribal descent, there are some contemporary Jews who trace their lineage back to the tribe of Levi (some even more narrowly to the subset of that tribe stemming from Moses' brother Aaron); apart from that group, however, "all other Jewish tribal identities have been lost."[2]

Well, back to Abraham: He had another son, Ishmael, older than Isaac, whose mother was Hagar. Muslims might point out that even in the book of Genesis (21.13), God is reported to assure Abraham about Ishmael, "I will make a great nation of him also, since he too is your son." Thus, the Jewish Holy Scriptures identify at least two great nations stemming from Abraham. One of them comes through Isaac; that is the nation of the Israelites, the Jews. The second comes through Ishmael. Muslims consider

---

2 Telushkin, *Literacy*, p. 656.

the Arabs as that second nation. This is the nation into which Muhammad was born; he is, therefore, like the rest of the Arabs, considered to be a descendant of Abraham over Ishmael.

In keeping with this, Arab Muslims consider themselves genetically as sons and daughters of Abraham. Today, Muslims of Arab ethnicity are in the minority. The majority of Muslims, probably as many as 80 percent or more, are non-Arabs. How do they relate to Abraham? Once again, the idea of adoption enters the picture. Non-Arab Muslims consider themselves as belonging to Abraham's family in the spirit of adoption.[3]

And Christians?

First, how about Jesus himself? He was born into a Jewish family; he was a descendant of Abraham over David, the second king of the Jews when their kingdom was still united. Jesus strictly observed the law as stated in the Torah.[4] All of his Apostles and all of his early followers were Jewish. To outsiders, the "Jesus movement" appeared initially as another subgroup of the Jews; a formal break between Judaism and Christianity occurred only several decades after the death of Jesus. Thus, early Christians considered themselves, just like Jews, genetically as descendants of Abraham.

If one considers contemporary Christianity as a whole, though, only a small minority of the more than two billion Christians would be able to claim a biological descent from these early followers of Jesus, and it is more than unlikely that one would even be able to identify who they are. How does the vast majority fit into the picture?

Once again, the idea of adoption must be considered. Whoever joins Christianity, no matter what his or her genetic, racial, or ethnic heritage may be, is considered by Christians as being adopted into Abraham's family. As St. Paul says, "Those who believe are sons of Abraham." (Gal 3.7)

Thus, Jews, Christians, and Muslims believe in the same one and only God who created them out of love and who wishes them to requite his love; further, they consider themselves as belonging to Abraham's family.

(III) A SOURCE OF GRIEF FOR PARENTS—APPLYING THE EXAMPLE

How should three groups of people sharing these beliefs regard each other?

Looking at their history and even at the contemporary situation in many places of the world, how did/do they regard one another? The way they ought to?

Think about it in terms of an example: Suppose a married couple has grown children who do not get along. I am not speaking about minor family squabbles which are unavoidable; I am speaking about

---

3 I hasten to emphasize that the word "adoption" must be qualified. It is meant to indicate that the "adopted" person is treated with the same love and concern as "literal" members of the family, not that a pretense is made of the adopted person's being genetically a member of the family, and his or her true ancestors being forgotten/ignored. Under this latter understanding, a conflict with Qur'an Surah 33.4 would arise, which states, "Allah has not made … those whom you assert to be your sons your sons" (based on Ali). Ali explains in his commentary on this passage that one of the customs it abolishes is "regarding the adopted son as if he was a real son" (p. 824). That there cannot be an objection to the qualified understanding of adoption becomes clear from the fact that Muhammad himself had an adopted son, Zayd.
4 He made the Pharisees angry, though, for they were sticklers for the details of the letter of the law while Jesus emphasized the spirit of the law.

actual enmity. The parents try to organize a celebration for their 45th wedding anniversary. When they contact their children to invite them to the event, each of them asks immediately, "Who else is coming? If so-and-so [a brother or sister] will be there, forget about me." How dreadful! Whenever the sons and daughters are together in one place, ugly fights break out. How devastating to the parents! Wouldn't you want to walk up to these children, grab them and shake them and tell them, "Try to get along—at least for the sake of your parents"?

Does one not feel like saying something similar to Jews, Christians, and Muslims? "Try to get along with each other, at least because of the one God of whom you believe that he created you out of love and for the sake of Abraham, the man you consider as your common ancestor."

(IV) AN OBJECTION

Someone might object at this point, "But Fritz, you are overlooking a very important fact. You speak as if there were no disagreements between Jews, Christians, and Muslims. To be sure, all three groups hold that God wants us to do his will; that he does not like it if we disobey him. What is God's will, though? Just look at the teachings of the three religions you are talking about, and you will find disagreements. Consider some simple—almost simplistic—examples: Muslims believe that God wants us to abstain from pork (Surah 2.173) and wine (Surah 2.219). Orthodox and Conservative Jews hold that we must abstain from pork (together with many other nonkosher foods), but not from wine. Christians consider both pork and wine acceptable. Many other similar examples could be given, such as the permission of polygamy the Qur'an contains (Surah 4.3) while Christians and contemporary Jews insist on monogamy.

"Thus, from the perspective of each single one of the three religions, the members of the other two violate God's will. Remember that God does not appreciate his will being violated; how, then, can he like someone who routinely acts contrary to his commands? How can a human like others of whom he or she is convinced that God does not like them? Do you see that logical thinking (a key ingredient of your day job) leads inevitably to the conclusion that Christians must dislike Jews and Muslims, that Muslims must dislike Jews and Christians, and that Jews must dislike Christians and Muslims?

"Maybe Osama bin Laden and al Qaeda got it right after all. However that may be, though, I am telling you, Fritz, that the tolerance between the three groups which you seem to advocate is a pipe dream, unrealistic, an impossibility."

(V) AN OBVIOUS DISTINCTION

What am I to reply?

The argument you just heard ignores a basic distinction which the following examples are to illustrate:

Suppose your car needed major repairs. Your friend had promised to give you a ride to work on Tuesday. He failed to show up, though. You ended up hiring a cab which cost a fortune, you arrived late at work, and your boss was mad at you. Whom might you have been angry about? Not difficult to guess. When you met your friend two days later and asked him about the matter, it turned out that he had been on his way to your place to give you the ride he had promised, but had seen a little restaurant that advertised a tasty breakfast special available only on that day. He had thought to himself, "Forget about picking my friend up," and walked into the restaurant to enjoy an early morning treat. Rather irresponsible, no?

Allow me to change the story: The beginning is the same—you ended up stranded at home and had to hire a cab. Now, it is different: Your friend showed up at your place on Wednesday instead of on Tuesday as he had promised. Wednesday happens to be your day off; you did not need a ride. The reason for his not having been there the day before turned out to be that he had had enormous pressure at work, his wife was sick at home, and one of his children was in the hospital with a serious disease; this accumulation of difficulties had confused him and caused him to believe that he had promised you a ride for Wednesday rather than for Tuesday. To top it all off, he came on Wednesday even though doing so was very, very hard on him with all the other difficulties in his life. If this is what happened, would it be just to continue being mad about him and calling him irresponsible?

The answer seems obvious, at least to me.

It remains true, however, that he did not keep his promise of giving you a ride on Tuesday, and isn't not keeping a promise wrong?

True, but the example shows that there is a tremendous difference between doing what is wrong out of laziness or negligence or just because one does not want to do what one knows to be right, as opposed to doing what is wrong on the basis of an honest mistake. Only the first does make the person *guilty* of wrongdoing; the second, while involving wrong conduct, does not involve any guilt on the part of the person who made the honest mistake. From the perspective of guilt, your friend's honest and sincere conviction that he had promised to give you a ride on Wednesday rather than on Tuesday excuses him, although his conviction turned out to be mistaken.

It is not difficult even for us puny little humans to see the distinction between doing wrong knowingly and doing wrong on the basis of an honest and sincere mistake.

The person who objected to my advocacy of tolerance seems to assume, however, that an all-knowing God would not be aware of that distinction. Isn't this a rather foolish assumption, though? If the God in whom Jews, Christians, and Muslims believe actually exists, would he not understand even better than any human that being involved in wrong conduct on the basis of a sincere but mistaken belief that one's conduct is right excuses a person from the guilt imposing itself on someone who does wrong, knowing full well about the wrongness of his conduct?

(VI) TOLERANCE—A START, BUT NOT ENOUGH

If this is so, each member of the three religious groups we examined in this course would have to say something like the following about his or her own group and about the others (I am formulating it from the perspective of a representative of the largest group, that of Christians):

"I am a Christian. Unless I want to begin having 'split personality disorder,' I must, of course, be convinced that Muslims are mistaken in their rejection of the belief in the Trinity and the divinity of Jesus, and that Jews are mistaken in their rejection of the belief that Jesus is the Messiah. Whenever

I think about Jews and Muslims I actually met, though, I remember that it is clearly not ill-will or dishonesty that makes them disagree with me; rather, without a doubt, they are honestly and sincerely convinced that they are right and that I am mistaken. If God is just—as we all believe—then he will not hold an honest and sincere mistake against anyone, including them. Who am I, therefore, to hold what I consider as their mistake against them?"

It seems that Jews would have to say something similar about Christians and Muslims, and Muslims would have to make a corresponding statement about Jews and Christians.

What is the result?

As a minimum, tolerance—true tolerance. True tolerance has nothing in common with the wishy-washiness of "What's true for me is true for me and what's true for you is true for you" attitude; it can coexist with firm convictions on the part of the one who is tolerant.

I said "as a minimum, tolerance" because I think the attitude Jews, Christians, and Muslims should have toward each other should go beyond mere tolerance. Tolerance is not more than "letting the other be"; it is no doubt preferable to persecuting someone because he or she has beliefs different from one's own. But tolerance is only a "first step." Suppose my next-door neighbor often has parties at his house with many guests; cars are parked all over the place, including in front of my house, and I say, "I tolerate his parties." This is not much of a positive attitude toward him, although he surely would prefer it to me giving him trouble.

It seems, however, that Jews, Muslims, and Christians, instead of merely tolerating each other, ought to take a much more positive attitude toward each other. That attitude should be motivated by a recognition of the fact that they do share truly significant beliefs, among them a belief in one and only one God, and a conviction that they belong to the extended family of Abraham. It seems that they should rejoice in that commonality. Further, it seems that this commonality could—and should—lead to a true community, a true friendship.

"Friendship between Jews, Christians, and Muslims? Are you serious, Fritz? How unrealistic can you get?"

Well, no doubt there are individual Jews, Christians, and Muslims who are friends, although each of them is strongly convinced that his or her religion is the truth, and that the others are mistaken in their alternative beliefs.

As far as I am concerned, I cannot start a mass movement; but I can try to convey to individual Jews, Christians, and Muslims that treating each other as friends does not require them to abandon the firmness of their convictions, and that they can acknowledge the "good faith," the honesty, the sincerity on the part of those with different convictions. You can do the same.

If one succeeds with conveying this thought—this attitude—to someone, it will become obvious to him or her just how regrettable enmity between these three faith communities is.

Convincing the one or the other individual to abandon hostility may seem like nothing if one considers the more than three billion Jews, Christians, and Muslims in the world, and the hostility which many of them continue to feel for one another.

What is to be preferred, though—cursing the darkness, or lighting a candle in one's backyard?

And if enough candles are lit—one by one by one by one—who knows what brightness it might lead to?

Who knows?

Bibliography

(I) PRIMARY SOURCES

Bible: For quotations from the Bible, the following translations are used: (1) *The New American Bible* and (2) the *New International Version*. For quotations from (1), only the book of the Bible, the Chapter, and the Verse are given (e.g., Lv 19.18); for quotations from (2), the book, chapter, and verse indication is followed by "NIV" (e.g., Mt 25.31–46 NIV). The abbreviations for Bible books are the same as those given in the Bible segment of the Christianity part of this text.

Qur'an: Quotations from the Qur'an are taken from the following English editions: (1) *The Holy Qur'an— English Translation of the Meaning and Commentary* by Mushaf Al-Madinah An-Nabawiyah, revised and edited by the Presidency of Islamic Researchers, IFTA, Call and Guidance; (2) *The Holy Qur'an, Arabic Text with English Translation and Commentary* by Maulana Muhammad Ali, first edition 1917, redesigned 2002, Dublin/Ohio, 2002. Both editions are in an old-fashioned language; I have taken the liberty of updating it, for example, by replacing "thee" with "you" and by similar changes. Quotations from (1) are identified as "based on An-Nabawiyah"; quotations from (2) are identified as "based on Ali."

(II) OTHER SOURCES

Armstrong, Karen. *A History of God.* New York: Ballantine Books, 1993.

Brown, Dan. *The Da Vinci Code.* Garden City, NY: Doubleday, 2004.

Carmody, Denise, and John Carmody. *Ways to the Center—An Introduction to World Religions*, Fourth Edition. Belmont, CA: Wadsworth, 1993.

Collins, Raymond F. *Introduction to the New Testament.* Garden City, NY: Doubleday, 1987.

Crawford, Paul F. "Four Myths About the Crusades." In *The Intercollegiate Review*, spring 2011.

Eusebius. *Church History.* In *The Nicene and Post-Nicene Fathers*, translated by Philip Schaff and Henry Wace, vol. 1. Michigan: Eerdmans, 1979.

Farnell, F. David. "Independence Response to Chapter 1." In *Three Views on the Origins of the Synoptic Gospels*, edited by Robert L. Thomas. Grand Rapids, MI: Kregel, 2002.

Gibb, H. A. R. *Mohammedanism—An Historical Survey*. New York: Oxford University Press, 1962.

Glazer, Nathan. *American Judaism*. Chicago and London: The University of Chicago Press, 1972.

Hughes, Thomas Patrick. *Dictionary of Islam*. Chicago: KAZI Publications, 1994. (Originally published in 1886.)

Jefferson, Thomas. *Writings*. New York: Viking Press, 1984.

Lammens, H. *Islam—Belief and Institutions*, translated by Sir E. Denison Ross. Haarlem: Frank Cass & Co. Ltd., 1968.

Lewis, C. S. *Mere Christianity*. San Francisco: Harper, 1980. (Originally published 1952.)

Linnemann, Eta. *Is There a Synoptic Problem?* Translated by Robert W. Yarbrough Grand Rapids, MI: Baker Books, 1992.

Maimonides. *A Maimonides Reader*, edited by Isadore Twersky. New York: Behrman House, 1972.

Panek, Richard. *The 4% Universe—Dark Matter, Dark Energy, and the Race to Discover the Rest of Reality*. Boston/New York: Houghton Mifflin, 2011.

Russell, Bertrand. "What Is an Agnostic?" http://www.davemckay.co.uk/philosophy/russell/russell.php?name=what.is.an.agnostic

Schmidt, Alvin J. *The Great Divide*. Boston: Regina Orthodox Press, 2004.

Spencer, Robert. *Islam Unveiled*. San Francisco: Encounter Books, 2002.

Stoldt, Hans-Herbert. *History and Criticism of the Marcan Hypothesis*, translated and edited by Donald L. Niewyk Macon, GA: Mercer University Press, 1980.

Tacitus. *Annals*. http://www.perseus.tufts.edu/hopper/text?doc=Tac.+Ann.+15.44&redirect=true

Telushkin, Joseph. *Jewish Literacy—The Most Important Things to Know About the Jewish Religion, Its People, and Its History*. New York: William Morrow and Company, 1991.

The World Almanac and Book of Facts 2014. New York: World Almanac Books, 2013.

"Touro Synagogue—National Historic Site," in *Newport History*, summer 1975, vol. 48, Part 3.

Trifkovic, Serge. *The Sword of the Prophet—Islam—History, Theology, Impact on the World*. Boston: Regina Orthodox Press, 2002.

Warren, Earl. "The Law and the Future," in *Fortune Magazine*, November 1955.

CPSIA information can be obtained at www.ICGtesting.com
Printed in the USA
LVOW09s2002150115

423006LV00002B/4/P